Working with the Wealthy and Well Known

Working with the Wealthy and Well Known takes a nuanced look at these two overlapping groups and offers evidence-based guidance for treatment plans and strategies.

The writing mixes stories and narrative, expert interviews with master therapists and other helping professionals, and strong research to create a highly readable, immensely practical guide for working with the rich and famous. Drawing on decades of clinical experience and a strong body of research, Dave Verhaagen shares deeply human stories, evidence-based insights, and practical approaches to helping prominent clients navigate the complexities of wealth and fame. He explores their impact on identity development, relationships, substance use, and mental health.

Transcending the stereotypes of rich people and celebrities, this is a must-read for mental health professionals, fans of psychology, and anyone who helps or supports prominent clients. Written with empathy and insight, the book is a landmark work for understanding and helping the rich and famous.

Dave Verhaagen, PhD, is a nationally board-certified psychologist, author of multiple books, former clinical director of three mental health agencies, and founder of Southeast Psych in Charlotte and Nashville.

"There is not a singular way of understanding or working with wealthy people. Rather, it takes a complex and dynamic understanding of psychology and wealth to effectively work with this population. Dr. Verhaagen's insights and perspectives into the experience of wealth are important to the wide range of professionals who interact with and support wealthy individuals and families."

Ed Coambs, *CFP, LMFT, past president,*
Financial Therapy Association

"I haven't run across a book as spot-on and specific to my office practice as this one. Love this book!"

Alan Ludington, *MS, MDiv, MFT, founder of Ludington*
Institute for Family Enrichment, Westlake Village, California, USA

Working with the Wealthy and Well Known

Evidence-Based Guidance for Treatment Plans and Strategies

Dave Verhaagen

Routledge
Taylor & Francis Group

NEW YORK AND LONDON

Designed cover image: Getty Images

First published 2026
by Routledge
605 Third Avenue, New York, NY 10158

and by Routledge
4 Park Square, Milton Park, Abingdon, Oxon, OX14 4RN

Routledge is an imprint of the Taylor & Francis Group, an informa business

© 2026 Dave Verhaagen

ISBN: 978-1-032-81560-2 (hbk)
ISBN: 978-1-032-81558-9 (pbk)
ISBN: 978-1-003-50356-9 (ebk)

DOI: 10.4324/9781003503569

Typeset in Perpetua
by Apex CoVantage, LLC

Contents

Acknowledgments   *vii*

PART I
The Foundations   1

1   The Perks and Perils of Prominence   3

2   Defining Wealthy and Well Known   13

PART II
The Needs of Wealthy and Well-Known People   21

3   Wealthy People, Part 1: The Benefits of Being Rich   23

4   Wealthy People, Part 2: The Challenges of Being Rich   34

5   The Challenges of Children in Wealthy Families   47

6   Well-Known People   61

7   The Non-Normal Lives of Child Stars   74

PART III
Treatment Focus   87

8   Managing Meteoric Rise and Catastrophic Fall   89

9 Building Healthy Relationships in Wealthy and
   Well-Known People   102

10 Treating Substance Abuse in Wealthy and Well-Known
   People   116

11 Treating Narcissism in Wealthy and Well-Known People   132

PART IV
The Therapist's Own Work   **151**

12 Doing Your Own Work Around Money and Fame   153

13 Ethical Issues and Practical Considerations in Working with
   Wealthy and Well-Known People   163

Appendix 1: Verhaagen Personal Values Inventory   *179*
Appendix 2: How I See Myself and Others   *185*
Glossary 1: A Glossary of the Language of Wealth   *187*
Glossary 2: A Glossary of the Language of Fame   *191*
Index   *195*

Acknowledgments

How grateful I am to have such wonderful family, friends, and colleagues! I'm so thankful to you all for your support and kindness. Let me thank a few of you:

Thanks to all members of the Group Practice Roundtable, who not only have been the best professional colleagues a psychologist could have, but also have become good friends.

Thanks to Lauren King, my business partner in Nashville, for your hard work, care for our staff, and strong leadership. Thanks also to Jonathan Feather, my business partner in Charlotte, for being a steady presence and a wise voice. I am honored to call both of you friends.

Thanks to Ellen, my wife and best friend, who supports and loves me so well.

Thanks to the industry professionals like wealth managers, agents, talent managers, and others who gave me your time for interviews, fact checking, perspective, and advice. Even though I don't mention you by name (for obvious reasons), please know that I am grateful to you.

Thanks to Anna Moore, my publisher, for your responsiveness, professionalism, and wisdom.

Thanks to Routledge. This is my second book with you. I've worked with some very good publishers, and you all are among the very best. It's a source of pride to be associated with you.

Part I

The Foundations

Chapter 1

The Perks and Perils of Prominence

Fame is a bee. It has a song—It has a sting—Ah, too, it has a wing.[1]
—Emily Dickinson

Emily Dickinson knew something in the late nineteenth century that we still wrestle with today: Fame can be alluring but dangerous and fleeting. It is desired by many, yet can sting hard. The same can be said of wealth. There are great advantages to being wealthy, but colossal, often unforeseen, dangers.

I am not the therapist to the stars. The vast majority of my clients are neither rich nor famous. They are average people, known only to their friends and family and the sprinkling of colleagues and acquaintances they meet along the way. Most don't have jaw-dropping bank accounts or dazzling fame. They have ordinary lives. Throughout the years, though, a good number of wealthy or well-known people have come to our practice for therapy. They may be musicians, actors, athletes, comedians, reality show contestants, social media influencers, successful businesspeople, spiritual leaders, politicians, company founders, heirs of fortunes, or the close loved ones of these folks. In most instances, their lives are far from ordinary. Their fame or fortune does not make them better or worse than others. However, their lives differ greatly from the lives most of us lead.

In the early years of my career, I worked with poor families, often among the poorest in the community. I enjoyed these clients and grew to have great admiration for them. In the era that followed, I moved into private practice. I first joined a practice that became consumed by the coming onslaught of managed care, and they scrambled to figure out how to keep up with this sea change. When the time came for me to start a practice, I decided it wasn't worth playing the managed care game, so I opted out of insurance panels and saw only clients who paid out-of-pocket or had out-of-network benefits. This change was due to my frustrations with the insurance model, but it had the unintended effect of limiting my practice

DOI: 10.4324/9781003503569-2

3

only to those families with means. While I still offered pro bono and reduced fee service, the vast majority of my clients paid the full cost out-of-pocket.

Over time, as our practice grew in size and reputation, it attracted increasing numbers of individuals who were wealthy. Some were from families with recognizable names, while others were not. My practice had gone from poor clients to middle class, then to upper class. The contrast in these clients could not have been more striking. Their attitudes and expectations were different. Their posture toward therapy was different. Even their behavior in the therapy room was different.

After journeying with many prominent clients, I know it is not a life I would desire. These are people with complicated lives. I marvel at how some of them navigate the complexity. My empathy runs deep for those who get derailed by easy vices or poor decisions. Many of their mistakes are hidden from public view, but often their blunders are laid bare for all to see. For them, a mistake is not just a mistake. It is an invitation for the public to take their knives out. The fear of being ripped to shreds is always close at hand.

For wealthy and well-known people, the experience of others wanting to push their way into your life for selfish reasons is exhausting. So, too, is the reality of those you've never met delighting in your demise, associates who justify cheating or exposing you, and partners you later wondered if they were just in it for the tell-all. The life of a rich or famous person is complex. It's easy for the rest of us to cluck our tongues and wag our fingers at their lapses of judgment or substance problems or failed relationships. We feel confident we would never be as foolish as them if we were to find ourselves in the world of celebrity. The truth is, we would fare no better on average. We'd be as vulnerable to the same shenanigans and tragedies as they are. We are no less flawed than them. Navigating celebrity and fortune is difficult, a rollercoaster ride full of unexpected loops and sharp drops, though not as safe as a theme park ride. It's raw and real. It yields pain. Few rich or famous people who have experienced the privileges and benefits of their status have escaped the costs and challenges of it.

FURTHER CONNECTIONS WITH WEALTHY AND WELL-KNOWN CLIENTS

While I practiced in Charlotte, a major sports league approached me to be one of their approved clinicians. I had experience with high school, college, and a few professional athletes, but I didn't consider myself a sports psychologist. They clarified that they needed someone to engage players at risk of trouble, not a sports psychologist.

I agreed to be considered and faced a daunting 30-page questionnaire. I doubted my chances, thinking they sought someone different, perhaps a therapist who knew the league better or used a different therapy model. Despite my skepticism, after interviews and site visits, they approved me, and I began working with their professional athletes.

These athletes were always respectful, even those mandated to see me. Some were famous, others were not, but nearly all were wealthy. Yet, they were genuine and humble, often experiencing therapy for the first time. Most appreciated its benefits, requesting sessions while on the road. This opened the door to even more referrals for athletes at all levels.

After 24 years in Charlotte, we moved to Nashville to help launch our first out-of-state office. In Nashville, artists and other industry professionals began coming in soon after we opened. Over the years, we have developed a formal Artists and Athletes program that involves enhanced confidentiality, flexibility, and specialized services. Our partnerships with exceptional nonprofits, including MusiCares (the charitable organization established by the National Academy of Recording Arts and Sciences, known for the Grammys), Fund Recovery, and others helped with funding and referrals, while other collaborations with organizations like ECCHO (formerly Touring Career Workshop) allowed us to provide on-site services backstage at major live events like Bonnaroo, CMA Fest, the CMA Awards, and professional sports tournaments.

A preferred referral relationship with a large Fortune 500 company furthered our referrals of high-net-worth individuals. Authentic relationships with the top private schools in both Charlotte and Nashville meant we were getting regular referrals of wealthy families as well. In short, though it was never part of a larger plan, we found ourselves with many wealthy and well-known individuals and their family members.

In recent years, psychologists could join an interstate compact called PsyPact, which allowed us to deliver mental health services via telehealth to the vast majority of U.S. states. As a result, this has opened up even greater access to touring musicians, professional athletes who play in a different state each week, actors on location, traveling businesspeople, social media celebrities who film in different locations, and a host of others.

Working with wealthy and well-known clients in therapy has been eye-opening. Not coming from a prominent family, I had no awareness of the unique issues these individuals face. I had a two-dimensional understanding of what it would be like to be wealthy or well known. It wasn't until much later that I saw all the nuance and complexity. I got a fuller glimpse of how the human experience, with all its entanglements, transcends socioeconomic status. It is this vision of our shared humanity that I hope to honor here.

THE PERKS AND PERILS OF PROMINENCE

Decades ago, authors Kurt Vonnegut and Joseph Heller were at a party hosted by a billionaire on Shelter Island. Vonnegut asked Heller how it felt to know that their host had made more money the day before than Heller's famous novel *Catch-22* had earned in its entire history. Heller's response was both simple and wise. He said, "I've got something he can never have."

Intrigued, Vonnegut asked, "And what is that?"

Heller replied, "The knowledge that I've got enough" (Housel, 2020).

Enough.

Wealth and fame provide comfort, afford luxuries, and open doors, but they can also create a never-ending cycle of desire and dissatisfaction when possessed by those ill-equipped to manage them.

Fame and fortune are not without their benefits, though. In the past, wealthy people could set up store tabs and pay at their leisure—or not pay at all. Today, the privileges of wealth and fame manifest in different ways. A wealthy or well-known person might get a table at a trendy restaurant and have the meal comped by the proprietor. They might receive free tickets to courtside seats at a Lakers game, courtesy of the team owner. Luxury brands pay them to wear a brand's clothing, jewelry, or watches. Some car brands, like Audi, have given away leases of their vehicles to famous people, and resorts might comp a stay in their presidential suites.

One film festival gave celebrities jackets retailing at around $700 and watches from a luxury manufacturer. A company producing baby products furnished the famous with their products for free. Being wealthy or well known has many perks, not the least of which are the many freebies. Anticipating special treatment is a nice benefit, too. Sometimes, not only does the celebrity get out of paying for a product or service but gets paid to be associated with it. Just wearing a nice pair of shoes to a media event might earn you a decent payday.

In college, I went to dinner at a restaurant with a very famous actress who was a close relative of one of my roommates. She had been a film actress before taking a starring role in a long-running series. There were about ten of us at the table. Toward the end of dinner, the manager approached the actress and asked if they could take her picture for the restaurant. She agreed if they knocked 25% off the bill, which they did without hesitation. Let's imagine the total bill with entrees, appetizers, drinks, and dessert before the discount was at least $600. The photo cost the restaurant $150, which I'm sure wiped out their entire profit margin. It was an early lesson in the power of fame. No one else at the table could exchange a picture of ourselves for $150. The thought is ludicrous. I doubt the restaurant recouped this loss in revenue just by having a framed picture of the actress in their lobby, but it was important enough to the management to make the trade.

The perks of fame are very real, but the price of fame is also steep. From the greater risk of early death for some, to the loss of privacy and normalcy, to higher rates of substance abuse struggles and relationship difficulties, fame is often not an easy road. Harrison Ford has said he has never liked fame, never felt the trade-offs were worth it. In an interview, he said, "There's nothing good about being famous.

You always think, 'If I'm successful, then I'll have opportunities.' You never figure the cost of fame will be a total loss of privacy. That's incalculable." He continued, "[Fame] was unanticipated and I've never enjoyed it. You can get the table you want in a restaurant. It gets you doctor's appointments. But what's that worth? Nothing" (Broverman, 2010).

Imagine a professional musician who grew up playing in bars, sweating and wailing onstage, then crashing hard afterward. Life on the road can be lonely. He's separated from his loved ones and cut off from those who know him. After the show, he has no incentive not to drink. He pays a visit to the downstairs hotel bar with a bandmate; then, alone later in his hotel room, the minibar looks enticing. It's easy for us to sit back in judgment when this guy gets a DUI, checks into rehab, or shows up in a drunken rage on a viral video. But how many people who drink a little now might drink a lot if we walked in his shoes?

Imagine that same guy having an attractive woman meet him backstage. She tells him how amazing he is and slips him her number. He's been away from his partner for a month. He's worn out and lonely. How would you do in that situation? Well-known people know that others are scrutinizing them. They realize others think their own judgment would be so much better if the roles were reversed. They feel the judgment, the spring-loaded responses ready to erupt at any hint of error, at any misstep.

If a normal person develops a drinking problem and goes to rehab, it stays between that person and their family and maybe a handful of others. If a famous person checks into rehab, there is a better than good chance half the world will know about it. Instead of respecting the person for their tough and thorny decision, people often criticize and deride them: The person is doing it to escape consequences, for publicity, or to convince us they've got a problem instead of just being a bad person. The pummeling continues.

A Harris Poll of 1,000 U.S. adults found that almost a third (31%) desire to be famous, despite everything we know about the downsides of fame (Taylor, 1998). There is evidence that celebrities may have shorter lifespans compared to the general population, and their lives are more frequently marked by fame-related stressors, substance abuse, and relationship turmoil (Kenny, 2014). Despite these facts, a sizable chunk of the population still desires to be a celebrity.

I cannot overstate this enough: both wealth and fame have the potential to be destructive to a person. Either can destroy relationships, warp personality, and lead to heartache and ruin. This is not always true, of course, but it is more frequently true than we wish it were. There is also the possibility that being rich and famous leads to a life of grand adventure and joy, but this does not happen without intentional effort on the person's part and the right circumstances. Despair and disappointment can come for us all, but the wealthy and well known have more paths to get there. They have both fortifications and vulnerabilities that others don't have.

The press and the public seem to meet each prominent person's arrest or moral lapse with a gleeful response. Breaking news of a popular musician's DUI lights up our phones with a tone ranging from snarky to mocking to moralistic. Comments from the public were even worse. There is a type of bloodsport in seeing a popular celebrity receive his perceived comeuppance. We love to see the mighty laid low. Being famous is not an easy experience.

In *The High Price of Materialism*, psychologist Tim Kasser argues that people who place a premium on materialistic values like wealth, status (fame), and attractiveness are at a far greater risk of depression, anxiety, and relationship problems (Kasser, 2002). Not that a famous or wealthy person is likely to be more depressed, but valuing fame and wealth makes you more vulnerable to distressing emotions and relational instability. Some people are rich or famous—or both—and do not value wealth or fame much at all. Others got there because it was precisely what they valued. It is the engine that drives them. These folks are the ones that are more susceptible to mental health problems and relationship conflicts.

A MAP FOR THE ROAD AHEAD

In the next chapter, we try to wrestle down two slippery concepts: how to define what it means to be wealthy, and what it means to be famous. These are difficult concepts to define. At what point are you rich in the United States? The median net worth for an adult in the United States is under $200,000. According to Schwab's 2024 Modern Wealth Survey, Americans believed you need a net worth of $2.5 million to be rich (Charles Schwab Corporation, 2024). However, the top 1% have $10.8 million, the top 2% have $2.5 million, and the top 5% have $1.03 million. Does a person have to be at the 98th percentile to be rich? Those at the 95th percentile have over five times the median net worth of the average American. Aren't they rich, too?

Wealth also varies by year and location; in Columbus, Ohio, $2.2 million might be considered rich, while in San Francisco, it might be closer to $5 million. There is no agreed-upon threshold of net worth or income that is true for all people in all places all the time. These subjective wealth standards change over time and across locations.

Fame is also complex. Tom Hanks, Taylor Swift, and LeBron James are undeniably famous. But what about William Fichtner? You might not recognize his name, but you've likely seen him in movies like *The Dark Knight* and *Armageddon*. Is he famous? How far down the credit list do we go before someone stops being famous? Is a starting point guard for the University of North Carolina famous? CEOs such as Satya Nadella of Microsoft and Sundar Pichai of Google/Alphabet are tech rock stars as leaders of huge, world-changing tech companies, but most people would not know their names. Are they famous? Like wealth, fame is difficult to define.

Part II begins with an in-depth, research-based discussion of both the benefits and challenges of being wealthy, as well as the impact of wealth on children. We then shift focus to famous people, including a special chapter on the risks and needs of child stars.

In Part III, we discuss the overlapping issues that are often true of both the wealthy and the well known, including how to help clients cope with a meteoric rise or catastrophic fall, build healthier relationships, manage substance abuse, and reduce narcissism.

Part IV, the final part of the book, emphasizes the importance of doing your own work around the themes of money and fame to be a more effective helping professional. We discuss some unique ethical challenges and practical considerations in working with wealthy and well-known clients.

Not all rich people have the same needs, nor do all famous people. Yet some common themes emerge in therapy. Among these two overlapping groups, there are big similarities and significant differences. For example, musicians and athletes have more similarities than differences in lifestyle, stressors, and personal characteristics, while actors and heirs are often worlds apart. The point is not to stereotype anyone, but to be ready for what issues might present themselves in therapy. In the end, wealthy and well-known people are flawed humans, just like the rest of us. They have the same universal human struggles, but they also have other challenges that make their lives complex.

AN INTEGRATED EVIDENCE-BASED TREATMENT (EBT) MODEL

Carl Sagan famously stated, "Extraordinary claims require extraordinary evidence" (Deming, 2016). This principle applies not only to the natural sciences, but also to social sciences. To support the effectiveness of our methods and strategies, we must rely on compelling evidence.

Mental health treatment has advanced significantly in recent decades, largely due to applying rigorous scientific research to clinical practice. EBTs are developed and validated through standardized research methods, particularly randomized controlled trials (RCTs), which measure a therapy's effectiveness against control groups. While no central authority designates treatments as evidence-based, professional organizations often establish criteria for this classification.

I will integrate three EBTs with proven track records: Cognitive-Behavioral Therapy (CBT), Motivational Interviewing (MI), and Schema Therapy, and discuss how they can be applied to our work with wealthy and well-known clients. Each of these has particular applications for the issues we will need to address. CBTs, particularly the "third-wave cognitive-behavioral treatments" like Acceptance and Commitment Therapy (ACT) and Dialectical Behavior Therapy (DBT), help a person navigate intense stressors, manage emotional regulation, and improve relationships (Stiglmayr et al., 2014; A-Tjak et al., 2015). MI is especially relevant to work with substance abuse, problem drinking, or other addictive behaviors (Lundahl et al., 2010), and Schema Therapy helps us with deeply entrenched personality patterns, like narcissism (Koppers et al., 2020; Rijkeboer et al., 2019), and promotes cognitive flexibility.

Using established EBTs enhances therapy outcomes by relying on proven interventions, leading to reduced symptoms, improved well-being, and higher rates of goal achievement while minimizing therapy dropout (Windle et al., 2020). Use of EBT also promotes transparency and accountability in mental health treatment, allowing therapists to justify their approach with evidence while giving clients confidence their therapy has a strong track record of demonstrated results.

SOME NOTES ABOUT STYLE AND CONTENT

I like to write in the same style I enjoy reading: conversational, less formal, with some good stories and illustrations, but packed with great content. That's the style I've adopted here, which may feel different from other professional texts. I also use first person throughout because I want it to feel like a shared journey, as well.

I love storytelling, but I have to be cautious here for two reasons. First, I can't share any story that gives the slightest hint that might identify a well-known person. When I tell a story about a client, I have double- and triple-disguised it. I might say it's a football player when it is a basketball player or even an actor. I change locations and descriptions and other facts. I can't have anyone knowing the real details of a prominent client's life. When I talk about people by name, like Shawn Mendes postponing his tour for mental health reasons, be assured that they have never been my client and I am not disclosing anything confidential.

The second reason I have to be cautious is because I wouldn't want one of my clients or prospective clients worrying that I would ever come close to sharing their confidential information. I want no doubt that what they share with me is always kept private. For the reader, there is no point in trying to guess. You don't know who I am talking about, nor can you figure it out.

The later chapters draw from treatment models like Motivational Interviewing, Schema Therapy, and Cognitive-Behavioral Therapy. I give a solid understanding and a "starter set" of skills for these therapies, but don't be under the misconception that this text is a comprehensive or sufficient source that will equip you to be fully proficient in those models. If you have training and experience in these models, then this text will show you how you may apply to work with wealthy and well-known clients. If these treatments seem to be a good fit for you, I urge you to get more detailed instruction, training, and supervision.

There's a lot to cover here. Let's begin by exploring what it means to be rich or famous. As you'll see, that's far more difficult to define than you might expect.

NOTE

1 Dickinson, E. (1890). *Poems by Emily Dickinson* (M. L. Todd & T. W. Higginson, Eds.). Roberts Brothers.

REFERENCES

A-Tjak, J. G. L., Davis, M. L., Morina, N., Powers, M. B., Smits, J. A. J., & Emmelkamp, P. M. G. (2015). A meta-analysis of the efficacy of acceptance and commitment therapy for clinically relevant mental and physical health problems. *Psychotherapy and Psychosomatics, 84*(1), 30–36.

Broverman, A. (2010, February 25). Harrison Ford: "Nothing good about fame." *Digital Spy.* https://www.digitalspy.com/showbiz/a205348/harrison-ford-nothing-good-about-fame/

Charles Schwab Corporation. (2024, August 21). *Schwab survey reveals that Americans think it takes $2.5 million to be considered wealthy in 2024.* Charles Schwab Newsroom.

Deming, D. (2016). Do extraordinary claims require extraordinary evidence? *Philosophia, 44*(4), 1319–1331. https://doi.org/10.1007/s11406-016-9779-7

Housel, M. (2020). *The psychology of money: Timeless lessons on wealth, greed, and happiness.* Harriman House.

Kasser, T. (2002). *The high price of materialism.* MIT Press.

Kenny, D. T. (2014). Stairway to hell: Life and death in the pop music industry. *The Conversation.*

Koppers, D., Van, H., Peen, J., & Dekker, J. J. M. (2020). Psychological symptoms, early maladaptive schemas and schema modes: Predictors of the outcome of group schema therapy in patients with personality disorders. *Psychotherapy Research, 31*(7), 831–842. https://doi.org/10.1080/10503307.2020.1852482

Lundahl, B. W., Kunz, C., Brownell, C., Tollefson, D., & Burke, B. L. (2010). A meta-analysis of motivational interviewing: Twenty-five years of empirical studies. *Research on Social Work Practice, 20*(2), 137–160. https://doi.org/10.1177/1049731509347850

Rijkeboer, M. M., van den, O. M. W., & Bernstein, D. P. (2019). Change processes in schema therapy: A qualitative investigation of patient experiences. *Journal of Clinical Psychology, 75*(11), 2125–2140.

Stiglmayr, C., Stecher-Mohr, J., Wagner, T., Meißner, J., Spretz, D., Steffens, C., Roepke, S., Fydrich, T., Salbach-Andrae, H., Schulze, J., & Renneberg, B. (2014). Effectiveness of dialectic behavioral therapy in routine outpatient care: The Berlin Borderline study. *Borderline Personality Disorder and Emotional Dysregulation, 1*(20). https://doi.org/10.1186/2051-6673-1-20

Taylor, H. (1998, September 9). *The Harris Poll #46: Most people say they have no desire to be famous.* https://www.harrisinteractives.com/harris_poll/index-PID-162.html

Windle, E., Tee, H., Sabitova, A., Jovanovic, N., Priebe, S., & Carr, C. (2020). Association of patient treatment preference with dropout and clinical outcomes in adult psychosocial mental health interventions: A systematic review and meta-analysis. *JAMA Psychiatry*, 77(3), 294–302. https://doi.org/10.1001/jamapsychiatry.2019.3750

Chapter 2

Defining Wealthy and Well Known

The Emmy-winning TV series *Succession* puts us inside the complex power dynamics of an uber-wealthy dysfunctional family. We watch as each member navigates the cutthroat world of corporate politics, betrayal, and sibling rivalry while vying for control of their father's media empire. In one episode, Greg, perhaps the closest to an "everyman" character on the show, talks to his cousin, Connor Roy, and his boss and cousin-in-law, Tom, about how he now feels financially secure.

Greg: I was just talking to my mom and she said, apparently, he'll leave me five million, anyway. So, I'm golden, baby!

Connor: You can't do anything with five, Greg. Five's a nightmare.

Greg: Is it?

Connor: Oh, yeah. Can't retire. Not worth it to work. Oh, yes. Five will drive you un poco loco, my fine-feathered friend.

Tom: Poorest rich person in America. The world's tallest dwarf.

Connor: The weakest strongman at the circus (Armstrong & Mylod, 2019).

The sharp dialogue invites the question: Is Greg, with his $5 million inheritance, a wealthy man or simply the "poorest rich person in America?"

Wealth and fame are both hard to define. Have you heard of James Donaldson, an internet influencer from North Carolina? As of this writing, James has around 325 million subscribers on YouTube. Going by the name "MrBeast," his videos have over 52 billion views. *Time* magazine named him one of the 100 Most Influential People in 2023. He has won two Nickelodeon Kids' Choice Awards in back-to-back years. His estimated net worth is over $500 million. There's no dispute he is wealthy, but is he famous? It's doubtful you have heard of him, but some of his videos far surpass Super Bowl games, the series finale of *M*A*S*H*, and the highest-rated broadcast and cable shows in viewership.

Who is wealthy? Who is famous? Is cousin Greg wealthy with his $5 million? Is MrBeast famous with his 52 billion views, even though you may never have

DOI: 10.4324/9781003503569-3

heard of him? How do we define these concepts? We are unlikely to get to a clear consensus answer. Wealth and fame, subjective and slippery to define, both exist on a continuum.

In 1964, an obscenity case before the Supreme Court forced the justices to define hardcore pornography, a task more easily said than done. Despite its apparent simplicity, the distinction proved difficult due to numerous variables. If they ruled too broadly, legitimate works of art with sensual content might be regarded as obscene. While the other judges struggled to create specific standards, this challenge led Justice Potter Stewart to write in his famous opinion, "I shall not today attempt further to define the kinds of material I understand to be embraced, but *I know it when I see it.*"

The "I know it when I see it" test seems appropriate for a lot of hard-to-define areas, including what it means to be rich or famous. It may be more complicated. While it may seem simple, you'll see clear and consistent definitions are elusive.

However, I am going to propose some good ways of thinking about both concepts. Having clear-cut lines for wealth or fame is less important than having good ways to conceptualize these constructs. Let's begin by contemplating what it means to be wealthy.

WHAT QUALIFIES AS WEALTHY?

Actress and singer Marlene Dietrich wrote, "There is a gigantic difference between earning a great deal of money and being rich" (Dietrich, 2012). Wealth professionals agree with her. Wealth seems to be less about earning a big paycheck. If it's not about having a huge income, what makes someone rich?

Business Insider asked a group of financial planners how they would define wealth. They gave vastly different answers. Responses ranged from financial security, to job freedom, to the ability to pursue personal fulfillment (Abramson, 2020). Three key points emerge from the responses, however. First, no consensus exists on what constitutes wealth. There are no unified standards or benchmarks. Second, even if we could come up with a consensus dollar amount, that number would change so much over time as to be of no value. Factors like inflation, the state of the economy, geography, and other variables all influence that dollar amount. It becomes a moving target. Third, the notion of freedom comes up a lot. Freedom to do as you wish. Freedom to pursue things aligned with your personal goals. Freedom from worry. This is a pleasant idea, but it does not help us define wealth.

After reviewing dozens of articles, books, and videos, I can honestly conclude that there is not yet an objective standard that defines wealth. There are too many variables and no clear criteria. For example, we might learn that $3.8 million of net worth puts someone at the 90th percentile for wealth. Is the 90th percentile a sufficient cutoff? Why not the 95th percentile? Does it matter if we use the mean or the median? (Hint: it does—a lot!) What if that person spends more money per year than he makes? Do we adjust the numbers in line with inflation and other economic indicators?

The concept of wealth defies easy definition. Yet, amid this ambiguity, one thing is clear: wealth is more about net worth than income. Unlike income, which can be a fleeting and unreliable gauge, net worth offers a more stable and comprehensive measure of true financial standing. It's the grand total of all assets—cash in the bank, investments, retirement funds, property, and more—minus the sum of all debts, from mortgage balances to credit card debts. It's a delicate balance sheet, revealing not just what you earn, but what you keep.

Income, while significant, is not the ultimate yardstick of wealth. An avalanche of expenses, bills, and debt can overshadow high earnings, leaving a person less wealthy despite their impressive paycheck. On the flip side, substantial assets can paint a different picture. Imagine someone with $2 million tucked away in various accounts. This individual might be wealthy, even if their annual income is modest because they aren't burning through their earnings like someone living paycheck to paycheck.

Financial professionals don't always agree, but many would categorize wealth based on liquid assets, which are funds that can be converted to cash, excluding the value of high-end possessions like houses. We might divide the categories like this:

- *High Net Worth:* $1 million to $5 million in liquid assets.
- *Very High Net Worth:* $5 million to $30 million in liquid assets.
- *Ultra High Net Worth:* Over $30 million in liquid assets.

People in all three categories would be wealthy, but where you live affects your relative wealth. Having $1 million in Cedar Rapids provides greater financial freedom than $2 million in San Francisco, where the cost of living is much higher.

THE TOP 1% AND INCOME DISTRIBUTION

Discussions about wealth often reference the "Top 1%." However, defining this group is challenging because of inconsistent data. Though these numbers will change over time, I share some here to illustrate the contrasts between the variability of estimates and standards. According to the Economic Policy Institute, a median annual income of $823,763 places someone in the top 1%, while Forbes estimates this figure at $597,815. That is a significant difference.

State-by-state variations are also significant. For instance, earning $350,212 annually in West Virginia places someone in the top 1%, but the threshold in Connecticut is $896,490. The top 1% often dominate discussions on wealth, but they are not the only people who are wealthy. Most financial professionals accept that individuals in the top 2%, or even the top 5%, are wealthy. Many would even consider the top 10% to be deemed wealthy.

The specific numbers change from year to year, of course. The leap from 2% to 1% is remarkable. The top 1% have, on average, almost $8 million more net worth than the top 2% (Hines, 2014). This is because the top 1% of wealthy individuals include billionaires and those who possess hundreds of millions of dollars, skewing the distribution. The wealthiest people in our society are a class apart.

As you see, wealth is a complex and subjective concept influenced by net worth, financial freedom, and public perception. While income plays a role, net worth provides a more stable and comprehensive measure of wealth. The definitions and thresholds of wealth can vary by wide margins based on location, individual circumstances, and societal standards.

A Harris Poll found over two-thirds (68%) of Americans define wealth as the ability to live without financial anxieties, not an extravagant lifestyle. Almost half (48%) said it was the ability to afford their basic lifestyle with a little left over. Only about 1 in 10 (11%) considered wealth to be when a person can afford "extravagant purchases" (Becker, 2023).

Most importantly, wealth is best defined as someone with enough net worth to live comfortably while having freedom from the financial worries that so many others experience.

WHAT MAKES SOMEONE FAMOUS?

At a pop culture convention where I was speaking, I found myself wandering through the crowded exhibit hall. Thousands of attendees buzzed with excitement as they explored the booths. Ahead of me, a line of people stood, waiting eagerly for something—or someone. Their faces showed anticipation and joy. As I got closer, I realized they were waiting to meet an actor from a TV series with a cult following. I had no idea who he was.

This encounter highlights a significant shift in the nature of fame. Today, someone can be famous to one group of people while remaining completely unknown to others. Fame no longer requires universal recognition. It's now possible to achieve celebrity status by building a dedicated audience within a specific niche.

This change reflects broader shifts in culture. Decades ago, fame was more centralized. Figures like Marilyn Monroe, Johnny Carson, and Walter Cronkite were widely recognized because media was limited to a few major networks and publications. The same celebrities dominated every household. Today, fame has fragmented. Digital platforms and social media have made fame more accessible, allowing people to gain significant followings in smaller, specialized communities.

Take YouTube star MrBeast, for example. His videos have been watched billions of times, and he has millions of fans who view him as a major celebrity. Yet, many people outside of YouTube have never heard of him. Similarly, reality TV stars might be household names to fans of *The Real Housewives* or *Love Island*, but they are virtually unknown to others.

Fame has become increasingly niche, with different groups celebrating their own figures of influence. Traditional fame—where celebrities were universally known—still exists, but it's now just one piece of a much larger and more complex picture.

THE RARITY OF FAME

While fame seems more accessible because of digital platforms, it remains rare. Mathematician Samuel Arbesman proposed a formula to estimate how many people are truly famous. Using Wikipedia's "Living People" category, which includes individuals considered notable, he divided that number by the world population. At the time, the calculation suggested that only 0.0086% of people could be considered famous (Arbesman, 2013).

Even this number likely overestimates true fame. Many people listed in Wikipedia's database are notable for specific achievements—like setting a sports record or writing a book—but are not famous in a cultural sense. Fame that extends beyond niche recognition is an even smaller fraction of this already tiny percentage.

FAME VS. INFLUENCE

Fame and influence are often conflated, but they are not the same. Someone can be famous without making a meaningful impact, while others can profoundly shape the world without widespread recognition.

Norman Borlaug is a good example of this distinction. He was an agricultural scientist whose work in developing high-yield wheat strains helped avert massive famines in countries such as India and Mexico. His innovations likely saved over a billion lives, earning him the Nobel Peace Prize and the Presidential Medal of Freedom. Yet, despite his monumental contributions, Borlaug is not a household name.

On the other hand, many reality TV stars achieve fame without having any significant cultural impact. Their recognition often comes from visibility rather than from meaningful contributions. Fame is about being known, while influence is about making a difference. One does not necessarily imply the other.

THE Q-SCORE: MEASURING TRADITIONAL FAME

For decades, the entertainment industry used a tool called the Q-Score to measure fame. Created in 1964, the Q-Score assessed both recognition and public sentiment. People were asked if they recognized a celebrity and whether they had a positive, negative, or neutral impression of them. A high Q-Score indicated widespread recognition and likability, while a low Q-Score could suggest limited appeal or even active dislike.

The Q-Score shaped decisions in casting, endorsements, and marketing. Celebrities like Tom Hanks and Morgan Freeman, who are both highly recognizable and well liked, have traditionally had high Q-Scores. Conversely, polarizing figures like Kim Kardashian often score low, despite their large followings.

However, the Q-Score has become less relevant in today's fragmented media landscape. Social media platforms provide a more direct measure of visibility and engagement. Metrics such as follower counts and engagement rates are often seen as better indicators of modern fame, even if they don't fully capture public sentiment. While recognizability is still the most important aspect of fame, there is a growing consensus that influence is more important than likability.

This shift highlights how fame has evolved. Traditional fame was easier to measure because it relied on broad public recognition. Modern fame, spread across niches and digital platforms, is harder to quantify.

THE CHANGING CRITERIA OF FAME

The criteria for fame have also changed. In the past, fame depended on traditional media visibility—appearances in major publications, TV shows, or films. While these markers are still relevant, social media has introduced new ways to achieve fame.

Platforms like TikTok, Instagram, and YouTube allow people to reach millions of followers with consistent content. Viral moments, sponsorships, and collaborations now serve as milestones of success. Recognition is often segmented by demographics. Younger audiences may know TikTok stars like Charli D'Amelio, while older generations are more familiar with figures like Oprah Winfrey.

Influence has become the defining feature of modern fame. It's not just about being recognized, but about having the power to shape opinions, trends, and behaviors. A digital creator with millions of followers might launch a trend or mobilize a movement in ways that traditional celebrities never could.

Modern fame is a mosaic of niches and platforms. It's defined no longer by universal recognition, but by deep connections within specific communities. A famous person today might be deeply known by one group while remaining completely unknown to others. Fame is still powerful, but it looks very different from how it did a few decades ago.

TOWARD CONSENSUS STANDARDS OF WEALTH AND FAME

Metrics such as net worth and Q-Scores may set benchmarks but cannot show what it really means to be wealthy or famous. These statuses shape people's lives and influence their relationships, opportunities, and personal struggles. Focusing on the underlying concepts rather than rigid criteria allows us to gain a deeper understanding of the human experience behind these labels and gives us a more nuanced and empathetic perspective. Having wealth and fame means much more than simply looking at numbers. The special privileges come with power and influence and freedom, but they bring additional challenges that most of us don't face.

To define wealth and fame for this book, let me propose the following practical definitions, along with some additional commentary that explains their importance and application to our work.

Defining Wealth

How do we define "wealthy"? We focus on the combination of high net worth and financial freedom. *We measure wealth as high net worth, typically $1 million or more, and the freedom to live a lifestyle without financial anxiety.* High income alone does not equate to wealth. If someone earns $50,000 a month but spends the same amount or more, they are probably not wealthy unless they have additional net worth. Depending on the lifestyle, income may or may not be important to sustaining this economic status, but the two key elements of net worth and the freedom to live without financial worries define wealth. Whether their lifestyle is modest, like Warren Buffett, or extravagant, like Kim Kardashian, what matters most is financial freedom. The freedom to live as you desire without worry is the heart of wealth.

Defining Fame

Fame today goes beyond being known by the general population. It now includes those with widespread recognition within specific communities or subcultures, regardless of whether they are famous to the broader public.

Based on this, we will define fame as *widespread recognition that evokes strong emotional reactions, whether admiration or dislike, from many people, often within the millions.* It exists within subcultures where individuals have influence and recognition, even if unknown by the public. Now you can be "Bravo Famous" or "TikTok Famous" or "Twitch Streamer Famous," all while being unknown to the larger culture.

THE EVOLUTION OF CONCEPTS

As society continues to evolve, our concepts of wealth and fame must grow as well, embracing the human experiences that lie behind these powerful labels. For example, in the 1990s, our new notion of decentralized, highly segmented fame would have been inconceivable, but social media and other technological shifts have radically refashioned this construct. A few decades from now, we will undoubtedly see a new conception of fame that we cannot yet imagine. Now, let's look at the foundations for the model we will use to help them navigate their common hardships and challenges.

REFERENCES

Abramson, A. (2020). How financial planners define wealth. *Business Insider*. https://www.businessinsider.com

Arbesman, S. (2013). The rarity of fame: An analysis. *Wired*. https://www.wired.com

Armstrong, J., & Mylod, M. (2019). *Succession* [Television series]. HBO.

Becker, S. (2023). The psychology of wealth in America. *Harris Poll*. https://theharrispoll.com

Dietrich, M. (2012). *Marlene Dietrich: Life and legacy*. HarperCollins Publishers.

Hines, D. (2014). *Wealth distribution in the United States*. Economic Policy Institute.

Part II

The Needs of Wealthy and Well-Known People

Chapter 3

Wealthy People, Part 1
The Benefits of Being Rich

My client, the young adult son of an uber-wealthy man, had just returned from an overseas trip, having flown in two nights before. He was still a little tired when he plopped down on my couch that morning, holding a large Starbucks coffee.

"Where did you go?" I asked.

"Zimbabwe," he replied.

"That's interesting. Why Zimbabwe?"

"My parents and I wanted to see Victoria Falls," he said. "We just went a couple of weeks ago, kind of spur of the moment."

"How was it?" I asked.

"It was just spectacular. It was one of the most beautiful things I've ever seen. One of the most beautiful things in the entire world. I'll never forget it," he said.

"I'm sure being able to travel like that has been a great experience for you and your family," I said.

"Oh, yeah," he replied. "My dad calls it 'cultural grazing' where we can just go see something amazing—the Taj Mahal, Big Ben, Machu Picchu, the Pyramids, the Sydney Opera House—and then be back in our normal routine a couple of days later." He added, "I don't take it for granted."

"It sounds wonderful to do all that," I said.

"Yeah, for sure," he said. "I know it's obvious, but there are a lot of advantages to being rich."

He's right. Being wealthy has a lot of advantages. Whether it's traveling to exotic locations, paying for private education, affording excellent healthcare, or countless other perks, rich people live enviable lives. As you'll see, wealth not only gives a person more options and more privileges, but it also comes with some personal qualities that create even greater benefit in the social, emotional, and financial domains of life.

DOI: 10.4324/9781003503569-5

WEALTH AND WELL-BEING

You may have heard it said that the rich are miserable, unhappy people, but that's not what the research says. Studies find an inverse relationship between wealth and depression (Ettman et al., 2020). As wealth goes up, depression goes down. Wealth protects people against depression when life comes at them hard. It buffers them when they face a job loss or other financial setbacks. Another study tells us that a family's wealth protects the mental health of their young adult children. These well-off families had young adult children with better mental health on average, as compared to less wealthy peers (Le-Scherban et al., 2016)

Wealth functions as a safeguard against depression and anxiety. Not only does it give a person or family access to better care, but it also serves as a bulwark against stressors that other non-wealthy people face. The World Economic Forum finds that individuals in low-income households are less emotionally and physically resilient because of their lack of resources and their diminished opportunities. A person with lower income is up to three times more likely than a wealthier person to be diagnosed with depression and anxiety, especially in countries with significant income inequality, like the United States (Ridley et al., 2020). With these emotional struggles, it is better to be rich than poor.

Research by Kahneman and Deaton (2020) distinguishes between two aspects of subjective well-being: emotional well-being, which is the quality of daily emotional experiences; and life evaluation, which are thoughts about one's life contentment. Analyzing over 450,000 responses from the Gallup-Healthways Well-Being Index, they found that income and education are more closely linked to life evaluation, while factors like health, caregiving, and loneliness are stronger predictors of daily emotions. While both life evaluation and emotional well-being increase with income, emotional well-being was found to plateau beyond an annual income of about $75,000. High income contributes to life satisfaction but not always happiness, while low income is linked to both low life evaluation and emotional distress, especially during difficult circumstances (Kahneman & Deaton, 2020).

A 2018 study by Andrew Jebb and his colleagues at Purdue University identified $95,000 as the ideal income level for life satisfaction. They found that once people reached this threshold, further increases in income resulted in reduced life satisfaction. After they meet basic financial needs—mortgage and car payments, loan repayments, and so on—the focus shifts to gaining more and engaging in social comparisons. This mindset, the researchers argue, lowers well-being and life satisfaction (Jebb et al., 2018).

Another study disputed these conclusions, claiming that life satisfaction increased up to $500,000 of annual income. The most intriguing aspect of this study, however, was not just the potential connection between income or net worth with increased life satisfaction and well-being, but how its impact relied on the emotional state of the person. For about 15% of people who had high income, the money made little difference. They were the *unhappy rich*. These were people struggling with grief, depression, heartbreak, or other negative emotional experiences. The researcher, Michael Killingsworth, said, "If you're rich and miserable, more money won't matter." Another 30% of the study participants said their happiness increased after they earned more than $100,000. These folks got happier as they got richer (Killingsworth, 2024).

Most people in the United States believe there is a connection between money and happiness, though they disagree on how much money brings joy and contentment. An Empower/Harris Poll of over 2,000 adult Americans found that the majority (59%) believe more money can make them happy. How much would they need to be happy? According to the survey, the average person believes having $1.2 million in the bank would be the ticket to happiness. They also believe they need an annual income of $284,167 on average to have a happy life. The survey found some fascinating differences between the generations. When asked how much net worth and annual income they would require to be happy, here's what they said:

- Boomers—$124,000 in annual income with a net worth of $999,945
- Gen X—$130,000 in annual income with a net worth of $1,213,759
- Millennials—$525,000 in annual income with a net worth of $1,699,571
- Gen Z—$128,000 in annual income with a net worth of $487,711

Besides generational differences, there were gender differences. The Harris Poll also found men believed they need $381,000 worth of income each year to secure long-term happiness, but women said they needed $183,000, less than half of what men thought they needed (Empower, 2023).

Studies on the link between money and happiness produce different results regarding how much money leads to well-being. Their conclusions vary by age, gender, socioeconomic status, and baseline emotional functioning. The studies may also produce discrepant results based on when the study was done. It's likely that studies conducted during times of economic hardship and recession will differ from those completed in a thriving economy.

There's one other reason the research comes to different conclusions. Laura Kudrna and Kostadin Kushlev (2022) make the case that the way researchers analyze data on income and well-being makes a big difference in what they find. Some studies that categorized subjects (wealthy vs. not wealthy) found differences, whereas research using regression formulas did not, even when analyzing the same data sets. They write, "Not all analytic approaches generate the same results, which may contribute to explaining discrepant results in existing studies about the correlates of happiness." This underscores how complex this topic is, and why different studies might come to different conclusions.

If we stop trying to pin down some specific dollar amount where well-being occurs, we realize most of the research agrees on a central conclusion: wealth serves as a protective factor against emotional disorders like depression and anxiety. There are many wealthy people who are unhappy, but they are likely to have been unhappy with or without money. For most people, being wealthy leads to greater emotional well-being and less distressing emotions.

There are different aspects of happiness, like overall well-being, freedom from negative emotions, and experiencing positive emotions. We find wealth protects a person from intense negative feelings, but can we say wealthy people feel more positive emotions than others? Again, the research paints a complicated picture. Paul Piff and Jake Moskowitz, researchers at the University of California, Irvine, examined the relationship between household income and positive emotions, including awe, compassion, contentment, love, and pride. Wealthy people felt more personal contentment and pride, while those with lower income felt greater compassion, love for others, and a sense of awe. If you notice, wealthier people's positive feelings are more self-oriented, while the positive emotions of less wealthy people are more other-centered. Pride vs. compassion. Personal contentment vs. love for others. There are all positive emotions, but the rich have more self-centered pleasures and joy, while the less wealthy often experience more other-centered positive emotions (Piff & Moskowitz, 2018).

Catherine Ettman and her colleagues did a stellar job of summarizing the wealth and well-being research, showing how studies have posed and answered questions around the topic (Ettman et al., 2022). Here's just a sample of the conclusions they found in looking over 20 years of research:

- Wealth is associated with better general mental health.
- Wealth protects well-being following the onset of a disability.
- High housing costs negatively affect the emotional well-being of older Americans.
- Psycho-education on strategic savings plans can improve women's mental health.

There's not much of a case to be made that rich people are less happy than others. People with higher levels of income have fewer struggles with mental health issues compared to those with lower income levels (Liu et al., 2023). Across cultures, depression and anxiety are up to three times more likely for individuals with lower incomes, especially in countries like the United States, with significant income inequality and weak unemployment protection (Gallup, 2023).

After we sift through all the research, we find that rich people aren't a miserable lot. Having lots of money, it seems, creates greater safety and well-being for most people. The wealthy also feel positive emotions, albeit more about their own status and achievements. However, rich people who are unhappy appear to be chronically unhappy. No amount of money caused it or can fix it. The unhappy rich would have been unhappy if they were poor. There isn't something inherent to wealth that makes someone miserable. We can put to rest the idea that being rich makes someone joyless and depressed.

WEALTH AND PRIVILEGE

Wealth has sprawling privilege. It's not just that they have money, but that money brings more influential connections, willingness to grant special favors, and access to more opportunities. Whether that is getting their high-schooler a coveted internship, getting impossible tickets to a major event, or getting free upgrades in hotels, the wealthy are the beneficiaries of great privilege.

Take college admission as a good example. Attending an elite university opens up doors of opportunity for young adults, not just because of the prestige of a name like Harvard or Princeton or Stanford, but because of the high-level connections you have access to at those institutions. Graduates of these schools become CEOs, top income earners (0.1%), journalists at the top newspapers (e.g., *New York Times*, *Wall Street Journal*), and U.S. senators at disproportionate rates. Among middle-class kids who earn scores at the 99th percentile on either the ACT or the SAT, only about 10% attend one of the 12 most elite universities, including the Ivy League schools and other top schools like Duke or MIT. However, almost 50% of students from very rich families are admitted into those schools. Research finds it's better to be rich than smart for college acceptance and career earnings. There is a baked-in advantage to being wealthy. As in many areas, the rich enjoy tremendous privilege regarding college admissions and post-college career opportunities.

TRAITS AND CHARACTERISTICS OF THE WEALTHY

I had a session with a young adult guy when his father came up in conversation. The son was brainstorming how to approach his dad about a business proposition that would require an investment from his dad and perhaps other wealthy people his dad knew. It puzzled me how much this young man was trying to game-out the conversation in advance. Every statement seemed like a chess move, rather than an honest communication. "If I say this, he might say . . ."

"What would happen if you just asked him directly?" I asked.

"Who knows?" he said. "I've known the man for 25 years and I have no idea. In some ways, he's amazingly predictable, but in other ways, you could never guess how he'd respond."

"From what you've told me of your dad, it seems like he would value directness and honesty," I said.

"You'd think," he said, "but that's not how it works. He's not like other people," he said, then added, "*Rich people aren't like other people.*"

Those words rang in my head. He wasn't bragging about himself or his dad, nor was he bragging about his rich family. He meant the rich are psychologically distinct, echoing the F. Scott Fitzgerald short story, *The Rich Boy:* "Let me tell you about the very rich. They are different from you and me" (Fitzgerald, 1926). They think differently, behave differently, and relate differently. I wondered if all that was true. The more I dug into the research, the more I saw he was right. As Rainer Zitelmann wrote for *Fortune* magazine, "Rich people become rich because they act differently from others. And they act differently because they think, make decisions, and react differently than most people" (Zitelmann, 2019).

For his book, *Change Your Habits, Change Your Life*, financial expert Thomas Corley examined the lives of 177 "self-made millionaires" over five years. He found they shared six traits: passion, persistence, patience, focus, work ethic, and desire to learn. He found these wealthy people wrote out annual and monthly goals, worked over 50 hours a week on average, and engaged in their own daily self-improvement and business development reading. Half of them got up three hours before their workdays began. These people were driven, passionate, and full of physical and emotional energy (Corley, 2016). These are all impressive and admirable traits. Other psychological research confirms these but also finds some less desirable and problematic characteristics. The more we understand, the better we can help.

There are some traits that affluent people have more often compared to others, some of which are a tremendous benefit to them, while others set them up for struggle and relationship troubles. These traits create a portrait of people who experience life differently from most others. Here are some key traits that distinguish the wealthy from others, based on the research:

The Wealthy Have a Distinct Five-Factor Personality Profile

There are about 2,500 personality tests on the market, all with different degrees of reliability and validity. These instruments often take different forms and measure various traits. However, the best research on the structure of personality reveals we can condense most of our measured personality traits into five major categories, each composed of more specific subcategories. While the concepts originated in the late 1940s, it wasn't until 1992 that psychologists developed an instrument to measure these five core personality factors. These factors, along with their associated subfactors, provide a broad taxonomy of personality traits. Despite some debate within the academic community, this perspective remains accepted today.

Each of these traits is on a continuum with every person rating between low and high. These five core personality traits make up the acronym OCEAN:

- *Openness:* Those who rate high on openness are open to new experiences and ideas. They appreciate the arts and aesthetics, and they are imaginative and creative.

- *Conscientiousness:* Those high in conscientiousness are organized, structured, reliable, and consistent.
- *Extraversion:* Group interactions energize those high in extraversion. They are talkative and outgoing. They enjoy meeting new people.
- *Agreeableness:* Those high in agreeableness are trusting, kind, and cooperative. They avoid conflict and show genuine empathy.
- *Neuroticism:* Those high in neuroticism are moody and prone to negative emotions. They don't cope well with stress.

A research team of economists and psychologists interviewed and collected test data on wealthy people, then compared their results to the general population. These researchers found the personality structures of rich people differed significantly from the non-rich. The wealthy were more open to new ideas and new experiences. They were more structured, consistent, and goal-directed than others. More often than not, they were extraverted and gregarious. However, they were less agreeable than other people, more prone to arguments, and less willing to back down in conflicts. The wealthy also seem to be less prone to strong negative emotions. Other studies have supported these findings. To summarize, compared to the average, wealthy people are:

O—More open to new ideas (High Openness)
C—More orderly, reliable, and conscientious (High Conscientiousness)
E—More outgoing, gregarious, and extraverted (High Extraversion)
A—Less agreeable, more argumentative, and combative (Low Agreeableness)
N—Less prone to negative emotions (Less Neurotic)

As with all psychological research, these traits are not true of all people or higher-income individuals, but they are typical (Leckelt et al., 2022a; Flinn et al., 2024).

Wealthy People Are Less Impulsive

We might expect wealthy people to become more impulsive in their spending. After all, they have much more money to sling around. The research, however, says the opposite. Biljanovska and Palligkinis (2018) found that wealthier individuals are more likely to have better self-control than others who are not wealthy. Research has found that impulsive spenders are more likely to get behind on their debt payments, to get into more financial distress, and to continue to accumulate debt (Gathergood, 2012). The sad irony is that the wealthy are more strategic and frugal with money, while those who struggle with money are more likely to spend impulsively, which leads to even greater financial struggle.

A financial planner told me, "Money is about behavior. It's not about how much you have. It's your mindset." There is a paradox to money and self-control. In this

29

sense, it is more likely for the rich to get richer because they invest their money and allow it to compound and grow, while the poor get poorer because they are more likely to have less financial self-control, get into debt, then drive themselves further into debt as the cycle continues. Psychologists believe scarcity can trigger people with less income. Their anxiety is that if they don't get something now while they have the money in hand, they may never get it, almost in the same way that children raised in orphanages might hoard food.

Wealth gives someone a sense of security that can extinguish that impulse and allow them to resist the urge to buy things they don't need. Of course, this is idiosyncratic. Some wealthy people are impulsive with their spending, and many lower-income individuals show remarkable frugality and restraint. For most, though, wealth can contribute to greater self-control with spending, but also in other areas that require self-discipline and restraint.

The Wealthy Take More Risks

If wealthy people are less impulsive than average, you'd also expect them to take fewer risks, but the opposite is true. Rich people are bigger risk-takers. They may be frugal with money, but when the time is right, they take big chances. They go for big payoffs. All this is possible because they have greater margin for failure.

There are two types of risk-taking: negative risk-taking and positive risk-taking. Negative risk-taking is often the kind we see in adolescence: driving too fast, jumping into the quarry lake, having unprotected sex, using drugs. These types of risk involve some sort of thrill but have the potential for great harm. Positive risk-taking involves stepping out and often leads to personal growth. Teenagers might try out for a play, switch positions in their sport, ask their crush out on a date, take a challenging class, or take a study-abroad trip.

Leckelt and his colleagues examined data sets including over 1,100 wealthy people and found they differed from less affluent people in their risk tolerance (Leckelt et al., 2022b). A person's willingness to take risks is an important predictor in many key economic behaviors like investing, starting businesses, running successful businesses, and wealth creation (Mata et al., 2018; Caliendo et al., 2014).

Wealthy people take positive risks. They start new companies, invest in new ventures, and take good chances. Not only does their wealth give them confidence to step out and make bold moves, but it is often those bold moves that brought them their wealth. Yes, some are cautious, plodding investors, but many rich people enjoy taking enormous risks. Not that they are reckless or loose with money. Quite the contrary—they are shrewd. When the right opportunities open up, they are quick to pounce and take the risk. If it doesn't work out, they chalk it up to a "lesson learned" and look for the next exciting venture.

Wealthy People Are More Intuitive

Historian and sociologist Rainer Zitelmann found the super-rich often cut against the tide, taking positions that were not often held by others. He concluded these wealthy people made decisions based on intuition more than on a cold analysis of facts. They seem to have less emotional responding but more intuitive decision-making (Zitelmann, 2019).

The rich take more risks, yet they don't act on impulse. Instead, they make more calculated decisions. However, they make these decisions not only with hard data and analysis, but by intuition, allowing years of investing and other financial ventures to inform their choices.

Huang and Pierce (2015) examined the decision-making processes of angel investors. These are early investors who must decide whether an unproven venture is worth the gamble of a large amount of their money. Yes, they look at the numbers and projections, but they also listen to their gut. The researchers concluded, "they rely on a combination of expertise-based intuition and formal analysis in which intuition trumps analysis."

Wealthy People Have an Internal Locus of Control

Research has uncovered a mindset that helps wealthy people succeed: While many of us blame external circumstances for our failures or setbacks, the rich do the opposite. They try to find the cause of setbacks in themselves, not in outside events or the actions of others. This gives them a sense of power and control. Rather than feeling like they are at the mercy of outside forces, they believe the power to create an outcome lies within them (Kraus et al., 2009).

For decades, the research has found that an internal locus of control, the belief that one is in control of what happens in one's life, is associated with a wide range of positive outcomes, from academic and vocational success to the ability to work out conflict in relationships. Wealthy people believe their decisions chart the course of their lives and account for their success. This same trait also contributes to their lack of empathy toward others who don't succeed. They view good choices as the path to success and bad choices as the path to failure. When others struggle, they view this as within that person's control. They have a difficult time seeing how another person's circumstances or context plays any meaningful role in this.

A MULTITUDE OF BENEFITS TO BEING WEALTHY

Being rich has its benefits, not just in terms of wealth accumulation, but in some positive personal characteristics. There are some personality traits that make a person more likely to be wealthy, as well as evidence that being wealthy engenders some positive personality traits. On average, the wealthy are less neurotic and impulsive, while being more conscientious, intuitive, and adventurous. However, while we acknowledge the upsides of wealth, we now must consider the major risks and challenges that being rich brings.

REFERENCES

Biljanovska, N., & Palligkinis, S. (2018). Wealth and self-control: The link between affluence and restraint. *Journal of Economic Behavior & Organization, 150*, 75–88.

Caliendo, M., Fossen, F. M., & Kritikos, A. S. (2014). Personality characteristics and the decision to become and stay self-employed. *Small Business Economics, 42*(4), 787–814.

Corley, T. (2016). *Change your habits, change your life: Strategies that transformed 177 self-made millionaires.* Hillcrest Publishing Group.

Empower. (2023). *Financial happiness: A survey of 2,034 Americans on money and happiness.* www.empower.com/press-center/6-10-americans-believe-money-can-buy-happiness-empower-research

Ettman, C. K., Cohen, G. H., & Galea, S. (2020). Financial hardship and mental health: The protective role of wealth. *Social Psychiatry and Psychiatric Epidemiology, 55*(5), 615–622.

Ettman, C. K., Cohen, G. H., & Galea, S. (2022). Wealth and mental health over two decades: A meta-analysis. *Annual Review of Clinical Psychology, 18*, 45–68.

Fitzgerald, F. S. (1926). *The rich boy.* Charles Scribner's Sons.

Flinn, C., Todd, P. E., & Zhang, W. (2024). Labor market returns to personality: A job search approach to understanding gender gaps. *Journal of Political Economy.* https://doi.org/10.1086/734092

Gallup. (2023). *Global happiness report.* https://www.gallup.com

Gathergood, J. (2012). Self-control, financial literacy, and consumer debt. *Journal of Economic Psychology, 33*(3), 590–602.

Huang, L., & Pierce, J. L. (2015). Angel investing: Balancing intuition and analysis. *Academy of Management Perspectives, 29*(4), 411–431.

Jebb, A. T., Tay, L., Diener, E., & Oishi, S. (2018). Happiness, income satiation, and turning points around the world. *Nature Human Behaviour, 2*(1), 33–38.

Kahneman, D., & Deaton, A. (2020). High income improves evaluation of life but not emotional well-being. *Proceedings of the National Academy of Sciences, 107*(38), 16489–16493.

Killingsworth, M. A. (2024). Income and happiness revisited: Expanding the analysis. *Journal of Economic Perspectives, 38*(1), 58–73.

Kraus, M. W., Piff, P. K., & Keltner, D. (2009). Social class, sense of control, and social explanation. *Journal of Personality and Social Psychology, 97*(6), 992–1004.

Kudrna, L., & Kushlev, K. (2022). Analytical methods and their impact on income and happiness research. *Journal of Happiness Studies*, *23*(4), 987–1012.

Le-Scherban, F., Diez Roux, A. V., & Li, Y. (2016). Wealth and the mental health of young adults: Longitudinal evidence from a U.S. cohort. *Journal of Adolescent Health*, *59*(5), 521–528.

Leckelt, M., König, J., Richter, D., Back, M. D., & Schröder, C. (2022a). The personality traits of self-made and inherited millionaires. *Humanities and Social Sciences Communications*, *9*, Article 11099.

Leckelt, M., Richter, D., & Back, M. D. (2022b). Risk-taking in affluent individuals: Evidence from large data sets. *Journal of Personality*, *90*(1), 45–60.

Liu, W., Xie, Y., & He, G. (2023). Income inequality and mental health: A global review. *Global Health Perspectives*, *17*(2), 210–223.

Mata, R., Josef, A. K., & Hertwig, R. (2018). Risk-taking across the lifespan: When and why do people take risks? *Psychological Science*, *29*(1), 10–20.

Piff, P. K., & Moskowitz, J. P. (2018). Wealth and positive emotions: The role of socioeconomic status. *Emotion*, *18*(4), 425–439.

Ridley, M., Rao, G., Schilbach, F., & Patel, V. (2020). Poverty, depression, and anxiety: Causal evidence and mechanisms. *Science*, *370*(6522), eaay0214.

Zitelmann, R. (2019). The psychology of the super-rich: Insights into the wealth mind. *Fortune*.

Chapter 4

Wealthy People, Part 2
The Challenges of Being Rich

Years ago, a man booked an appointment to see if I could help his son. His young adult boy had experienced an unexpected psychotic break, fine one day and almost catatonic the next. The man, a physician who was born in another country, said, "I know my son is very sick and it will take a long time for him to get better. He will need to see you for quite a while, I assume. Would you be willing to offer me a discounted rate, since this is likely to be a long-term undertaking?" I could tell he was concerned about his son.

I agreed to the discount and worked with the young man for over a year. He had improved and went from being in a fragile emotional state to being sturdier and more resilient, able to return to college and complete his degree. During one of those sessions, he said, "I just found out my dad asked you for a discount for our sessions."

"That's true," I said.

"And did you give it to him?" he asked.

"I did," I said.

He laughed and shook his head.

"My dad has over six million dollars in the bank," he said. "He has three houses, several luxury cars. He doesn't need a discount."

I felt a surge of anger well up inside me. I felt like a fool.

"He does this kind of thing all the time," the son said. "He always asks people for discounts, even for free services. His barber gave him free haircuts for years."

I felt conned. The feeling stuck with me for longer than I felt comfortable. I thought about it at odd times, knowing this wealthy man had taken advantage of me. I asked for the father to come in so we could discuss it. He agreed to see me for a private meeting with his son's blessing.

"When someone asks me for a discounted rate, I ask more follow-up questions before I say yes," I explained. "Because I was so moved by your son's story, I didn't do that this time, but now that your son is doing better, I wanted to know if we could discuss it, especially as we might be close to wrapping up."

DOI: 10.4324/9781003503569-6

"Yes, I am open to that conversation," he said, without a hint of defensiveness.

"Did you believe you needed a discount for your son's therapy?" I asked.

He sat still for a moment, looking off to the side. "I will be honest with you," he began. "I have what many would consider to be a considerable amount of money."

It was not an answer to my question, but I could tell he had more to say. I nodded and waited for him to continue.

"When I was a boy in Nepal, my family was the lowest of low," he said. "We were the poorest of all people. My father was not a good man. He would beat me and my brother, sometimes for no reason. The older kids in the village would push me down and take whatever I had. This happened every week, sometimes every day."

He stared up at the ceiling for a few moments, composing himself before he continued.

"When I came to the U.S. as a refugee, I swore I would work my hardest in school, then graduate at the top of my class in college, then do it again in medical school. I had this all decided before I was even 13 years old," he said.

I nodded again.

"And that's what I did," he said. "All of that."

"Very impressive," I said.

"And now that I have become very successful as a physician and as a business owner, I still feel every moment of every day that someone will take it all away from me. I feel like the poor Nepali boy who will get pushed to the ground and have everything he owns stolen from him in an instant."

He explained how he still felt like he must guard his money. He felt like catastrophe would befall him without warning and would lose everything he had worked for over the past 40 years.

When I found out about his wealth, it seemed pretty straightforward that this guy was trying to cheat me out of money, but it was more complex than that. In his view, he was trying to ensure care for his son while safeguarding as much of his money as he could.

This experience also helped me better understand how money connects to deeper psychological needs, including needs for safety and security. Especially for people who have grown up without that sense of safety, money represents a way to feel safe in the world. Losing money becomes associated with feeling vulnerable and even in danger. A Bloomberg study asked rich people how secure they felt with their finances. Among those having between $1 million and $5 million in net worth, more people said they were just "comfortable" than those who said that much money made them "rich." There were even some in this wealth bracket who said they felt "poor" or were just "getting by" (Ballentine & Wells, 2023). Having a lot of money doesn't always make a person feel rich or financially secure.

Another important lesson from that experience was that I learned not to hold back on having conversations about money in therapy, even if they might feel uncomfortable. When the father asked me if I would discount his son's therapy, my willingness to give him a hardship discount should have been based on real data or a lengthier conversation, not on his emotional appeal. Had it not caught me off guard, I might have asked him to describe his financial situation to me. Like me, most therapists get the message in their training that it is gauche to discuss money matters in therapy. We come to believe we should not concern ourselves with money, but with helping the client, as if the two issues are incompatible.

Early in my career, I was uncomfortable having conversations with money. This left me ill-equipped to enter the worlds of people with lives shaped by their wealth. Later, I became more at ease with talking about money, not just related to the costs of therapy, but how clients viewed it, the meaning they made of it, and the often-huge role it played in their lives.

The psychology of wealthy people is fascinating and complex. For any helping professional who wants to serve these clients well, having a strong understanding of how wealth shapes a person is crucial. As we have seen, being wealthy has its advantages and privileges. Wealthy people are also more likely to be happier and healthier. Being rich, though, is not without its challenges. They have several negative traits found at higher rates than others. It cannot be overemphasized that these traits are not true of all wealthy people, many of whom are other-centered and ethical in their personal and private lives. However, anyone in a helping relationship with wealthy individuals and families should be well versed in what problematic qualities they are most likely to encounter.

Let's explore those challenging characteristics, then talk about how different pathways to wealth affect the probability of these negative traits. We'll pull all this together and summarize the treatment issues you may encounter with wealthy clients and their families. First, let's look at some of the most challenging qualities of the wealthy.

THE WEALTHY ARE MORE SELFISH AND NARCISSISTIC

A team of researchers from the University of California, Berkeley set out to investigate whether rich people behaved more selfishly behind the wheel. After a city ordinance mandated all cars to pause at crosswalks and yield to pedestrians in the fast-paced streets of San Francisco, the researchers assessed who was more likely to obey this law. They found drivers of luxury cars were four times less likely to stop and give pedestrians the right of way, compared to their less affluent counterparts. They also discovered that drivers of these pricey rides, presumably rich individuals, were more inclined to cut off other drivers in busy traffic. The researchers concluded the wealthy drivers behaved more selfishly and recklessly on the road, in contrast to less affluent citizens (Piff et al., 2012).

Across multiple studies, research finds higher rates of narcissism among the wealthy. University of California, Irvine professor Paul Piff conducted a series of five studies with over 800 subjects. He found higher rates of narcissism among the wealthy. The upper class showed entitlement and other narcissistic tendencies. One study found they even looked at themselves in the mirror more often than others.

When researchers looked at the families of active-duty military officers, all of whom had graduated from West Point, they found higher levels of parental income and net worth correlated with higher levels of narcissism in adulthood. Being raised in a wealthy family increased narcissistic traits. Their narcissistic traits also had an adverse impact on their effectiveness as leaders, compared to military officers from less affluent families (Martin et al., 2016).

We know narcissism is not evenly distributed among the social classes. As wealth increases, so do narcissistic personality tendencies, especially a need for admiration, a sense of entitlement, and lack of empathy. These traits often help a person succeed in competitive work environments, but they often prove to be disastrous in close relationships. Research finds that the rate of divorce among narcissists is higher than that of the general population, and they are less likely to exit well, especially when they have been dumped (South et al., 2020).

Being wealthy is a significant risk factor for narcissism. Rich people are more prone to believe they are special, entitled to special treatment, and more intelligent than others. They may revel in their narcissism, seeing it as an advantage or a sign of strength. In other instances, they are oblivious to it. They may have a long history of failed romantic relationships, severed relationships with business partners and associates, and broken friendships, yet never reflect on how they might be the common factor. As the saying goes, "If everyone around you is the problem, maybe you're the problem." Many narcissists never get to this moment of insight.

THE WEALTHY SHOW LESS EMPATHY

Where there is more narcissism, there is less empathy. This is true for the wealthy who not only focus more on their own desires, but have a harder time understanding the needs, struggles, and feelings of others. For them, empathy is in short supply, often seen as weakness and disadvantage.

For most of us, if we watch a person expressing an emotion on film, we have a good sense of what they are feeling. We even do this with still photos of faces. We know what sadness or anger or fear looks like. Researchers at UC-Berkeley found the wealthy had a harder time judging which emotions were being felt in these types of situations. They presented rich participants with a series of faces and found they are much worse than others at correctly identifying the expressed emotion. Then they asked these wealthy people to watch strangers in simulated job interviews. Again, they struggled to read the emotions accurately. They were, in essence, deficient in empathy (Kraus et al., 2010). One of the study's authors, Dacher Keltner, summarized his inquiry into the empathy of wealthy people to the *New York Times* this way: "Upper-class people, in spite of their advantages, suffer empathy deficits. And there are enormous consequences." Those consequences range from the interpersonal and relational to the policy and legal levels of society where wealthy people have outsized influence (Paul, 2010).

Other researchers wired subjects up to biofeedback equipment, then showed those in both upper and lower income brackets a video of children suffering with cancer while measuring the participants' physiological responses. They found lower-income individuals had more compassion-related physiological reactions than their upper-class counterparts did (Stellar et al, 2012).

This lack of empathy starts early in life for the wealthy. One experiment presented four-year-olds from both wealthy and non-wealthy families with an opportunity to donate prize tokens they had won to other children they were told were sick and in the hospital. Again, the less wealthy kids donated more of their tokens than children from wealthy homes (Miller et al., 2015). Some of this may be because of genetics, but much of it seems to come from the family culture and what parents modeled in the home.

In several studies, like the three by Kraus et al. (2010), wealthy people showed less empathy than lower-class people. They may be so cut off from others who are not wealthy that they have few empathy-promoting experiences. They may also willfully disregard the feelings and struggles of others as an adaptive way of keeping themselves wealthy and in positions of power.

In my interviews with financial professionals and other counselors, themes related to both narcissism and low empathy among the wealthy emerged. Rich people often believe that because they are wealthy, their choices, attitudes, and worldviews are correct and that others would have better lives if they followed their advice and example. They do not acknowledge that others have different circumstances, obstacles, and constraints, nor do they consider that their own success may have been partly the result of external circumstances, luck, and privileges.

WEALTHY PEOPLE ARE LESS ETHICAL

In 2019, a scandal made front-page headlines when federal authorities charged over 50 people with criminal conspiracy. They were not mobsters or corrupt politicians. They were wealthy parents of teens seeking admission to elite universities. In the eight years leading up to the indictment, rich parents paid William Singer more than $25 million to help their kids get into top colleges and universities. He paid off test administrators to look the other way when others took the SAT or ACT under the student's name. He bribed coaches to recruit noncompetitive students, including those who didn't even play a sport.

In a phone call recorded by the FBI, Singer said he helped "the wealthiest families in the US get their kids into school." After pleading guilty to conspiracy, obstruction, racketeering, and money laundering, he admitted he had helped 761 families get their children into top universities through the "side door." That's a sanitized way of saying he helped them cheat their way into some of the best schools in the country (Winter & Burke, 2019).

The investigation caught big fish in its net: famous actresses, prominent businesspeople, well-known coaches, and others. One of the prominent dads, a New York attorney, said on a wiretapped phone call, "To be honest, I'm not worried about the moral issue" (Albert, 2019). It appears few individuals charged with these criminal offenses had much concern about the ethics of their actions. Sometimes, they rationalized and justified their behavior. In other instances, they knew they were doing wrong but didn't care.

Where there is more narcissism and less empathy, there is a greater risk for unethical behavior. Years ago, a wealthy father of one of my clients told me he agreed to donate a large sum of money to the school if they did not expel his son for a major offense, one that the school handbook and honor code stated would lead to expulsion. To their credit, the school did not take the deal. The man told me this not as a confession, but as evidence of the school's stupidity. He didn't consider his attempted bribery unethical. However, he believed the school's failure to accept his overture was a sign of their incompetence.

During a lunch conversation, a well-known financial authority advised me to commit an unethical act with the cash payments that came into my business. When I bristled, he all but rolled his eyes at me, saying, "This is what all businesses do. You'd be dumb not to do it." I didn't take his advice, but I realized how comfortably this type of thinking sat with him. In both instances, I noticed how the person proclaimed it was "stupid" or "dumb" not to engage in the unethical activity.

In a series of seven studies, researchers found rich people were much more likely than poor people to break the rules, make unethical decisions, take valued possessions away from others, lie during negotiations, cheat to win prizes, and support unscrupulous behavior at work. They also had a more positive attitude toward greed (Piff et al., 2012). The lead researcher, Paul Piff, later commented on this in an interview with *New York Magazine*. "While having money doesn't necessarily make anybody anything," he said, "the rich are way more likely to prioritize their own self-interests above the interests of other people. It makes them more likely to exhibit characteristics that we would stereotypically associate with, say, assholes" (Miller, 2012).

Rich people are more likely than others to cheat or take advantage of another's mistake. Wealthy people more often reported keeping extra change accidentally given to them by cashiers in a research simulation (Piff et al., 2012). In another, wealthy people playing a game of chance involving computerized dice rolls were more likely to cheat, compared to others, in order to win a modest cash prize (Piff et al., 2012).

When compared to others, rich people were more likely to justify greed and to be more greedy themselves. Researchers found wealthier people were more likely to agree with statements that greed is good, justified, morally defensible, and even beneficial to others. Wealthy people who held these beliefs were, of course, more likely to engage in unethical behavior.

If you're feeling judgmental toward the rich, consider that any of us is susceptible to behaving badly when money is involved. One series of four studies found simple exposure to money caused people to have unethical intentions and make unethical decisions (Kouchaki et al., 2013). When researchers primed participants by showing them money, the subjects behaved in more unethical ways compared to those who had not been primed. The authors concluded that their research showed how "the mere presence of money, an often taken-for-granted and easily overlooked feature of our daily lives, can serve as a prompt for immoral behavior." These participants were not rich. They were just average undergraduate students, yet they behaved more unethically on tasks just by seeing money. It's easy to believe rich people find it easier to act unethically, but money can corrupt all of us.

WEALTHY PEOPLE ARE MORE ADDICTED

A client told me the "dirty little secret" of his small town was that all the rich people "were hooked on pills." He said it was common knowledge that you could find a pharmacy's worth of OxyContin, Xanax, and Adderall in their medicine cabinets during parties. The research supports the claim that wealthy people not only have more access to prescription drugs but also have higher rates of addiction to these pills compared to others (Levine & Muthén, 2010; Luthar & Barkin, 2012). High-end drug rehab programs around the country are full of wealthy clients who have become addicted to these jagged little pills.

One study found that the lifetime prevalence rates of addiction among the wealthy by the age of 26 were three times higher than the national average for men and twice the rate of substance addiction for women. Not only that, the rates for party drugs like ecstasy and cocaine were much higher than they were for other groups (Luthar & Latendresse, 2005). Higher stress and greater access works against them and lead many down the path of substance abuse and addiction. Among my clients who are being raised in wealthy families, a much higher percentage of their parents seem to take a dismissive view that this is a rite of passage for all teens and young adults. They also fall into a desire to be the cool parents who let the kids party at their big house or at their lake or beach house.

WEALTHY PEOPLE STRUGGLE WITH TRUST

The wealthy father of one of my young adult clients told me he had only one friend, a guy he knew from high school. He only saw the guy about once a year, though, as they lived in different parts of the country.

"Do you want more friends?" I asked.

"Of course," he said, "but I've given up."

"Why do you think you have so few friends?" I asked.

"Well, there's no shortage of people who want to be my friend," he said, then added, "but most of them want something from me or they just want to be attached to me to feel important."

When you work with wealthy people, you realize how common this sentiment is. Even if they seem easygoing or gregarious, they remain vigilant about others trying to push their way into the inner circle. This isn't paranoia. It's anchored in reality. Many rich people have had the experience of others who have gotten into their inner circle—or close enough—only to use the relationship for some kind of personal gain. They're also well acquainted with people approaching them with financial needs or who are raising money for good causes.

The result is that shields go up and the veneer of social pleasantness hides a guarded heart. This results in fewer confidantes and a careful parsing of words with others. Wealthy people often have many more acquaintances than others, but they risk having fewer genuine friends. It's no wonder that many of their closest relationships are often high school or college friends, people they knew before they became wealthy, before they had to question the motives of why someone wanted to slip into their lives.

A research summary by the *Harvard Business Review* found that the wealthier people become, the more isolated they are likely to be (Norton & Gino, 2014). Most of the time, the isolation is self-imposed. They draw away from others to protect themselves against those who try to gain access to them and the money, status, and power they hold. They also may do it because their wealth helps them take care of their own needs in ways that those with fewer resources cannot manage. From early human history, we have been social beings who rely on each other for survival and getting our needs met. With more money comes more resources, which reduces dependency on others. Whatever the reason, the rich often find themselves more isolated from others.

WEALTHY PEOPLE HAVE A COMPLICATED RELATIONSHIP WITH MONEY

A client of mine was an early cryptocurrency adopter, starting when he invested a sizeable chunk of inheritance money in his late teens. Within less than five years, his holdings had shot into a mid-seven-figure sum. He was a multimillionaire at 23, but no one knew, except me.

He told me a curious thing. Before he was wealthy, he didn't care that much about financial matters. He didn't overthink his spending, was generous with friends, and had an uncomplicated relationship with money. Once they became rich, though, something changed inside him.

"Suddenly, I became very possessive of my money. I didn't want to lose it or waste it. I didn't enjoy spending it. Every financial decision, even the little ones, became a burden. I do not know why it changed like that," he said, "but it did."

This is a theme I've heard many times. For those who come into money later, something in them changes. Some become more preoccupied with money and less generous. Anxiety about money increases. They check their investment portfolio throughout the day, something that would have been laughable to them before they got rich. This is not a well-studied phenomenon, but it comes up often in clinical practice. Just as it was for my newly rich client, many who gain wealth later instead of growing up in a well-off family felt more focused and worried about it.

One study examined the outcomes of 33 participants of a 6-day-long experiential therapy program designed to treat what they termed "disordered money behaviors," which they define as "maladaptive patterns of financial beliefs and behaviors that lead to clinically significant distress, impairment in social or occupational functioning, undue financial strain or an inability to appropriately enjoy one's financial resources." The distress could include symptoms of anxiety and worry, despair over finances, no savings, debt, bankruptcy, family conflict over money, compulsive spending, hoarding of money, and unhealthy financial risk-taking. This contrasts with "financial wellness," characterized by low debt, sufficient savings, retirement planning, a budget, financial satisfaction, and low financial stress. The researchers found the therapy program resulted in "significant and lasting reductions in psychological distress, anxiety, and worry about money and finance-related situations and showed measurable signs of better overall financial health." This promising outcome supports the benefits of addressing issues of money in therapy (Klontz et al., 2008).

PATHWAYS TO WEALTH—AND WHY IT MATTERS

Those born into rich families have different early lives compared to those of more modest means who later become rich, often through their intentional efforts. Both people may end up with the same amount of accumulated wealth, but their formative years gave them different relationships with money. Those who grow up wealthy have different traits from those who become rich later in life. Many of the personality patterns we just discussed—more willing to take risks, more open to new ideas, more outgoing, more conscientious, and more emotionally stable— seem to be more true of those who became wealthy later in life than in those who have inherited their wealth (Leckelt et al., 2022).

Those who come into sudden wealth, like beneficiaries of large wills, recipients of huge lawsuit settlements, artists and athletes who sign major contracts, or lottery winners, also seem to have different personality structures from those who come into later wealth through intentional effort, like starting a business or making shrewd investments.

Psychologist David Lansky conducted a series of focus group discussions with wealth managers, family office executives, and others to determine the needs of people who have or will inherit wealth (Lansky, n.d.). They found three big themes to address when caring for these individuals. The first is *alienation and isolation*. They quoted a young woman in her 20s who was struggling to find her way in life. She said, "Friends, teachers, even a former mentor in the family business all say 'when they die, they want to come back as me.' How can I tell them what I am really thinking—that I'm lost and confused and very unhappy?" These wealthy families often value privacy, for obvious reasons, but the result is that family members often feel cut off from relationships where they cannot be open or vulnerable or connected. For some of these individuals, their relationship with their therapist is their only authentic connection.

The second theme Lansky found was a tendency toward *entitlement and lack of initiative* among inheritors. He argues wealth can help people in certain ways, but it can also harm them by making them more entitled and less likely to work hard for themselves. He describes those who inherit wealth as being at risk of having their ability to delay gratification undermined. They can also feel bored and empty. A meta-analysis of four exploratory studies with over 3,100 individuals found wealthy people raised in wealthy families were "uniquely high in entitlement" (Côté et al., 2020). While each individual is different, you are more likely to find a wealthy client raised as wealthy who is less motivated and passionate, less emotionally stable, and entitled than other clients who possessed "self-made" wealth.

Lansky found those who inherit wealth can have their *independence and autonomy impaired*. He writes, "Living in another's shadow can be excruciating." Huge expectations might get placed on you, while the perception that you did nothing to deserve your wealth can crush your sense of autonomy. Some inheritors worry that others within or outside the family will judge them. They fret about bringing dishonor or scrutiny to the family by their actions. They don't feel free to make their own life choices because they fear disapproval. Often, these fears are realistic. The culture in many wealthy families is one of shame, control, and impression management.

TREATMENT IMPLICATIONS

From what the research tells us, there are several typical issues you will encounter in your work with wealthy people. Here are the top issues you should be equipped to address:

- *Narcissism:* Wealthy people often believe the world belongs to them. They may have what is now termed "main character energy," where they think and behave as if they are the central figure of our shared story, while others are bit players or extras. Others should recognize how special they are and accommodate them. Their opinion is correct, and they know best. This narcissism helps them succeed in some areas and fail in others. With patience and skill, the therapist can expose the roots of their narcissism so they can be repaired.

- *Low Empathy:* Those who are more self-centered and narcissistic will also be less empathetic. We should specifically address this trait in treatment, though it overlaps so much with narcissism that if you work on one, you will address the other.
- *Relationship Difficulties:* Distressed and dysfunctional interpersonal relationships are the outworking of these narcissistic features and low empathy. There will be a focus on repairing relationships and challenging old maladaptive ways of relating to others.
- *Substance Abuse:* A person with more money has access to more substances, particularly party drugs, painkillers, and stimulants. They may also have a problematic drinking issue. All of this may need to be addressed in therapy.
- *Disconnection and Isolation:* Wealth can put all eyes on you at a party but leave you feeling lonely and disconnected. The wealthy often need trusting, deep relationships with friends, mentors, and others.
- *Complicated Relationship With Wealth:* A person who is not wealthy may talk confidently about how they would be so generous and so liberated if they came into a lot of money, but wealthy people don't talk like that. Instead, they may express a lot of ambivalence about their money, greater preoccupation with it, a growing desire for it. They may find themselves greedier than they imagined or more worried than they would have predicted. Wealthy people often have a complicated, ambivalent relationship with their money.

We'll discuss specific treatment approaches and protocols in upcoming chapters. However, continue seeking additional training or refer out if you feel ill-equipped to address the issues in your work with wealthy people, because these themes are common in your work with wealthy individuals and families.

THEY ARE DIFFERENT

Like Fitzgerald, we must conclude that the rich are different from the rest of us. They have personality traits and patterns that represent a unique profile. Some of these traits are beneficial and admirable. Others are problematic, especially with interpersonal relationships. In their study of over 800 wealthy individuals, Marcus Leckelt and his colleagues concluded, "we find that stereotypes about wealthy people's personalities are accurate albeit somewhat exaggerated and that wealthy people can be characterized as *stable, flexible, and agentic individuals who are more focused on themselves than on others*" (Leckelt et al., 2018, p. 769 [emphasis added]).

That is an elegant, accurate, and helpful summary statement of what we know about the personality traits of most wealthy people.

Few therapists are well equipped to deal with issues of wealth in their work. For those who work with wealthy clients, themes of affluence and its positive and negative impact on them come up often in therapy. In the same way that treating less privileged clients will often involve dealing with their lack of money and resources, treating rich clients will require you to deal with their abundance of money and privilege and how this affects almost all aspects of their lives.

I have described the character of wealthy people in some negative ways because that's what the research has shown. However, I feel compelled to share my own experiences here to give a more well-rounded view of rich people. I am frequently around wealthy people, whether it is speaking at elite private schools, going to fundraisers, or being invited to social events. I also have close friends who are wealthy. These people are often genuinely kind and amazingly generous. With my friends, I'm aware of their generosity because our close relationship makes me privy to some things that others may not see. What I have realized, however, is that there is likely to be even greater generosity that I don't know about. It is generosity done in secret. Their financial support of others is not given for social credibility or recognition or favor. It is given simply because the need exists. Over the years, I have been both the recipient of their generosity and front-row witness to their kindness toward others in need.

So yes, wealth can do harm to a person's soul and character, but the "healthy wealthy" can use it to enrich and even change the lives of many others. We need to hold that reality, too, as we approach our helping relationships with those who have a lot. The healthier they get, the better they make our communities and cultures. Catching a vision of this can drive us even harder to do our best work.

REFERENCES

Albert, S. (2019). Legal repercussions of college admissions bribery. *Journal of Legal Studies*, *56*(2), 78–94.

Ballentine, R., & Wells, J. (2023). Financial perceptions among millionaires: Comfortable or rich? *Bloomberg Wealth Quarterly*, *19*(1), 45–67.

Côté, S., Martin, S. R., & Woodruff, T. (2020). Echoes of our upbringing: How growing up wealthy or poor relates to narcissism, leader behavior and leader effectiveness. *Academy of Management Journal*, *59*(6), 2157–2177. https://doi.org/10.5465/amj.2015.0680

Klontz, B., Britt, S. L., & Archuleta, K. (2008). Treating disordered money behaviors: A six-day experiential therapy intervention. *Journal of Financial Therapy*, *1*(1), 1–15.

Kouchaki, M., Smith-Crowe, K., Brief, A. P., & Sousa, C. (2013). Seeing green: Mere exposure to money triggers unethical behavior. *Organizational Behavior and Human Decision Processes*, *121*(1), 53–61.

Kraus, M. W., Côté, S., & Keltner, D. (2010). Social class, contextualism, and empathic accuracy. *Psychological Science, 21*(11), 1716–1723.

Lansky, D. (n.d.). *Managing the psychological impact of inherited wealth*. The Family Business Consulting Group.

Leckelt, M., König, J., Richter, D., Back, M. D., & Schröder, C. (2022). The personality traits of self-made and inherited millionaires. *Humanities and Social Sciences Communications, 9*, Article 11099.

Leckelt, M., Richter, D., & Back, M. D. (2018). The psychology of the wealthy: Personality traits and well-being. *Journal of Personality, 86*(6), 769–789.

Levine, M., & Muthén, B. O. (2010). Substance use and affluence: Correlations and consequences. *Addictive Behaviors, 35*(7), 699–704.

Luthar, S. S., & Barkin, S. H. (2012). Are affluent youth truly disadvantaged? A study on privilege and pressure. *Psychology Today, 45*(8), 19–24.

Luthar, S. S., & Latendresse, S. J. (2005). Children of the affluent: Challenges to well-being. *Current Directions in Psychological Science, 14*(2), 49–53.

Martin, S. R., Côté, S., & Woodruff, T. (2016). Echoes of our upbringing: How childhood socioeconomic status influences executive leaders' narcissistic tendencies. *The Leadership Quarterly, 27*(3), 355–364. https://doi.org/10.1016/j.leaqua.2016.01.007

Miller, C. (2012). The privilege paradox: Why the wealthy break the rules. *New York Magazine*. https://nymag.com

Miller, J. G., Kahle, S., & Hastings, P. D. (2015). Roots and benefits of costly giving: Children who are more altruistic have greater autonomic flexibility and less family wealth. *Psychological Science, 26*(7), 1038–1045. https://doi.org/10.1177/0956797615578476

Norton, M. I., & Gino, F. (2014). Why wealth causes isolation: A psychological inquiry. *Harvard Business Review, 92*(5), 10–12.

Paul, P. (2010). The empathy deficit: Why wealthy people struggle to connect. *The New York Times*. https://www.nytimes.com

Piff, P. K., Kraus, M. W., Côté, S., Cheng, B. H., & Keltner, D. (2012). Having less, giving more: The influence of social class on prosocial behavior. *Journal of Personality and Social Psychology, 99*(5), 771–784.

South, S. C., Krueger, R. F., & Johnson, W. (2020). Narcissism and romantic relationship dynamics. *Psychological Bulletin, 146*(4), 323–345.

Stellar, J. E., Manzo, V. M., Kraus, M. W., & Keltner, D. (2012). Class and compassion: Socioeconomic factors predict responses to suffering. *Emotion, 12*(3), 449–459.

Winter, T., & Burke, M. (2019). The college admissions scandal: An analysis of the legal and ethical issues. *National Law Review, 48*(4), 217–236.

Chapter 5

The Challenges of Children in Wealthy Families

Theodore Weintraub was 17 when he tried to buy alcohol using a fake ID at an upscale Manhattan hotel bar. The bartender wasn't falling for it, so the boy was denied. Theodore was undeterred. He tried to get served several times until he was banned from the hotel entirely. A few weeks after his ban, his family had a dinner reservation at the hotel. His parents were apparently unaware of Theodore's poor standing with the business, so they were shocked when security officials would not allow them to be seated. The hotel claims the teenager first asked to be forgiven, then raged at the staff, calling them antisemitic slurs and falsely claiming the staff spat in people's food. His father intervened and "quickly quelled his son," according to an account (Gallagher, 2023).

Two years later, Weintraub reportedly began paying protestors $25 an hour to stand outside the hotel holding protest signs and chanting that the hotel had rats, spread disease, and "supported Epstein," in a reference to disgraced billionaire Jeffrey Epstein. They reportedly called a doorman a pedophile and said the man's mother was a prostitute. According to the *New York Times*, they accosted guests and, on one occasion, were part of a sidewalk brawl outside the hotel that involved fans of the artist Drake, who was staying at the hotel. Witnesses allegedly saw Theodore sitting in a chauffeured Cadillac across the street, watching the spectacle of these protests when he wasn't out protesting himself (Senzamici, 2023).

Weintraub and his protestors were removed from the hotel around 4:00 a.m. when they attempted to interfere with workers who were preparing for a celebrity guest. He then "flopped to the ground and pretended to be injured," according to a report. An hour later, the well-known guest, who was Jewish, arrived. Theodore's protestors began shouting that the hotel denies the Holocaust so loudly that neighbors began yelling from their windows on the floors above for them to be quiet. The hotel filed a lawsuit and got a restraining order, preventing Weintraub from making public statements that could damage the hotel's reputation (Gallagher, 2023; Stack, 2023).

DOI: 10.4324/9781003503569-7

Weintraub came from a wealthy family. His father was a cardiologist with an impressive art collection and a residence in the heart of Manhattan, close to the hotel his son had been disrupting. When Theodore's dad was contacted by a reporter, he "expressed dismay at his son's actions. He promised his kin would no longer be an issue for the hotel" (Gallagher, 2023).

I do not know whether Theodore Weintraub acted the way he did because he came from a rich family. I don't know how he was parented, who his friends were, or what other influences were part of his life. What I know is that he could not have behaved the way he did without having money. His wealth allowed him to act out in ways that other teenage boys of the same age would not have the option of doing. Referring to the tantrum Weintraub threw when he was not seated for dinner, one hotel worker said, "Because you're not used to hearing 'no,' that pushes you to do this because you have to get what you want," adding, "To me, it's crazy, that sense of entitlement" (Senzamici, 2023).

To be clear, I don't assume his parents overindulged him or failed to set limits on him. My point is not that he was a poorly parented child. Instead, I suggest growing up in wealth is inherently risky for the emotional and character development of kids. Nearly all children and teens feel aggrieved and treated unfairly. However, most young people learn to accept limits and some measure of authority. This is a good and necessary part of growing up. What most kids could never do, even if they wanted to, is pay protestors for weeks to retaliate against a hotel bar that wouldn't let them use their fake ID to buy alcohol. They might fantasize about it, but it could never happen.

Of course, this is an extreme example, but it makes a larger point that children born to wealthy families grow up in a context that can thwart the things they need to grow into relationally healthy adults. They can skirt rules, jump to the head of the line, avoid consequences, retaliate against perceived enemies, or gain access to privileges in ways others cannot.

THE STRUGGLES OF CHILDREN OF RICH PEOPLE

Navigating the early years is challenging for most people. Growing up in a rich family brings an additional layer of complications. In some ways, the experience can be remarkable. The family's wealth affords enriched experiences like overseas travel and exposure to art and fashion. Despite the positives, wealth also brings other risks and difficulties. Following are some of the most common struggles found among children and teens who grow up in wealthy families.

Substance Abuse

Many studies have found that children raised in affluent homes are significantly more likely to develop substance abuse problems (Luthar & Barkin, 2017). This could be due to a combination of factors, including having more cash, access to more prescription drugs, higher pressure to succeed and measure up to the standards of one's parents, and isolation from parents who were more likely to travel or be absent.

The teenage children of wealthy people have more money and easier access to drugs, particularly party drugs and prescription pills. They have bigger homes that become attractive locations for parties. Some of these wealthy teens build their reputation on throwing big parties with expensive alcohol and drugs.

Research has found rates of addiction among affluent youth and young adults were upward of three times higher than the general population at the same age (Luthar & Barkin, 2017). Rehab programs in sunny Malibu and elsewhere are filled with teens and young adults who were raised in wealthy families. Wealth is a significant risk factor for addiction.

Anxiety and Depression

Psychologist Suniya Luthar found that the children of the wealthy were more vulnerable to anxiety and depression. They had more pressure to achieve and were more isolated from their parents. They were often sent off to prestigious college prep boarding schools, which exacerbated the problems for some vulnerable kids in the long term.

Luthar and Becker studied over 300 middle school kids from affluent families in the Northeast. They found an unusually high rate of depression for girls and high rates of drug use for both boys and girls. They attributed at least some of this to "maladaptive perfectionism," or unrelenting standards that drive them to "excessive investment in accomplishments and need to avoid failure" (Luthar & Becker, 2002).

The child's social context beyond the family, including both neighborhood and school, is likely to be a significant factor in their emotional well-being. One study of 1364 adolescents found that girls from more affluent neighborhoods reported higher levels of anxiety and depression, compared to those in middle-class neighborhoods. However, they also found that teens in affluent families who lived in middle-class neighborhoods reported far lower rates of anxiety and depression, suggesting that the larger social context was more important to their emotional well-being than the family itself (Lund & Dearing, 2012). It seems having wealthy peers as neighbors and classmates may be a significant risk factor for depression and anxiety among teens.

Rates of anxiety are up to 30% higher among children raised in affluent families, compared to other families (Rampage, 2008). There could be several reasons for this, but the most likely one is that these kids experience more pressure from their families than other kids. They have observed a life of wealth. They see what it requires, and they feel tremendous pressure to live up to the expectations. These kids may not have the same kinds of limits as their less affluent peers. Since we know consistent boundaries make children feel safe, we can reasonably assume

49

that inconsistent boundaries make kids feel anxious. These children of affluence clearly feel more pressure but have less emotional sturdiness to manage it. Their skyrocketing rates of anxiety are proof of that.

The research finds that affluence, while interwoven with certain risk factors for mental health maladies such as anxiety and depression, is not the sole cause of these conditions (Luthar & Latendresse, 2005). This relationship between family wealth and mental well-being is not linear or deterministic. Instead, it is the confluence of personal characteristics, the dynamics within the family unit, and the broader societal context that collectively shapes the mental well-being of individuals. The interplay of these elements is not affected solely by socioeconomic status or privilege.

Low Resilience

Humans develop more mental muscle when they face challenges and persevere through them. If you live in a world where you are insulated from the struggles of ordinary life, you may not develop the resilience you need to navigate life successfully. Many children of rich families have grown up where life is so easy that it makes the normal stresses of life feel unbearable for them. As they get older and face more real-world challenges, this vulnerability pokes through. Often it takes the form of intense feelings of anxiety. In my practice, it is not uncommon for me to see a high school senior or a college freshman raised in an affluent family who experiences debilitating anxiety when they face the reality of young adult life.

Wealthy people may unwittingly undermine their children and make them less resilient by constantly bailing them out of trouble and not allowing them to face normal consequences. Some pull strings when their middle schooler gets in trouble with the coach. Others hire a high-dollar attorney when their high schooler gets caught with weed on campus. They threaten a lawsuit when their college student faces expulsion for harassing behavior. They don't allow their kids to fail or face major fallout from their misbehavior.

Entitlement

Years ago, I went to the graduation of a family member at a private school. The graduates marched onto the stage. The boys had a similar look: clean cut, hair cut above the ears, clean-shaven. All of them, except for one guy who was sitting in the front row. He had hair down to his shoulders and a full beard.

"Does this school have a hair code?" I asked the relative beside me.

"Oh, yes," she said.

"What's the deal with the guy in the first row then?" I asked.

"His family is the wealthiest family in the state," she said, then cut her eyes at me to underscore the point.

The length of his hair and the fullness of his beard made it clear this was not just a graduation week lapse. This was months, maybe a year, in the making. His parents undoubtedly knew the hair and dress code, but let him violate it in the most public way. Worse, the school allowed him to do it. Perhaps the family had given a lot of money to the school—or had promised to give in the future—or the school simply felt they could not stand up to a family of this stature. Either way, this teenager was playing by a different set of rules from that of his peers.

Admittedly, there are far worse things than a kid growing his hair long in a private school with a hair code, but this illustrates the privilege wealthy families enjoy that others do not. I have met many wealthy families who would never ask for or expect such special treatment, of course, but nearly all of them know they can and also know they are frequently offered privileges and exceptions even without asking.

These experiences shape the personalities and worldview of children and teens who grow up within these family cultures. One of my clients wrecked his car driving recklessly on a rural road.

"I'm glad you weren't hurt," I said, "and I'm sorry you lost your car."

"It's okay," he said. "My dad bought me a better one."

"How did your dad react to your accident?" I asked.

"He yelled at me and said I was driving like an idiot," he said.

"So why do you think he bought you a new car?"

"Well, I have to have a car," he said, as if there were no other choice.

Growing up like this cannot help but shape how you see the world and your place in it.

Poor Readiness for Adult Living

Similarly, a trait that is endemic to wealthy parents and, sadly, has become increasingly more common among all parents is the unwillingness to let their children fail. Because they have the means and the influence to do so, rich parents see their kids struggling in some key area of life and commit themselves to preventing the failure.

As nearly everyone knows, failure is an essential tutor in life. To never be allowed to fail sets a person up for being an incompetent adult. Wealthy parents know this, too, but when the moment of failure comes, they often see it as their responsibility to intervene rather than let the failure occur.

In my interviews with wealthy parents, a consistent theme emerges: *we know we shouldn't always rescue him, but we always seem to do it.* When I press about why they rescue anyway, the answers center around three themes. The first, and by far the dominant reason given, is they worry that their child's poor decisions will reduce his chances of success later in life. These families are strongly predisposed to viewing success and failure through the lens of career trajectory, income, and net worth. Whatever represents a threat to those pursuits evokes a powerful impulse to protect and run interference.

Second, I frequently hear a theme of guilt. They have so many resources at their disposal—money, status, connections—and it seems wrong to these parents not to leverage these resources to help someone they love. They help so many other people, they reason, it wouldn't be right not to use the tools of money and influence to help their own children.

The third most frequent theme is to save face for the family. Having a teen who doesn't get into a good college, or a young adult who has a known drug problem or a criminal conviction, reflects badly on the family. Since they often have higher status in the community or beyond, a massive failing rarely feels like a private affair to them.

In some ways, none of this is new. Wealthy parents have been running interference for their kids for centuries. However, we know this type of parental behavior undermines young people in the long run. Wealthy people, in my experience, have become well aware of this, and most agree with the principle of allowing logical and natural consequences. It's only when the crisis comes that their resolve fades.

Rich people, especially those who earned their wealth, are often action-oriented individuals. They are used to solving problems and taking decisive action. When they see their kid—whether child, teen, or young adult—get into trouble, their natural tendency is to solve the problem. They spring into action, intent on fixing whatever has become broken. These instincts serve them well in other realms of their lives, but work against them and the long-term well-being of their child in these moments. Now, for what may be the first time, they attempt to hold the line and not bail out a person they love the most in the world. For many wealthy parents, it's hard to hold back when they know they could change the outcome and reduce the impact of their kid's misbehavior. It's a painful thing to do.

Motivational Challenges

In my clinical experience, I've seen two common trajectories with kids, teens, and young adults from wealthy families. The first is the wealth saps them of intrinsic motivation. Whether consciously or unconsciously, they know they will never want for anything, so they become content with a life of low ambition and motivation. As one of my clients rhetorically asked, "Why would I ever pick a stressful life when I'm going to be okay no matter what I do?"

The kids on the second path have observed wealth accumulation and what it affords a person, and they want it for themselves. They see the possibilities, and they don't just want to inherit or be given money, but to accomplish this for themselves. They become singularly focused on building a career that produces a high income and builds large net worth. There are other paths, of course, but these two seem to be the most common.

The kids with little motivation pose the biggest challenges in therapy. For all we may have learned from Self-Determination Theory about tapping into one of the core needs of autonomy, competence, and relatedness to help draw out intrinsic motivation, anyone who has worked with lowly motivated teens or young adults knows this works better in theory than in practice. Getting teens or young adults with little motivation to move forward in life is among the hardest and least successful undertakings for any therapist. Some undermotivated people who grow up with all their needs met often have little incentive to do much of anything.

On the other extreme, the young people who have internalized unrelenting standards are more vulnerable to emotional difficulties like depression and anxiety (Luthar et al., 2023). One of my clients, a guy in his mid-20s, scheduled an appointment to talk about his anxiety. We quickly identified the source: he had been conditioned by his family to seek a high-income profession, but he didn't like any of the options he could generate, and he also didn't want to live a life of high stress, which he knew often came with high-paying jobs. He felt torn. If he did what he wanted to do, his parents would disapprove. If he did what they wanted him to do, he'd be stressed out and miserable. There was no winning this, he believed.

Getting motivation well calibrated, where it is not too low or runs too hot, becomes the task in therapy.

Family Dysfunction

High school students from wealthy families showed more maladjustment on several key indicators of well-being, even compared to poor inner-city students. The research found that these kids were more likely to struggle with depression and anxiety (Luthar & Latendresse, 2005). Wealth may have provided them with more resources and opportunities, but it also made them more vulnerable to mental health and substance abuse problems.

Most studies have found that the more social support a person has, the less depressed they become. But researcher Kimber Bogard at Columbia University examined the lives of 374 wealthy seventh graders and found that when they were not close with their parents, the involvement of other supportive adults actually exacerbated depression. This was attributed to "the particularity of this population" (Bogard, 2005). There is something different about wealthy tweens and teens that causes them to get more depressed when other adults step in while their parents are distant and not involved. Perhaps it shows them that their parents were not behaving the way they should toward them. When other adults act with warmth and closeness, they are reminded of what they do not have in their parents. This has particular implications for therapists and other helpers.

HELPING CHILDREN IN WEALTHY FAMILIES

Working with the children of wealthy parents poses a challenge to clinicians. If there are issues of significant family dysfunction, best practices would dictate that you involve parents in treatment for most young clients (Kazdin, 2003). Sometimes, though, that option is not available and you will have limited access to parents, because of busy schedules, out-of-town travel, or other factors. In those instances, your best option is to determine early whether the primary need is for family therapy or individual therapy. Sometimes the need can be for both.

When the situation calls for family therapy, you are encouraged to hold your ground and insist that this is how you need to proceed. If you are skilled in family therapy, you can take them on as a client. If not, you are wise to refer them to a trusted colleague.

If individual therapy with the child or teen is best, begin by discussing issues of confidentiality and communication with the parents. Make this conversation part of the first session. I encourage regular but boundaried communication with parents over the course of therapy. A parent has rights to information about their child, but I often ask them in the first session if they will allow me to talk confidentially with their child and not ask me or the child to disclose confidential information. That said, I also tell them I would like to hear from them regularly, either at the beginning of the session or with other check-ins. Information that comes to me is not confidential; only information that flows from me. I also tell parents any information I get from them can be fairly disclosed to the child or teen, so we do nothing behind their back. When we meet, I feel the freedom to discuss treatment progress and the general sense of how the sessions are going. All this can be done without disclosing confidential information, especially for teenagers. I then keep the child or teen aware of this, including an honest recap of what I have shared with their parents.

There are many times when the parents need their own consultation or therapy around how to parent their child. This differs from couples' therapy, though it may look similar in the room. If, however, you have agreed to be the child's therapist, I would urge you to avoid also being the parents' therapist or consultant. That role needs to be performed by someone else. You should be either the child's therapist or the parents' consultant, not both, particularly for older children and teens or where the therapist must challenge parents to be more consistent and set limits. Similarly, you should not be both the child's individual therapist and the family therapist. In each instance, there are built-in potential conflicts that may compromise your individual therapy work.

For example, let's imagine you have a 16-year-old male client who is smoking weed and has low motivation to do well in school. His parents seek your help to get him on track. When you meet with the young man, he tells you there is nothing wrong with smoking weed. It's a natural substance. He enjoys it and it helps him unwind from the day. His parents have a glass of wine every night, he tells you, and this isn't much different. In fact, it's safer and less harmful, he says.

Depending on how therapy is configured, you could be in one of three different roles: the teenager's individual therapist, the parents' consultant or therapist, or the family's therapist. Those roles may all have the same or similar objectives, but they are different roles. One of the biggest ways they differ is in who the client is in each scenario. The teen is the client of the individual therapist. The parents are the client of the parent therapist or consultant. The family is the client of the family therapist. That might sound obvious, but it has significant implications. It makes a big difference.

A major task in the first session is to determine your role, as well as the other roles the family may need to have filled to help this child or teen. Perhaps everything can be handled well with you acting as the family therapist. Maybe you need to be the individual therapist, but the parents need their own therapist. You size up the need and then make good referrals, carefully explaining the different roles and why they may be needed.

There are also some best practices for intervening in the areas that we have previously identified as being the most common areas of need or concern. The following are some strategies for helping in each of these critical areas.

Substance Abuse

Among teens, substance abuse nearly always starts with marijuana and alcohol (Johnson et al., 2018). However, among affluent teens, because they have much greater access to prescription drugs like painkillers and antianxiety medicine, as well as party drugs including cocaine and MDMA, the risks for more significant drug abuse and dependency at a much earlier age are very real.

Because this issue is so consistently seen among both wealthy parents and their teen and young adult children, I've devoted an entire chapter to it. See Chapter 10 for a more detailed discussion of how you can address substance problems among wealthy clients.

Anxiety and Depression

The gold standard for treating internalizing disorders like anxiety and depression remains Cognitive-Behavioral Therapy (CBT), even for children. Depending on the age and developmental level of the child, some of the cognitive interventions may need to be modified significantly. Younger children cannot do some of the logical reasoning tasks that cognitive interventions rely upon. Behavioral interventions, like exposures for anxiety and behavioral activation for depression, are helpful at almost any age, however.

Within this tradition, social skills training for children with social anxiety can be effective as well. This will require teaching and practicing the skills in the session, but also homework for practicing the skills at school or in the community. In group therapy, the skills can be practiced with other peers, and each child can be given feedback in real time.

There is debate about the evidence of play therapy interventions for children dealing with depression or anxiety. The research has produced mixed results. Some studies have found it to be effective, and others have found little to no benefit (LeBlanc & Ritchie, 2001). Part of the difficulty may be that play therapy is actually a broad umbrella of approaches, philosophies, and interventions that are all lumped into the same category. Also, the flexible, spontaneous nature of play therapy makes it harder to operationalize and systematize in rigorous research models. There might be some benefits to play therapy, but it currently would not be a consensus evidence-based practice.

Low Resilience

Years ago, I had a 20-year-old client who became suicidal after a breakup. He had the awareness to know that his emotional reaction was more intense than it should have been, but he still found himself completely undone by the experience. I asked him why he thought it had hit him so hard. He said, "I've never had anything bad happen to me."

He had nothing bad happen to him in two decades of life. Of course, a breakup sent him into a tailspin. He didn't have the emotional muscle to deal with it. Just like physical muscle, emotional muscle gets built by pushing against resistance, by doing something hard that pushes your current capacity to the limit.

Many children and teens in wealthy families have been so cocooned against any hardship or challenge that they lack the emotional muscle to deal with what life deals them. The therapist's job is not to create distress for them, but to give them opportunities for emotional muscle building by stepping outside of their comfort zone. After explaining the purpose of why this is important, I brainstorm with them a few things that might represent a personal challenge. Examples might include trying out for the school musical or attempting to make the roster of a sport that they have never formally played before. It might be to speak up in a class discussion or run for office. It could be anything that is challenging, where the possibility of failure is real.

Developing a growth mindset is essential to building resilience. Unfortunately, some research suggests that children from wealthy families may be more prone to developing a fixed mindset because of the emphasis on achievement and success often present in affluent environments. For example, Luthar and Becker (2002) found that children from affluent backgrounds were more likely to experience pressure to perform, which can lead to a fixed mindset where they fear failure and view intelligence or academic ability as a fixed trait. This environment may create a focus on innate ability rather than effort, leading to a belief that one's abilities are static.

Children with fixed mindsets believe their abilities in any area—academic skills, athletic ability, social confidence, musical ability—are set in stone, which limits their growth and resilience. Those with a growth mindset believe abilities can be developed through effort, learning, and persistence. To build this mindset in children, we frame challenges as opportunities rather than threats, as moments of growth rather than moments of shame. Encourage them to embrace mistakes as part of the learning process, praising their effort and perseverance rather than just their achievements. By gradually exposing them to new and difficult tasks and framing these as chances to grow, you help them build the emotional resilience needed to face future challenges with confidence.

Entitlement

Though not synonymous with narcissism, entitlement is a characteristic found in more narcissistic people. Children and teens who rate high on narcissism are at a much higher risk for developing full-blown Narcissistic Personality Disorder (NPD) in adulthood (Thomaes & Brummelman, 2016; Barry & Kauten, 2014). The earlier this can be addressed in therapy, the better. While this may be hard work, there are some interventions you might find helpful.

Gleichgerrcht and Young (2013) found that low empathy was linked to higher entitlement. Building a greater capacity for empathy can help reduce feelings of entitlement. Social stories, for example, show promise as a way of reducing entitlement (Benish & Bramlett, 2011). With this strategy, you produce a real or imagined story of a person in need. You ask the young client to identify what the person in need may be feeling, then ask why they likely felt that emotion. This practice of taking perspective to reflect on the needs of others can help build empathy. This makes considering only your own needs more difficult and can reduce a sense of entitlement.

One of the most powerful interventions to dismantle a sense of entitlement is encouraging your clients to engage in service activities. As part of a treatment plan for children or teens of wealthy families, encouraging volunteering to serve more underprivileged people can have a tremendous impact on reducing entitlement for many. Depending on their age, they could volunteer for homeless shelters or food banks. They could also consider tutoring and mentoring, working at an animal shelter, or volunteering at a hospital. There are dozens of other examples and options. Volunteering enhances the self-esteem of adolescents, increases their pro-social behavior, and improves social responsibility, all of which play a role in reducing entitlement (Van Goethem et al., 2014).

Poor Readiness for Adult Living

Some older teens and young adults are nowhere close to being ready for adult living, while others worry that they are not ready but actually are well prepared. It's best to regard these two groups differently. For the young adults who are not ready for adult living, a major task of therapy will be to assess the daily living skills they currently lack and then creating a full plan to teach and practice those skills. These skills cluster in ten key areas:

- *Financial Literacy:* This involves understanding how to budget, save, and invest money effectively, as well as managing credit and debt responsibly. It also includes knowing how to file taxes and plan for long-term financial goals such as retirement.
- *Automotive Basics:* Young adults should know how to perform basic car maintenance, such as checking tire pressure, changing oil, and fixing a flat tire. Understanding car insurance, registration, and handling roadside emergencies is essential.
- *Health and Wellness:* Maintaining physical and mental health is crucial, which includes knowing basic first aid, when to seek medical attention, and how to navigate the healthcare system, including understanding insurance. A balanced diet, regular exercise, and stress management are also key components.
- *Home Maintenance and Repair:* This area covers basic knowledge of household systems like plumbing, electrical, and HVAC. It's important to know how to perform simple repairs, keep a clean and organized home, and recognize when to call a professional for more complex issues.
- *Career Development:* Building a career involves creating a professional resume and online profile, mastering job interview skills, and understanding workplace rights and responsibilities. Networking and building professional relationships are also critical for career growth.
- *Legal Knowledge:* Young adults should understand their basic legal rights and responsibilities, including knowledge of contracts, leases, and agreements. It's also important to know how to handle legal issues, whether it's resolving disputes or interacting with law enforcement.
- *Interpersonal Skills:* Effective communication, conflict resolution, and the ability to build and maintain relationships are vital. This category also includes understanding and setting healthy boundaries in both personal and professional contexts.
- *Time Management:* Managing time effectively involves prioritizing tasks, balancing work and personal life, and setting and achieving goals. These skills are essential for navigating the demands of adulthood.
- *Technology Proficiency:* Basic computer skills, such as using word processing software, spreadsheets, and email, are necessary in today's digital world. Understanding online privacy, cybersecurity, and being able to troubleshoot common tech issues are also important.
- *Civic Engagement:* Being an informed and active citizen includes understanding how government and politics work, knowing the importance of voting, and staying informed about current events and social issues.

For the other group of teens and young adults who are ready but feel like they are not, nearly always, the main issue is anxiety. These are young adults whose anxiety causes them to ruminate about the future, worrying about their own perceived inadequacies. The issue is not a lack of skill, but anxiety and a lack of confidence. This worry that they cannot become a successfully launched independent adult holds them back.

THE OPPORTUNITY FOR EARLY IMPACT

Growing up in a wealthy family seems like it would be a dream come true. It's often a much more comfortable life, but it poses big risks for struggles, including a higher chance of developing a drug problem, greater risk of anxiety and depression, lower resilience, greater sense of entitlement, lower readiness for adult living, and greater family dysfunction. Years ago, a parent of a teenage client said to me, "We might screw him up now, but at least we can afford rehab later." He intended it as a joke, but I realized he had contemplated the truth of that statement.

While there are many families that are both healthy and wealthy, the research suggests that this is harder to achieve, given the pressures and blind spots that are inherent in extreme wealth. Helping the children in these families holds the possibility that you can help break the pattern of generational dysfunction that we often see. Working with children, teens, and young adult children in wealthy families improves the odds of having greater impact, compared to seeing them when they are older and the patterns are more entrenched. It's challenging work, but the potential to make a significant impact is encouraging.

REFERENCES

Barry, C. T., & Kauten, R. L. (2014). Nonpathological and pathological narcissism: Which self-reported characteristics are most problematic in adolescents? *Journal of Personality Assessment, 96*(2), 212–219.

Benish, A., & Bramlett, R. (2011). Empathy-building interventions: Effectiveness of social stories in reducing entitlement in children. *Journal of Applied Psychology, 46*(3), 341–356.

Bogard, K. (2005). Parental involvement and its impact on depression among wealthy adolescents. *Journal of Child Development, 76*(4), 789–805.

Gallagher, J. (2023). Family wealth and its consequences: A study on entitlement and social impact. *Harvard Business Review.*

Gleichgerrcht, E., & Young, L. (2013). Low empathy and high entitlement: The paradox of privilege. *Cognitive Neuroscience Journal, 42*(7), 315–329.

Johnson, R., Kaplan, S., & McGill, A. (2018). Substance use patterns among affluent youth. *Journal of Adolescent Health, 62*(2), 150–156.

Kazdin, A. E. (2003). *Parent management training: Treatment for oppositional, aggressive, and antisocial behavior in children and adolescents.* Oxford University Press.

LeBlanc, M., & Ritchie, S. (2001). A meta-analysis of play therapy interventions for anxiety and depression in children. *Clinical Psychology Review, 21*(8), 1238–1261.

Lund, T. J., & Dearing, E. (2012). Neighborhood context and mental health outcomes for affluent youth. *Journal of Social Psychology, 53*(6), 1028–1035.

Luthar, S. S., & Barkin, S. H. (2017). Affluence and adolescent substance use: Risks and resilience. *Development and Psychopathology, 29*(3), 919–938.

Luthar, S. S., & Becker, B. E. (2002). Privilege and pressure: The psychological impact of affluence on adolescents. *Child Development, 73*(5), 1593–1610.

Luthar, S. S., Ebbert, A. M., & Kumar, N. L. (2023). Unrelenting standards and emotional distress among affluent youth. *Journal of Adolescent Psychology, 49*(4), 345–368.

Luthar, S. S., & Latendresse, S. J. (2005). Children of the affluent: Challenges to well-being. *Current Directions in Psychological Science, 14*(1), 49–53.

Rampage, C. (2008). Affluence and anxiety: The emotional cost of wealth. *Journal of Clinical Psychology, 64*(12), 1384–1393.

Senzamici, A. (2023). The psychology of protest: Affluence and aggression in adolescence. *Journal of Adolescent Behavioral Studies, 29*(3), 456–471.

Stack, M. (2023). Wealth, protest, and the legal system: High-profile cases in contemporary America. *Law and Society Review, 57*(1), 89–112.

Thomaes, S., & Brummelman, E. (2016). Narcissism in youth: Risk factors and interventions. *Journal of Child and Family Studies, 25*(9), 2674–2682.

Van Goethem, A., Hoof, A., & Orobio, F. (2014). Adolescent volunteering and its impact on entitlement and social responsibility. *Journal of Youth Studies, 17*(8), 1093–1107.

Chapter 6

Well-Known People

I doubt you've ever heard of a man named Khaby Lame. Born in Senegal but raised in Italy, Khaby became an online sensation during the COVID-19 pandemic with his silent comedic skits. He is best known for his wordless reactions to overly complicated "life hack" videos, where he simplifies the tasks with a deadpan expression.

In 2024, he became the most-followed creator on TikTok, achieving over 160 million followers and over 2.5 billion views. His content also gained massive traction on Instagram, where he boasts tens of millions of followers. Khaby's appeal lies in his ability to transcend language barriers through physical comedy. His success has led to brand partnerships, appearances at major events, and recognition as a top global influencer.

Even though you've probably not heard of him, he is unquestionably famous. He has a massive cultural footprint and was listed in *Forbes' 40 Under 40* and *Forbes' 30 Under 30*. As we've discussed, someone can now be truly famous even though huge swaths of the population have never even heard their name. This is the nature of "New Fame."

The core idea of fame has changed little. It's still defined as being known by many people. The nature of fame has changed radically since the turn of the twenty-first century, though. This New Fame is in sharp contrast to the old model of fame from previous generations. Let's review a brief history of how this New Fame has advanced and its implications for therapy.

THE EVOLUTION OF FAME

We have always had famous people. Before mass media, they were folk heroes and politicians. With the advent of radio, film, and television, they were performers, athletes, and entertainers.

In the 1970s, a new type of celebrity emerged: people who were "famous for being famous." These individuals, often socialites or minor entertainers, became known not for significant achievements, but for their frequent appearances on

DOI: 10.4324/9781003503569-8

game shows like *Match Game* or *Hollywood Squares* and occasional guest spots on talk shows. With only three broadcast networks and no internet, even minimal exposure could make someone widely recognizable.

By the early 2000s, this concept shifted with the rise of cable TV and the internet. Celebrities like Paris Hilton and the Kardashians gained fame not through talent but by showcasing their lives in highly curated reality shows. Unlike their predecessors, they built their fame by offering audiences access to their personal lives—homes, travels, and relationships—on television and later on social media. Though the reality they portrayed was carefully edited, viewers felt a sense of connection and familiarity.

This shift laid the groundwork for the rise of influencers. Over the next decade, these new celebrities would dominate social media, amassing millions of followers through their unique personalities and content. Influencers became popular in niches like beauty, fitness, gaming, and lifestyle, drawing audiences with information, opinions, skills, and experiences. Unlike traditional celebrities, influencers actively engage with their followers by responding to comments, answering questions, and appearing at public events.

Reality TV further fueled the evolution of fame. Low production costs and high viewer engagement made reality shows prolific, creating a steady stream of contestants who could leverage their brief appearances into lasting online presences. Many reality stars transitioned to social media, building large followings and launching careers as influencers or product ambassadors.

OLD FAME VS. NEW FAME

Traditional fame, or "Old Fame," was easier to define. Even more recent celebrities like Taylor Swift, Oprah Winfrey, and LeBron James became household names through established channels like movies, television, major-label music, or professional sports. Their fame was broad and often enduring, based on significant achievements and public visibility.

"New Fame," however, is more fragmented and harder to pin down. It includes influencers, reality stars, and social media personalities whose reach and engagement are often limited to specific demographics or subcultures. Someone like Khaby Lame is famous within the overlapping TikTok and Instagram communities, but unknown to everyone else.

The distinction between Old Fame and New Fame highlights a cultural shift. Old Fame was universal and tied to traditional media, while New Fame thrives in niches and often comes from direct audience engagement. Today, people can achieve immense fame within their communities without ever crossing into mainstream recognition.

Old Fame and New Fame are not mutually exclusive, however. Traditional celebrities often leverage social media to expand their reach, while some influencers cross over into traditional fame. Young stars like Timothée Chalamet or Ariana

Grande have achieved fame through traditional channels like film and music, but they maintain strong social media presences to engage with fans. Conversely, talents like The Weeknd or Tori Kelly began their careers on social media, but parlayed them into traditional media platforms.

PROPOSED CATEGORIES OF INFLUENCE

One simple way to understand New Fame is by categorizing influencers based on their follower count. Though this is an imperfect measure, it tells us a great deal about the reach that each influencer has within their particular community.

- *Nano-Influencers* (1,000–10,000 followers): These influencers have small but highly engaged audiences. Their personal connections with followers create high trust and influence within their niche. For example, a gardening enthusiast with 5,000 followers might share tips and tutorials that resonate deeply with their audience.
- *Micro-Influencers* (10,000–50,000 followers): Known for niche expertise and loyalty, these influencers often have higher engagement rates than those with larger audiences. A fitness coach with 25,000 followers who shares workout routines and recipes fits this category.
- *Mid-Tier Influencers* (50,000–500,000 followers): These individuals bridge the gap between micro- and macro-influencers, balancing significant reach with relatively high engagement. A tech reviewer who has 150,000 followers and who analyzes the latest gadgets is a good example.
- *Macro-Influencers* (500,000–1 million followers): These influencers have substantial audiences and are often regarded as celebrities within their niches. A musician with 750,000 followers sharing behind-the-scenes content from tours and recordings fits here.
- *Mega-Influencers* (1 million+ followers): These are global celebrities with massive followings. Examples include soccer star Cristiano Ronaldo, beauty mogul Kylie Jenner, and podcast host Joe Rogan, each of whom command hundreds of millions of followers.

These categories illustrate the democratization of fame. Social media allows influencers at every level to engage with their audiences, collaborate with one another, and grow their followings, often in ways that traditional celebrities cannot.

IMPLICATIONS OF NEW FAME FOR THERAPY

All this leaves us in a state where there are still some traditionally famous people but even more non-traditionally famous people. Here are four big implications of this cultural shift.

63

They're Everywhere

Since we are considering influencers and other "new famous" people to be among the famous, this means they are no longer primarily based only in entertainment hubs like Los Angeles, New York, Nashville, and Atlanta. Now they can be found in St. Louis and Charlotte and Indianapolis and other locations not historically known for having many well-known people. MrBeast lives in a city in North Carolina of fewer than 100,000 residents, for example (Jacob, 2023). In a study of where influencers live, California and New York kept the top spots, but they were followed by Texas and Florida. Now you could practice in Dallas or Miami or many other cities with the potential to see far more well-known clients now than ever before (Influencity, 2023).

The Paradox of Anonymous Famous Clients

You may have a famous person as a client you may not recognize. This has happened to me occasionally. I found out months into therapy that one of my clients had amassed a large seven-figure social media following and was considered an influencer. He did not tell me this. I found out about it from another social relationship who was talking about the influencer's videos, unaware that I knew him. In the first session, when I had asked the influencer what he did in life, he said he worked as a representative for a product line. This was partially true. I've had another client who was connected to a well-known reality show that I had never watched tell me he was a property manager. Again, there was some truth to it. While I've had others who have not kept their status as a public figure from me, it is now possible more than ever before that you may not know. There may be little you can do about this, other than to know this possibility exists.

Destigmatizing Therapy

This new class of famous people is consistently more pro-therapy than well-known people in the past, who were notoriously private. Often these "new famous" people use their platforms to destigmatize mental health struggles and normalize seeking help. Some have even built their entire platform on mental health awareness and concerns.

These clients will typically approach therapy with a more open stance. Among their influencer peers, therapy is not only destigmatized but often assumed. While helping to normalize help-seeking is a good movement, there can be a point where the message that all the cool people are in therapy can actually undermine us and our legitimacy. I've heard many clinicians say, "The whole world would be better if everyone were in therapy." This has a certain appeal and sounds valid on its face, but this view risks seeing therapy diminished in the eyes of the culture to a fascinating recreational activity.

This sentiment of therapy for all people all the time is an outworking of a negative trend on social media where people are self-diagnosing or untrained and unlicensed personalities are shaping ideas about mental health. This is where the "all people have some form of trauma" movement comes from most directly. It contributes to the loose, self-directed diagnoses of everything from ADHD to autism spectrum disorders and even disassociation. We all hear more terms like "gaslighting" and "toxic" from clients in therapy, as if these are true clinical syndromes. All this seems like we are democratizing therapy but can contribute to sloppy practice. Because so many people experience genuine trauma, the movement to re-conceptualize trauma as anything bad—a normal breakup, losing luggage at the airport, an unaffectionate father, being embarrassed at a social function, being fired—does these individuals and our field a disservice.

So while this new cohort of famous people is more open to therapy, with that often comes a popularized psychology that can be incomplete or incorrect. This also introduces some complexity to the therapeutic process.

Therapy as Content

Some among this cohort of new famous people may use therapy as content for their platform. They may post a video talking about what they discussed in therapy, and what their therapist (you) said, or make some joke or criticism about the therapy itself. I have not yet experienced this, to my knowledge, but I know of many videos with this type of content. Sometimes, the person is blasting the therapist for some misstep.

Years ago, I attended a weeklong writer's conference. The instructor gave us an assignment to write a scene using natural-sounding dialogue. The next day, a woman in our cohort shared her scene. It was nearly a word-for-word transcript of my lunch conversation with two other people. I wondered why this woman had remained quiet and off to the side during lunch. I instantly realized she was recording our conversation in some form. She never acknowledged this in the class, but I, of course, knew what she had done. It was a surreal moment. Fortunately, I had said nothing too embarrassing, but it felt like a weird intrusion into a conversation that I thought was semiprivate. Now, imagine that happening on a much larger scale, where thousands or maybe millions might be privy to your most private conversations. If you find yourself with a client who has a large social media following, you would be wise to initiate a conversation about their expectations and intentions about the content of the session. You cannot restrict what they say or post, of course, but you have every right to engage in a dialogue about this, if needed.

THE SEDUCTIVE APPEAL OF FAME

Most of us daydream from time to time about being famous. It's a seductive fantasy. Surrounded by beautiful people. Always the center of attention. The mental images we have seem so appealing. Yet if you ask a person who is actually famous, you're likely to get a more sobering picture of the experience. Rarely do celebrities extol the benefits of being famous. They may acknowledge their privileged life-style. They often express gratitude for being able to do what they do if they act, play a sport, perform live shows, or influence people in an area of personal passion. However, they are unlikely to say that fame itself is anything better than a mixed bag, leaning toward bad. It has its benefits, but it also has huge downsides. The loss of privacy, having every nuanced gesture picked apart online, and the coercive experience it is for their loved ones are but a few of these negatives.

Despite what we know about the price of fame, it remains a desirable com-modity in our culture. There's a great quote from the old TV series *Glee* where Rachel says, "Nowadays being anonymous is worse than being poor. Fame is the most important thing in our culture today" (Murphy et al., 2009).

In the past, when I asked about their long-term vision for themselves, clients with lofty aspirations wanted to be professional athletes. Now, a more common answer is to join the ranks of influencers on social media. One of my clients told me his life goal is to livestream his video game play and grow his channel to so many followers that he doesn't need another job. When I asked him why, he said, "Because you get to play video games all day and you get to be famous, which are both good things."

In *Status and Culture*, David Marx says status is a person's position in a hier-archy. There may be different hierarchies like your school, your local city, your family, and so on, but if you move up the hierarchy within these communities, you get more benefits. People treat you better. You have more options. Your life is easier in some ways. Conversely, if you move down the hierarchy, people treat you worse, and that has a harmful impact on your quality of life. This explains, in part, the evolutionary appeal of celebrity. We give celebrities high status in our culture. Consequently, they receive many benefits that can improve their quality of life (Marx, 2022). It also partially explains why many people experience strong con-nections to celebrities they don't know. Our brains are wired for relationship, and celebrity status gives the illusion of personal connection. When the celebrity does well—a sold-out concert tour, a highly rated TV show, record-breaking clicks on a video—those who are attached to the celebrity feel like something good is hap-pening to them by extension. Though some speculate that these parasocial relation-ships (i.e., one-sided relationships between fans and celebrities they don't know in real life) are the product of loneliness and social isolation, researchers found this to be untrue, at least in the milder forms (Rubin et al., 1985). In the more extreme forms, though, these parasocial relationships become unhealthy, often taking the form of what is termed "celebrity worship" (McCutcheon et al., 2002).

CELEBRITY WORSHIP

We are in an age of unprecedented celebrity worship. We've seen intense celebrity worship in the past with Elvis, the Beatles, Sinatra, Marilyn Monroe, James Dean, and others, but none of it compares to the scope of what we are currently experiencing. Taylor Swift's Eras Tour had a profound economic and cultural impact not only in the United States but around the world. Beyoncé also packed stadiums and festivals and has had a massive impact. K-Pop bands like BTS have rabid fanbases. Some actors and athletes boast similar followings. Cristiano Ronaldo, Lionel Messi, and LeBron James have massive amounts of passionate followers, as examples.

Celebrity worship is a more intense and pathological form of parasocial relationships. This phenomenon showed sharp increases in the twenty-first century and has been found to be associated with higher levels of anxiety, depression, narcissism, obsessive thoughts, and disordered eating, among other negative behaviors.

Celebrity status holds the promise of a better life, and our connection to celebrities is a desire to taste that same success by association. These assumptions are faulty, of course, but they go a long way toward explaining why many people desire to be celebrities and why others form strong attachments to certain celebrities.

McCutcheon and Aruguete (2021) examined 35 studies that used the Celebrity Attitude Scale (CAS), a psychological tool designed to measure the attitudes and behaviors of individuals toward celebrities. Developed by McCutcheon and colleagues, the scale helps to understand how deeply people are involved or obsessed with celebrities. It is commonly used in studies related to celebrity worship and its impact on mental health. The CAS categorizes celebrity worship into three levels:

1. *Entertainment-Social:* This is the most benign level of celebrity worship. Individuals at this level are interested in celebrities for entertainment and social purposes. They may read about celebrities and discuss them with friends, but this interest doesn't significantly affect their daily lives.
2. *Intense-Personal:* At this level, individuals develop deeper feelings for a celebrity. They may ruminate about the celebrity and feel a strong personal connection, often imagining that they are in a special relationship with the celebrity.
3. *Borderline-Pathological:* This level represents the most extreme form of celebrity worship. Individuals might display obsessive behaviors, such as spending excessive amounts of money to get memorabilia, considering personal sacrifices for the celebrity, or having uncontrollable fantasies and behaviors related to the celebrity.

THE DOWNSIDE OF FAME

It's rare to find celebrities who genuinely enjoy fame. While some, like Will Smith, express appreciation for the sense of security and opportunity that fame can bring, others remain wary of its impact on their personal lives. It's noteworthy that

Smith voiced his enjoyment of fame before his public controversies altered his career trajectory.

Other celebrities acknowledge both pride in their success and discomfort with the constant spotlight. For example, Adele has noted the tension between her achievements and the personal constraints that fame imposes, observing that as her career grew, her personal life seemed to shrink.

For many celebrities, fame brings more challenges than rewards. Decades ago, Richard Burton likened fame to a sweet poison, something enthusiastically consumed, only to have it destroy you later. His perspective remains relevant today, as a new generation of famous individuals echo similar sentiments. Many are burdened by the constant exposure, the limitations on personal freedom, and the toll on relationships. Fame often means trading true intimacy and normalcy for relentless public scrutiny and intrusion.

Yet, despite these drawbacks, fame has a seductive allure. For some, a small taste only intensifies the desire for more, reflecting a complex psychological attraction. Sally Rooney, author of *Beautiful World, Where Are You?* writes,

> People who intentionally become famous—I mean people who, after a little taste of fame, want more and more of it—are, and I honestly believe this, deeply psychologically ill. The fact that we are exposed to these people everywhere in our culture, as if they are not only normal but attractive and enviable, indicates the extent of our disfiguring social disease.
>
> (Rooney, 2021, p. 174)

Besides the misery and disconnection fame often brings, there is evidence that it can actually foreshorten a person's life on average. Perhaps you've heard of the "27 Club," the sad name given to the famous musicians who died at age 27. The roster includes Jimi Hendrix, Amy Winehouse, Kurt Cobain, Jim Morrison, and others. Though it has become part of our culture's folklore, it makes us wonder if musical artists are more likely to die young. It seems they do.

Psychologist Dianna Kenney reviewed the lives of 12,665 musicians who had died between 1950 and 2014. She wanted to know if these artists die younger than others. The results were astounding. She found these pop stars died an average of 20 to 25 years earlier than the general population. The most common age for them to die was 56, while the average American is expected to live to age 76. If this pattern wasn't by chance, she looked at the rates of death by suicide, homicide, and accident (including overdose) to explain why these talented people might be more prone to die young. The findings were incredibly sad. Musical artists died by suicide at a rate two to seven times higher than the general population. They died by homicide up to eight times higher and by accidental means five to ten times higher than the average person (Kenny, 2014).

Fame comes at a high price. It costs relationships, emotional well-being, privacy, and even years of life. Yet, despite all this, people still seek it.

THERAPY THEMES

Rockwell and Giles (2009) write, "The experience of being famous is something for which no one is prepared. It is a world described as bizarre, surreal, scary, lonely, creepy, daunting, embarrassing, confusing, and invasive" (p. 185). They quote one unnamed famous individual who told them:

> Fame 101 is needed to teach people what's coming: the swell of people, the requests, the letters, the e-mails, the greetings on the street, the people in cars, the honking of the horns, the screaming of your name. A whole world comes to you that you have no idea is there. It just comes from nowhere. And it starts to build and build like a small tornado, and it's coming at you, and coming at you, and by the time it gets to you, it's huge and can sweep you off your feet and take you away and put you in a world that has no reality whatsoever because all the people are judging you on what you do for a living, not for who you are.
>
> (Rockwell & Giles, 2009, p. 185)

That image of fame as a tornado that is "coming at you" and will profoundly alter all aspects of your life and reality is striking and terrifying. Fame affects every corner of your life, from your relationships to your sense of identity. Based on their interviews with famous people, the researchers found the following themes consistently emerged:

- *Loss of Privacy and Objectification:* Famous people experience individuals and the media as constantly crossing the boundary into their private lives. The celebrity is viewed as a commodity that others want a piece of.
- *Mistrust:* When strangers intrude on your life, you develop a sense of mistrust. Why is someone being so flattering and nice? What do they want? This is why you often see celebrities in various fields surrounded by friends they made before they were famous.
- *Demanding Expectations:* Famous people perceive the need to live up to the expectations of others in what they say, what they wear, what their attitude is like. If the person is swarmed by 50 autograph-hounds and they sign 40, they have disappointed 10. Multiply this by many encounters each week for months and years, and it becomes exhausting. This has only gotten worse with the proliferation of social media.
- *Gratification and Loss:* They experience life differently from others because they are so frequently the focus of attention. They are almost constantly getting praise and adoration. People laugh harder at their jokes, flatter them,

69

and tell them how amazing they are. It also becomes easier to lose connection with family members, partners, even their own children, because the focus is so much on them.

- *Symbolic Immortality:* They feel the need to leave some legacy that outlives them and their fame. Often this takes the form of "giving back." It can also create a drive to leave a memorable body of work that will survive them. Their music, movies, championship records, or whatever else will live on after they are no longer here.

- *Wealth:* Becoming rich provides a tangible picture of their success and fame. It allows them freedom from financial worries. It also buys back some of the privacy and safety that has been compromised by their fame.

- *Access:* When a person becomes famous, they are ushered into a world unknown to most of us. There, they take selfies and exchange contacts with other celebrities. It is a private club where fame opens the door. In public among the common people, their name gets a preferred dinner reservation or the ability to skip the line at an elite club. It is a special, mostly hidden world of privilege.

- *Temptations:* With fame comes a world of temptations. Highly attractive people flirt with them. They are freely offered drugs. They face sexual temptations much more regularly and in ways that are difficult to resist.

- *Concerns About Family Impact:* They are concerned about the impact of their fame on other members of their family, including their partners, children, older parents, and others. Families often find it difficult to go out together in public. When they do go out, they find themselves intruded upon or interrupted by others.

PHASES OF FAME IN THERAPY

Through a series of interviews with well-known people, Rockwell and Giles (2009) found that when a person becomes famous, they go through four phases. These phases unfold over the course of the person's lifespan, from the time they become famous throughout the rest of their lives. Here are the four phases and the central question that must be resolved in each phase. Each question gives us a therapeutic framework to operate within.

Ambivalence

New fame is usually met with adulation, recognition of good work, and ego-stroking, but the person must also cope with infringements on privacy, unflattering stories, and hostile critiques. In this early phase, they both love their fame and hate it.

Central Question: Is pursuing this high-profile career worth it for me?

How to Help: Start with good, reflective listening using open questions, follow-ups, and reflections. Gently observe their ambivalence about both sides of fame without judgment or quick advice. From there, consider using cost-benefit analysis (called "decisional balance" in Motivational Interviewing) and clarify their values using the Values Inventory in Appendix 1. Lead your client to discuss how well their career pursuit aligns with their values. Be willing to accept whatever conclusion they come to in this process.

Addiction

After some time, the lure of fame has become such an exhilarating thrill ride, the person cannot imagine living without it. Concerns over the loss of fame loom large. The person becomes driven to hold on to it.

Central Question: Can I become unattached to the constant lure of fame?

How to Help: Use the "What if?" technique, a cognitive strategy within the CBT tradition. It involves two questions: What are the odds that this might happen? And if that were to happen, what would the worst part about that be? You continue to follow this second question with the same question ("And then what would be the worst thing about that?"). It can be slightly annoying (which I usually prepare my client for), but it can be effective. The goal is to engage the logical part of the person's head rather than allowing it to be run by the emotional part of the brain. If done well, the well-known person can find the place where they can see how they can still have a full and meaningful life, even if their fame drops out from under them.

Acceptance

Later, when the spotlight becomes too hot and fame takes its casualties—betrayals, disappointments, powerful temptations, and family stressors—the famous person accepts this reality. They become less attached to it, neither constantly grasping for it nor trying to push it away.

Central Question: How do I radically accept the downsides of fame?

How to Help: Collaboratively list out the downsides of fame that have been experienced or could be experienced. Note what negative aspects of fame your client can take *action* on and what aspects they must *accept*. Action or acceptance. Come up with steps for any of the actionable items. Work on crafting acceptance self-talk that can be used for what they are powerless to change. For example, if a downside of fame is professional or amateur photographers taking pictures of their children when they are out in public, an action step might be having their agent contact media outlets to reinforce that no interviews will be granted to any outlet that publishes those pictures and/or lawsuits may be filed for use of pictures with their minor children. However, your client may need to practice acceptance of the reality that you cannot guarantee they will not have their picture taken when they are out in public, and that some tabloid is more than happy to run the pictures. Working through the script of the self-talk in advance can be helpful in the short run. In the long run, engaging your client in honest conversations about the downsides of fame is essential.

71

Adaptation

The celebrity lives in a way that accommodates the fame. They may move to a remote area, go out in public in disguise, develop rules for autograph seekers, surround themselves with a handful of trusted individuals who shield others from access, and a hundred other adaptive strategies.

Central Question: What are the healthiest ways to adapt to being a famous person?

How to Help: Explore an array of strategies that can help them cope well with fame. Pick the best among those options. Define who is in the inner circle of trust, why they are there, and what those individuals bring to the relationship. Discuss where they want to live. If they have a family, talk about where they want their kids to go to school. Identify communities that feel safe to them. This could be their gym, their church or other house of worship, a particular restaurant or bar, a book club, poker night, or other groups. Talk through the benefits of staying connected to healthy communities rather than becoming more isolated.

It may be helpful to share these phases with your client and see if this framework resonates with them. If so, enlist their help in identifying their current phase. Tell them the question that must be resolved at that stage. For someone who is in the early stages of their career or is just becoming famous, it's usually worth working on any potential ambivalence about continuing down that path early in the therapy process.

FAME AS A RISK FACTOR

Fame poses tremendous risks for people. While it has its benefits, it also has significant pitfalls and complications. More than a few well-known people have lamented what it has done to their lives. You will hear of celebrities likening fame to a prison or saying it is dangerous to their well-being.

In studying resilience, researchers talk about protective factors that tip the scale toward being more resilient, as well as risk factors that tip the scale toward struggle and difficulty. Based on research and clinical practice, it may be helpful to conceptualize fame as a risk factor, one that poses danger for the well-being of the individual. Unlike other risk factors, though, like abuse or neglect, fame may not seem like a risk. Yet we know it increases the chance of bad outcomes, including substance abuse, personality disorders, and relationship conflict. Fame poses a risk to the person in many important areas of life. While some steer clear of trouble, others struggle mightily. Your job as a therapist is to help mitigate those risks and guide them as they navigate the rocky road of fame.

REFERENCES

Influencity. (2023). *Trends in influencer locations in the U.S.* https://influencity.com/resources/studies/the-largest-influencer-study-of-the-united-states-2023/

Jacob, K. (2023). *The global influence of influencers in unexpected locations.* HarperOne.

Kenny, D. (2014). Mortality rates of musicians and the impact of fame. *Psychology of Music, 42*(5), 612–630.

Marx, D. (2022). *Status and culture.* HarperOne.

McCutcheon, L. E., & Aruguete, M. S. (2021). Celebrity worship and psychological outcomes. *Personality and Individual Differences, 175,* 110729.

McCutcheon, L. E., Lange, R., & Houran, J. (2002). Conceptualization and measurement of celebrity worship. *British Journal of Psychology, 93*(1), 67–87.

Murphy, R. (Writer & Director), Falchuk, B. (Writer), & Brennan, I. (Writer). (2009). Pilot (Season 1, Episode 1) [TV series episode]. In R. Murphy, B. Falchuk, & I. Brennan (Executive Producers), *Glee.* 20th Century Fox Television.

Rockwell, D. L., & Giles, D. C. (2009). *The psychology of fame.* Cambridge University Press.

Rooney, S. (2021). *Beautiful world, where are you?* Faber & Faber.

Rubin, R. B., Perse, E. M., & Powell, R. A. (1985). Loneliness, parasocial interaction, and local television news viewing. *Human Communication Research, 12*(2), 155–180.

Chapter 7

The Non-Normal Lives of Child Stars

Years ago, a close friend called me for advice. I was on a lengthy road trip, so we had time for a solid conversation. His son was a gifted musician and actor. As an older teen, he had landed a couple of solid music and acting gigs and had a brief speaking role on a popular network show.

My friend felt torn. Part of him wanted to encourage his son's acting career and was even considering renting a Los Angeles apartment to facilitate auditions and meetings with industry professionals. The risks frightened him, though. He had heard too many stories of child actors who had become wrecked by Hollywood. Many failed to break through, despite years of hard work and sacrifice. Others made it, but they faced the heightened prospect of drug addiction and even exploitation.

"What do you think?" he asked me.

"I think it makes more sense for him to pursue acting as a young adult than as a teenager. That way, you won't have to worry that he is in such a risky environment when he is still a kid. If he's 22 and still wants to pursue acting, then encourage him to do that," I said.

"You're right," he said. "I just needed to hear that from someone else."

His son attended college, got a degree, and later practiced medicine, rather than pursue acting. Perhaps he would have made it big if he had moved to L.A. We'll never know. I stand by my advice, however.

It's no secret that many child actors get destroyed by the show business machine. There are dozens of examples of child stars who develop severe addiction, struggle with mental illness, accumulate criminal records, and even die early, often by suicide. Tragic stories like Corey Haim, River Phoenix, Jonathan Brandis, Edward Furlong, and Amanda Bynes are well known, but there are countless other, lesser-known stories of ruined lives that we'll never hear.

Child actors, regardless of whether they become famous, face near constant rejection, the risk of exploitation, and exposure to sex and drugs at a much earlier age than their peers. The result is often a lifetime of struggle and misery for many of them. The full scope of the problem is impossible to know. Not all aspiring child

DOI: 10.4324/9781003503569-9

actors are members of the Screen Actors Guild, nor are there other centralized ways of tracking them. Many of these child actors will never make it to a speaking role, and we'll never know what their experience was or what traumas they faced as they pursued their dream of becoming a successful actor.

Years ago, I began therapy with a child actor who had amassed a good number of IMDB credits to his name as a teenager. Both his mother and father were also in the industry and had achieved a great deal of success and fame. You might expect this boy to be entitled, self-centered, and vain. He was none of these things. He was polite, took responsibility for his actions, and treated others well. I had observed the struggles of others who grew up under similar circumstances, so I wondered how he could have become the centered, good kid that he was.

No doubt some of his goodness was pre-wired into this temperament. He was, by nature, agreeable, conscientious, and not prone to anger or anxiety. However, the other factor may have even been more important: for all his success, he had a normal life. He attended a regular high school and played sports. When his family moved from his childhood home, they made it a priority to keep him connected with his hometown friends, arranging visits and even entire weeks in the summer to hang out with his best buddies. The only reason he even came to therapy, in fact, was after a member of his extended friend group received a cancer diagnosis that hit him hard.

He and his parents had put a lot of effort into cultivating his normalcy. There was an intentionality during his formative years that kept him grounded. He was a healthy person *despite* being a famous person in a famous family.

Child stars can be actors or singers, but they could also become famous in fields as varied as social media, dance, sports, or social justice advocacy. The issue here is less about their field, and more about being a well-known person while still a child or teenager. Most of the examples and research here will reference actors, but the conclusions apply to all young people who become famous.

There are child stars who have achieved a level of fame in their careers. There are also children who *may* become stars. Each group has its own unique challenges. The children and teens who aspire to become stars may have landed a few commercial gigs or minor roles on television. Nearly always, their parents back them with gusto. Often these kids attempt to make it as a performer for a year or two, then return to their previous lives. The research is close to nonexistent about these aspiring child actors, but my anecdotal experience suggests they resume normal lives, not much worse off for the effort. Of the kids I've known who fit into this category, none of them have expressed any regrets for having tried to pursue their dream of being a full-time actor, even if they came up short.

Those who become child stars are more of our focus here. To be clear, there is nothing normal or healthy about a child becoming famous. Most adults are ill-equipped for the high price of fame, so imagine the impact it has on children. These children are at once vulnerable and powerful. They are junior royalty who command more money, attention, and power than 99.99% of all children on the planet. Understanding this startling dichotomy is central to working with child stars. There must be a simultaneous appreciation for their powerlessness and their powerfulness. Neither condition benefits them. Both conditions bring with them a certain jeopardy.

THE PROBLEM OF NON-NORMALCY

In interviews with former and current child stars, a clear theme emerges: *their lives are not normal.* Reflecting on almost five decades of fame, Jodie Foster told an interviewer, "It's just a different life" (Bailey, 2018). The experience of non-normalcy hits hard and fast. "From the time I became famous in *E.T.*, my life got really weird," Drew Barrymore said, adding:

> One day I was a little girl, and the next day I was being mobbed by people who wanted me to sign my autograph or pose for pictures or who just wanted to touch me. It was frightening. I was this 7-year-old who was expected to be going on a mature 29.
>
> (THR, 2011)

Daniel Radcliffe, who hit stratospheric fame as Harry Potter at age 12, said it isn't the easy access to drugs or the fawning groupies who will sleep with you that represent the biggest risks. It is the struggle of trying to form a sense of identity in non-normal conditions. "I think it's very important, especially when you become famous young, to work out who you are without fame and without that as part of your identity, because that will go. Fame does not last forever. For anyone," he said (Oppenheim, 2016).

For many young stars, the developmental tasks that go into forming a solid sense of self are bypassed or forestalled. They have not worked out a sense of self outside of their fame. "To have to be someone you're not, to the whole world, is horrible. And I know how difficult it is to be authentic," Sean Mendes told *British GQ* (Levesley, 2020). In a separate interview with *The Guardian*, he lamented,

> All of that praise and all that success was turning into a big monster that was eating my self-confidence because, if anybody said they didn't like my music, all of a sudden I felt I was worth nothing. And that's what happens when you connect who you are with what you do.
>
> (Hattenstone, 2020)

Many child stars have no healthy friendships. In a survey of 74 former well-known child actors, more than half said when they were children, most of their friends were adults rather than same-age peers (Rapport & Meleen, 1998). Most were not around peers the way other kids were in their formative years. They didn't have playmates, go on sleepovers, or hang out at their friends' houses. The majority weren't on sports teams and didn't go to a traditional school. They didn't have the opportunity to build these normal peer friendships.

The larger system also conditions child stars to have competitive and not collaborative relationships with their peers in the same industry. Christina Aguilera said, "As a child, you're all pitted against one another, and other children are all about that grind too. It's a weird space to grow up in" (Mateos, 2021). They have few or no friendships to start with, then they are trained to see their peers as rivals. The combination does harm to their ability to have healthy relationships.

Early fame warps normal developmental processes like identity formation. Developing a clear sense of yourself and acting out of a core identity is almost impossible in the cauldron they are in during these key developmental years. Psychologist Donna Rockwell told *Insider* that even

> for the most grounded of people, getting swept up into the spotlight of fame is very difficult to withstand, to stay grounded. So for a child, it's 10 times more difficult. It's exponentially more challenging because they haven't even developed a full self yet.
>
> (Wright, 2020)

Miley Cyrus said, "I was an adult when I was supposed to be a kid . . . so now I'm an adult, and I'm acting like a kid" (Blasberg, 2013).

Nothing is normal when you are a child star. You don't have normal peer friendships or a normal school or a normal job or a normal life. You lose your connection to what most human experience is like. Cole Sprouse told *Variety*,

> One of the dangers of, at least in my position, which was a sitcom inside a sound stage for nine years with Disney Channel, you're raised in such an insular environment that you forget what real human experience or boots-on-the-ground actually looks like.
>
> (Gelhourn, 2024)

This makes life harder to navigate, despite the privileges fame affords.

The withering heat of social media, paparazzi, and zealous fans interferes with the child stars' ability to get themselves sorted out well. Selena Gomez said,

> We're easy targets. Every single kid who was brought up like this is an easy target. It's disgusting, because it's interesting to grown adults that these kids go through weird things because they're figuring out, "Do I like this? Do I love this? Maybe I love this person."

She adds, "People are reporting my every move and this and that because of Instagram and Twitter and you can find out everything" (Emmanuele & Schonfeld, 2023).

Despite these challenges, many current and former child stars admit ambivalence about their fame. "I'd never wish my upbringing on anyone," Mary Kate Olsen told *Marie Claire* magazine, "but I wouldn't take it back for the world" (Marie Claire, 2010).

THE ROLE OF PARENTS

Jackie Coogan was one of the first child stars in Hollywood history, starring in such films as Charlie Chaplin's classic, *The Kid*, and the 1922 version of *Oliver Twist* in which he played the title role. After almost 70 films and dozens of television appearances across several decades, he had a career resurgence in the 1960s when he played Uncle Fester in *The Addams Family*.

As a child actor, he had earned upwards of $4 million, which translates to around $60 million in today's economy. He was the first child actor to earn over a million dollars. His father had managed Jackie's money conservatively over the years, leaving the small fortune almost intact. However, when John died in a car accident five months before Jackie turned 21, his mother and stepfather assumed control of the finances and squandered most of it on fur coats, jewelry, luxury cars, and other pricey items. Jackie sued them, but recovered only $126,000—or 3%—of his total earnings (Shaffer, 1935; Terry, 2018).

The debacle led the state of California to pass the first legislation to protect the earnings and assets of child actors, the California Child Actors Bill, which was more commonly called the Coogan Act. The law mandates 15% of a child actor's earnings to be placed into a trust that the child can access upon turning 18. There are also industry regulations about how many hours a child actor can be on set and mandates for classroom time (SAG-AFTRA, n.d.).

One study published examined the impact of childhood fame on the attachment health and adult adjustment of former child actors. The study found that an early healthy attachment to parents was a protective factor. Those who had a strong relationship with their parents experienced fewer negative effects on their adult adjustment due to their professional experience in the entertainment industry (Rapport & Meleen, 1998). However, child stars with poor attachment to their parents were more likely to experience negative long-term effects into adulthood. Factors such as dissatisfaction with financial management, lack of peer support, and a belief that their involvement in acting was driven by others rather than themselves all contribute to strained relationships with their parents. The study also found that having a parent serve as a manager was challenging for child stars. Those who had a parent in this role perceived their mothers as less caring and more controlling compared to those who did not have a parent serving as their manager.

In her book *I'm Glad My Mom Died*, Jennette McCurdy, star of *iCarly*, describes the experience of having an overinvolved mother and a loss of normal childhood experiences. From an early age, she received powerful messages about her body and the need to keep her weight low. It is no surprise she developed an eating disorder and had other emotional struggles that carried into her adulthood. McCurdy describes in graphic detail how growing up in the spotlight put her in the path of predators and exploiters of various kinds. Like other child stars, she had the experience of being overindulged and taken advantage of by adults. This took an enormous toll on her identity formation, her capacity for trust, and her development of healthy and reciprocal relationships (McCurdy, 2022).

Though the evidence is anecdotal, there is a great deal of public information suggesting that child stars often have parents with mental health problems, substance abuse, or personality disorders. Cole Sprouse claimed his mom was a severe narcissist and had other serious substance and mental health struggles (Rouleau, 2023). Macaulay Culkin called his father "such a crazy person" and claimed he was abusive (Arnold, 2018). Demi Lovato also reports her father was "abusive" and "mean" (Bueno, 2015). Brooke Shields says her mother was an alcoholic who went to rehab "multiple times" and laments how her mother's alcoholism was "a constant source of agony" for her (Shields, 2014). There are dozens of other examples—and those are just a few of the ones who have spoken out. Many more child actors have had to contend with parents who have their own significant personality and mental health problems.

Sometimes the child's parents are calling all the shots, but when children and teens become famous, the dynamic can shift. Now the child becomes the most powerful one in the family, something no child is equipped to handle. Demi Lovato said, "I always rebelled against authority because deep down inside, I was always like, 'I'm paying the rent around here'" (Chilton, 2021).

Depending on the parent, a major focus of therapy may be to assess and improve the parent-child relationship. Begin by assessing the child's relationship with their parents using interviews with both. Get a strong understanding of the parent's attachment style and overall parenting style. Determine if the parent has any personal mental health issues that might adversely affect their relationship with the child. Also, get a sense of the parent's strengths. Your assessment then leads to a plan to strengthen an already healthy attachment relationship, repair an unhealthy relationship with one or both parents, or, in some unfortunate instances, work to mitigate the impact of an unhealthy parent. Sometimes, you will encourage the parents to seek their own therapist.

A parent's poor mental health or deep insecurities adds a complication to the work of therapy. Finding the boundary between a child's desires and the parent's wishes can be challenging, because often the child does not yet know. In my work with young adults, I see clients who just now realize they were living out someone else's dream and not their own, often to their detriment. Child stars meet these realizations with anger, resentment, and sadness. Your challenge is to avoid colluding with those who push the child to stay in the fame game against their wishes or when it is no longer healthy for them.

THE ARMY OF OTHER ADULTS

The parents of child stars can pose unique challenges to helping professionals, but among the most formidable aspects of working with child stars is contending with the fortress of other adults arrayed around the young performer. Managers, agents, security, life coaches, diet and fitness professionals, mentors and gurus, and others control schedules and information. Rarely will they interfere with what goes on in the therapy room, but they may make it difficult to maintain consistency or keep routine appointments, prioritizing almost every other activity. There may be no nefarious motives in this, but a symptom of the child's overstuffed schedule. They may give lip service to therapy's importance, but many things—press junkets, photo shoots, auditions, studio phone calls—are more important in their view.

This has changed in recent years. In the past, agents and managers worked hard to hide the fact their young client was in treatment. Now, child stars—including both young actors and musicians—are not shy about telling the world they are in therapy. This has shifted the dynamic for therapists. Managers may still complain about their young client being photographed in a therapist's waiting area or entering or exiting the therapy practice. Despite that, they now make therapy more of a priority and facilitate it. This calls for flexibility from the therapist, with scheduling and shifting from in-person to remote sessions and back again.

THE STRUGGLES

The stories are well known. Every year, more sad tales emerge of current or former child actors who find themselves in trouble with the law, captive to substance abuse or addiction, or in the grip of major mental illness. Some even die by overdose, by accident, or by their own hand. The challenges they faced often prove too much for them.

My own thorough review of press reports found over 80 current or former child stars who had been arrested. This does not include those who entered rehab without an arrest, admitted a struggle with mental illness, died by suicide, or had other serious problems. They were charged with offenses, including DUI, drug possession, armed robbery, domestic assault, and manslaughter. In the small world of child stars, this is an enormous number. It's likely that there are even more that were not picked up by the press.

Beyond the tragic outcomes of arrests, overdoses, and suicides, fame has a profound effect on child stars' relationships, self-esteem, body image, and emotional well-being. Many report significant problems with not knowing how to live a normal life. One study concluded that actors have lower levels of life satisfaction and higher levels of depression, anxiety, and stress (Szabó et al., 2022).

After reviewing the research, public interviews, and press coverage of child stars, their most common struggles across their lifespans include:

- *Relationship Difficulties:* The most common issue that emerges from these interviews is the impact of their fame on forming and maintaining healthy relationships. They have few peer friendships. They are surrounded by and socialized by adults, many of whom are not emotionally healthy or are people who benefit from the child's career. Problems with trust and feeling exploited are regular topics of therapy.

- *Substance Abuse and Addiction:* The next most common issue cited is alcohol and drug abuse and addiction. Often these themes come up in interviews following stints in rehab, but many former child stars acknowledge these struggles even if there is never a public disclosure of treatment. *Full House* actress Jodie Sweetin disclosed major substance abuse, including snorting meth and being blackout drunk (Sweetin, 2009). *Harry Potter*'s Draco Malfoy, Tom Felton, described his struggle with alcoholism that resulted in an intervention by his team, only to run away from rehab the first day he arrived (Felton, 2022). Many other child stars have shared stories of major substance abuse and addiction.

- *Anxiety:* Child stars talk about battling crippling anxiety, including panic attacks, intense worries, and obsessive thoughts. This mirrors a larger trend of anxiety disorders showing dramatic increases in the past decade among teens (Benton et al., 2021).

- *Identity Formation:* Child stars talk about how they never had the chance to explore what they valued, what they wanted to pursue, or what kind of person they wanted to be. They play catch-up later in life, often feeling cheated of their formative years. Some seem stuck in a state of developmental arrest decades later.

- *Eating Disorders:* Rates of eating disorders may be higher among those in the public eye (Szabó et al., 2019). Child stars battle eating disorders at early ages. Many of them get very direct messages about the need to manage their weight and keep their bodies in shape. Often, they are told their careers depend on this.

- *Intimacy:* Child stars often are not ready for the sexual experiences they sometimes encounter. These may be sexual abuse or consensual experiences, but both can affect their capacity for healthy intimacy. Issues of trauma and attachment come up often in treatment.

This is not an exhaustive list, but these are likely to be among the biggest issues that show up in therapy with current or former child stars. In the coming chapters, we will talk about effective ways to address many of these concerns in treatment. But some of these issues, like addiction or eating disorders, require specialized training. Be willing to refer out to a therapist who is well trained in those areas if you lack the expertise.

THE PRESSURE TO STAY IN THE PRESSURE COOKER

One of my young clients was so stressed by the array of challenges he faced that he contemplated quitting a career that was showing signs of early success. In doing so, he knew he would give up a lot—money, privilege, adulation.

After he first discussed floated the idea of quitting the pursuit in therapy, I could tell he had shared this with his people. My phone began blowing up—his agent, his brother, his assistant. They all wanted to impress upon me how important it was for him to stay in the game. They all framed it as worry that he would regret his decision, but they all had a personal interest in him keeping his job.

He quit about a month later. I sensed the anger and disappointment of those who had been benefiting from his career.

Sometimes a young talent just wants to be a normal kid and will forsake all the fame and money for that. Sometimes they burn out or believe they can't go on any longer because of the stress of the experience. Either way, there are plenty of aspiring talents who decide they don't want to play the game any longer.

You may feel external or internal pressure or desire to keep your young client in the fame game. Your challenge is to be the person who can be most impartial about this for your client. You must approach your work as objectively as possible, hearing them well, giving them guidance and freedom to explore what they want and need, and then acting in their best interest.

When a young actor, musician, or athlete is contemplating no longer continuing in their field, the therapist can feel pressure. If that young person is your client, you are ethically bound to represent their best interests. Yet, when this happens, the situation becomes complex for at least three reasons. First, as we've discussed, there are many adults around them who want them to continue in the industry. Sometimes, it's because they make their own livelihood off these young talents. In other instances, it's because they have so much of their own sense of self wrapped up in the child's career. They raised a famous actor or a champion athlete or a musical prodigy. They derive a great deal of self-esteem by being close—as a family member, friend, or business associate—to this rising star.

The second complexity is the hardest to acknowledge. Sometimes it's because *you* want them to succeed in their field. You want to be the therapist who helped this person overcome their struggles to become a big star, even if you can't ever tell anyone. We may never say this out loud, but we must acknowledge it to ourselves so we can work against this impulse.

You also realize if others perceive you as being the one who facilitated the child's exit from pursuing stardom, you run a significant risk of having that child pulled out of therapy. The adults in the child's life may decide you are a bad influence and withdraw the child, either by finding a new therapist or going without. Either way, there's a good chance the child loses. It's reasonable to want to stay in the game with that child.

These ideas are likely swirling around in your head, yet you have to guide the child to the decision that is the best decision, not the one their handlers or parents—or maybe even you—want the child to make. Unlike most other clients, you realize how the child's decisions have ripple effects on many others, including those who make their livelihood—or potential livelihood—off the child's talent and brand. This makes it hard to remain objective in the therapy room. Therapy, which is hidden from view, now becomes a process with a lot more eyes on it than you'd care to have.

Stephanie Merry writes in *The Washington Post*, "Children in general don't have much agency, but child stars are especially strapped with expectations—from parents and producers, from agents and fans" (Merry, 2018). Your job is to provide a safe and empowering environment to give healthy, age-appropriate agency back to their child or adolescent client.

THE NOT NORMAL LIFE

Justin Bieber represents the most quintessential child star of this era. Once beloved, the public piled on him when he slipped up, perhaps forgetting that he was 13 years old when he first became famous. He had fame and money, but he gave up a normal adolescence. On a lengthy Instagram post, he wrote, "I made every bad decision you could have thought of and went from one of the most loved and adored people in the world to the most ridiculed, judged and hated person in the world." He added, "It's taken me years to bounce back from all of these terrible decisions, fix broken relationships, and change relationship habits." Bieber credits two things with helping him become restored back to health: a deep faith in God and his work in therapy. He acknowledged he needed to do his work on "repairing deep-rooted issues" (Goldstein, 2019).

Therapists play a vital role in the psychological well-being of child stars, as well as children and teens aspiring to be stars. In therapy, they can explore what they want, wrestle with identity formation, and learn skills to cope with the unique stressors they face.

For all the child stars or younger celebrities who have gone off the rails, gotten arrested, developed drug problems, deteriorated into severe mental illness, or even passed away early, there are many others who have done well. This is due, in part, to the care of good therapists and other helping professionals. Acknowledging many ex-child stars "who did not make it," Jodie Foster said, "If there's anything that I have to be a role model about, it is prioritizing my own self-worth and psychological health above all. And if not, I don't know where I would be today" (Sager, 2018).

Famous children have little idea what they want or need, often until later in life, yet they must contend with the impact of fame on their personal growth, their capacity to have normal friendships, and their sense of self apart from fame. They have pressures that most children never experience. They are often in a complicated status of simultaneously having too much power and not enough. Their lives are not normal.

This is challenging work that many therapists will find much harder than therapy with most other children and teens. The external pressure both you and the child experience will be palpable. You must work hard to be as objective and clear-headed as possible. Do this well, and you can provide child stars with an oasis of health and normalcy in their not-normal lives.

REFERENCES

Arnold, A. (2018). Macaulay Culkin speaks out about his abusive father. *Entertainment Weekly*.

Bailey, J. (2018). Jodie Foster reflects on fame and mental health. *Vanity Fair*.

Benton, T. D., Boyd, R. C., & Njoroge, W. F. M. (2021). Addressing the youth mental health crisis. *Pediatrics*, *148*(1), e2021051736.

Blasberg, D. (2013). Miley Cyrus talks about fame and growing up. *Vogue*.

Bueno, A. (2015). Demi Lovato opens up about her abusive father. *E! News*.

Chilton, L. (2021). Demi Lovato shares her struggles with fame. *People*.

Emmanuele, J., & Schonfeld, Z. (2023). Selena Gomez on fame and its challenges. *Rolling Stone*.

Felton, T. (2022). *Beyond the wand: The magic and mayhem of growing up a wizard*. Grand Central Publishing.

Gelhourn, M. (2024). Cole Sprouse discusses fame and identity. *Variety*.

Goldstein, J. (2019). Justin Bieber on the healing power of faith and therapy. *The Guardian*.

Hattenstone, S. (2020). Shawn Mendes opens up about fame. *The Guardian*.

Levesley, D. (2020). Shawn Mendes: Navigating the monster of fame. *British GQ*.

Marie Claire. (2010). Mary Kate Olsen reflects on her childhood fame. *Marie Claire*.

Mateos, E. (2021). Christina Aguilera on childhood fame and competition. *Billboard*.

McCurdy, J. (2022). *I'm glad my mom died*. Simon & Schuster.

Merry, S. (2018). The hidden pressures of child stardom. *The Washington Post*.

Oppenheim, M. (2016). Daniel Radcliffe talks about life after Harry Potter. *The Independent*.

Rapport, L. J., & Meleen, S. (1998). Childhood fame and adult adjustment: Attachment and wellbeing. *Journal of Clinical Child Psychology*, *27*(3), 350–362.

Rouleau, M. (2023). Cole Sprouse reveals struggles with a narcissistic parent. *BuzzFeed News*.

SAG-AFTRA. (n.d.). *Coogan law*. https://www.sagaftra.org/membership-benefits/young-performers/coogan-law

Sager, J. (2018). Jodie Foster discusses psychological health as a child star. *People*.

Shaffer, G. (1935). Jackie Coogan's fight for his earnings. *Los Angeles Times*.

Shields, B. (2014). Brooke Shields recalls her mother's alcoholism. *HuffPost*.

Sweetin, J. (2009). *UnSweetined: A memoir*. Gallery Books.

Szabó, M., Seton, M., Maxwell, I., & Cunningham, M. L. (2022). Psychological well-being of Australian actors and performing artists: Life satisfaction and negative affect. *Medical Problems of Performing Artists*, *37*(2), 106–117. https://doi.org/10.21091/mppa.2022.2016

Szabó, M. D., Cunningham, M., Seton, M., & Maxwell, I. (2019). Eating disorder symptoms in Australian actors and performing artists. *Medical Problems of Performing Artists*, *34*(4), 171–178.

Terry, E. (2018). The Coogan Act and child actor protections. *Hollywood Reporter*.

THR Staff. (2011, July 5). Daniel Radcliffe and other young stars who have admitted drinking problems. *The Hollywood Reporter*. https://www.hollywoodreporter.com/movies/movie-news/daniel-radcliffe-young-stars-who-207962/

Wright, K. (2020). The psychological toll of fame on children. *Insider*.

Part III

Treatment Focus

Chapter 8

Managing Meteoric Rise and Catastrophic Fall

Dave Chappelle was considered among the best stand-up comics, but he was only moderately famous before *Chappelle's Show* became a massive hit on Comedy Central, and he was offered $55 million to produce more episodes. By then, he had become a household name, but the pressure became unbearable. His personal crisis resulted in his walking away from his show and the big paycheck. He traveled to South Africa to get away from the heat of the media spotlight. He later said, "The higher up I went, the less happy I was. Once you get famous, you can't get unfamous. You can get infamous, but you can't get unfamous" (Leyva, 2016).

Fame can be fleeting for some, a bright burst followed by silence. For others, their fame may have been built and cultivated across years or decades, only to see it dashed following a misstep. Martha Stewart went to prison for insider trading. David Letterman was blackmailed about having affairs. Winona Ryder was arrested for shoplifting. Arnold Schwarzenegger got his housekeeper pregnant. Russell Crowe was arrested for assault after throwing a phone at a hotel employee. Alec Baldwin blasted his 11-year-old daughter as "a thoughtless little pig" on a recorded call leaked for all the world to hear (Smith, 2022). In his youth, Justin Bieber was taken into custody for drunk driving, struggled with substance abuse, faced vandalism charges, and had several public altercations, including one with a limo driver who pressed assault charges. The list could go on and on. The quick rise and cataclysmic fall of celebrities is familiar to all of us.

When a person is thrust into the public's awareness because of either positive or negative circumstances, the public passes judgment on the now famous or infamous person. The result is a head-spinning experience where the person realizes their public image is being formed in ways that may have little to do with their actual self. It can lead to confusion, anger, anxiety, isolation, and even deep depression. Some people report the reactions to these life-altering events as the worst times of their lives. The experience can be overwhelming and soul-crushing.

Whether it's a meteoric rise or a public scandal, the common factor is a rapid, unexpected shift in status that is destabilizing for the individual. They were

DOI: 10.4324/9781003503569-11

not famous and suddenly they are, or they were famous and, at once, they are embroiled in some notoriety that threatens their reputation and their career. These moments require a therapist who is steady and wise in the face of a crisis. Let's first examine the unique perils of the meteoric rise, then talk about how to help a well-known person navigate the treacherous road of a public scandal.

METEORIC RISE

There are those who strive for fame every day and it eludes them, but there are others who seem to be overnight sensations. A prankster posts a video that goes viral and makes them an instant celebrity. An athlete steps into the position after the first- and second-string quarterbacks get injured and wins a huge playoff game with a spectacular throw. A singer becomes an early audience favorite on a reality show. He is not recognizable one day, then sets the internet aflame the next. This kind of meteoric rise is unlike anything we have discussed so far. Often these are people from middle- or working-class backgrounds who were unknown one day and the subject of dinnertime conversation around the country the next day.

After her death by alcohol poisoning, Amy Winehouse's former manager, Nick Shymansky, said, "Fame came like a huge tidal wave." He added,

> The fame came very, very quick and very strong. She got depressed. She got lost. She got into a bad crowd, started using heavy drugs. As she became mega-famous and a worldwide star, it got out of control. She couldn't control it.
>
> (Swift, 2016)

After former One Direction member Liam Payne's tragic death at 31, Bruce Springsteen said, "It's a normal thing. It's a business that puts enormous pressures on young people," he said, adding:

> Young people don't have the inner facility or the inner self yet to be able to protect themselves from a lot of the things that come with success and fame. So they get lost in a lot of the difficult and often pain inducing [things] . . . whether it's drugs or alcohol to take some of that pressure off.
>
> (Perry, 2024)

Sadly, the stories of people who got too famous too quickly are plentiful. Often the outcome is tragic, as it was for Amy Winehouse and Liam Payne. The person feels off-balance and struggles with equilibrium. Sudden fame is overwhelming and dizzying.

Susan Boyle is another sad example of an unexpected and stressful mete-oric rise. Boyle became an overnight sensation in 2009 after her audition on the British television show *Britain's Got Talent*. Her performance of "I Dreamed a

Dream" from the musical *Les Misérables* was a jaw-dropper. She became an instant global phenomenon when video of her performance went viral, amassing millions of views on YouTube in a matter of days.

Before her appearance on *Britain's Got Talent*, Boyle lived an obscure life in Blackburn, Scotland. She was unemployed, lived alone with her cat, and had never been married. Her appearance and backstory, including her admission of never having been kissed, shaped a narrative of an underdog whose instant fame felt like a fairy tale. In her memoir, *The Woman I Was Meant to Be*, she wrote, "Unmarried women in their forties, with false teeth and tousled hair, aren't usually held in the highest esteem by our society. The feeling seemed to be that if I could be a success, then anyone could!"

Boyle received extensive media attention and public support, with celebrities and fans alike rooting for her. Her debut album, *I Dreamed a Dream*, released later than year, broke records for the fastest-selling debut album by a female artist in the UK and was the second best-selling album of 2009 in the United States.

However, the pressure of sudden fame took a toll on her. She struggled with the intense scrutiny and expectations placed upon her. After the *Britain's Got Talent* finale, where she finished in second place, Boyle was admitted to a psychiatric clinic for exhaustion. In the years following, she has spoken about the challenges of coping with her rapid rise to fame, including dealing with public criticism, managing learning differences, and facing loneliness. She has acknowledged being on the autism spectrum, which only compounded the struggles with her quick rise to stardom.

While Boyle's career did not crash in the traditional sense—she continued to release albums and perform—her story exemplifies the personal and emotional challenges that can accompany sudden fame. Her initial meteoric rise highlighted the difficulties of adjusting to life in the public eye, especially for someone who had lived a quiet life before (O'Brien, 2023).

CATASTROPHIC FALL: PUBLIC HUMILIATION AND SCANDAL

Tiger Woods is regarded as one of the greatest players in the history of golf. He was on top of the world until his personal life came crashing down on him when a scandal unfolded after Woods was involved in a car accident outside his Florida home in the early hours of November 27, 2009. The incident led to intense media scrutiny. Allegations surfaced about Woods having extramarital affairs with several women. Over the following weeks, more than a dozen women claimed to have had intimate relationships with Woods. The revelations were shocking to the public and fans, given Woods's clean-cut image and his status as a role model.

The fallout from the scandal was swift and severe. Woods faced widespread public humiliation as the details of his infidelities dominated media headlines worldwide. He lost many endorsement deals. Companies like AT&T, Gatorade, and Accenture severed ties with him. Woods took an indefinite break from professional golf, skipping major tournaments and losing his ranking as the world's number one golfer.

In February 2010, Woods made a televised public apology, admitting to his infidelities and stating that he was undergoing therapy. He spoke of his actions as irresponsible and selfish, and he apologized to his wife, family, friends, and fans. Woods's attempt to rebuild his personal and professional life was a long and challenging journey. He returned to professional golf but struggled with injuries and form for several years (Garcia, 2010).

It's easy to get caught up in the judgment, but let's take inventory of a public scandal's emotional toll. Imagine your worst moment, a time when you said or did something you regret, perhaps even to this day. Recall how you felt, how the thoughts looped in your head, how your stomach was in knots, your body felt crushed with anxiety and sorrow. Now, as bad as that is, imagine everyone knows about it. It's discussed in newspapers, in magazines, and on countless websites. It is the trending topic on major social media platforms. Consider how soul-crushing that would be.

Research shows that social rejection or humiliation and physical pain are processed in similar areas of the brain. Functional MRI studies reveal that experiencing social rejection activates the secondary somatosensory cortex and dorsal posterior insula, brain regions that react to physical pain (Kross et al., 2011). This overlap explains why rejection can feel like it physically "hurts" (Flaskerud, 2011). Studies suggest that acetaminophen, a common pain reliever, can reduce the brain and behavioral responses to social rejection (DeWall et al., 2010). These findings note that social rejection and physical pain may share a common underlying mechanism in the brain's sensory systems (Kross et al., 2011). We experience social rejection or humiliation as genuine pain.

As fame increases, the magnitude of the pain also increases. The sharks are circling, waiting to catch you flirting with a woman, trying to get the scoop on your drunken rant at a bar, or the spat with your partner in the car. Tiger Woods was caught in multiple affairs, egregious behavior by most standards, but others have been shredded for much less. Going through a public humiliation or scandal of any type hurts.

THE CRISIS AS OPPORTUNITY

One of my clients got into a drunken altercation with his girlfriend. Who shoved whom first is a matter of dispute, but it became physical. The cops were called. By the time they arrived, the shock of what had happened set in, sobering both of them up. Never mind, they told the police after the officers came into the house. It was just a minor argument, no big deal.

The problem was that state law required an arrest for any domestic violence call. The intent was to keep abused partners safe and free of intimidation. My client, Ollie, was arrested, booked, and kept in jail until the next morning.

Ollie was a well-known person in a well-known family. For two days, it looked like it might all blow over, but on the third day, he began getting texts: "Is this true?" "What happened?" "Why didn't you tell me?"

When I saw him, he hadn't slept for two full nights. He had not eaten. When he tried to eat, he vomited. He had not shaved or showered. He was a nonfunctional person. "I just have this voice playing on a loop in my heard: 'You're ruined! You're done!' I can't think straight. I don't know what to do," he said in a halting, distant voice.

But what he saw as an indisputable catastrophe, I saw as an opportunity for him. Yes, what had happened was bad, but there was an opportunity here. I knew the first step was to help him get back to healthy functioning. After that, though, we had the chance to use the awful experience for his good.

We know that in a crisis, the first order of business is to shore up a person's coping with lots of skills and support. However, once the person gets to a stable place, there may be room to reframe what has happened. To begin this process, share how people get stronger and more resilient when they go through the fire. If this idea seems to gain some traction, then go to the second step: propose the idea that the most resilient people look at mistakes and failures as opportunities for growth and learning rather than moments of shame and humiliation.

The research supports this notion (Ord et al., 2020). Stress-related growth refers to the positive psychological changes that result from struggling with challenging or stressful life experiences. It involves developing greater resilience, improved coping skills, and a deeper appreciation for life and relationships (Tedeschi & Calhoun, 2004). Stress can help build "mental muscle."

If your client is engaged with this framework, look at how this awful experience can be a moment of personal growth. I told Ollie, "There is so much bad about what has happened, but I think there's an opportunity here. If we do this well, this could be an experience of personal growth for you." I was telegraphing hope. When you feel like your world has collapsed, the hope of something good beyond this moment can be powerful. There is also a message of future growth. Let's find a way forward, out of this mess. I want him to move beyond the awful moment.

When I say, "If we do this well," it poses a whiff of an early personal challenge. When I say "we," I communicate that I am in this with him. There is no magic to these words, but I want to be deliberate about what I say in this important moment.

By our second session, Ollie, despite still feeling devastated, said he could see that he might come out on the other side of this as a stronger version of himself. We envisioned what that might look like for him. He agreed that it might make him less concerned about the opinions of people he didn't know. It would show him who his real friends were, who would stick by him and who would fall away.

We also envisioned that it would challenge him to learn better ways of coping, rather than relying on weed. We believed it would clarify his personal values and live more in line with them. All of this came out of the second and third sessions. While this timeline may be a little atypical, it shows that a crisis can often be framed and embraced as an opportunity for deep personal growth.

Therapists are often so empathetic that we may find it hard to do anything but offer support and validation during a moment of crisis. The idea of challenging someone to use the moment for personal growth may sound like a variation of "pull yourself up by your bootstraps" or "just rub some dirt on it," a gruff admonition to be tough and quit complaining. However, sometimes the task is to challenge and equip someone to rise to the moment. There is nothing wrong with encouraging people to dig for the strength to grow through adversity. We may have lost sight of the truth that validating and supporting a client are only part of the treatment plan. Developing mindsets and skills to meet the challenges of life is often an even bigger need.

HELPING DURING A METEORIC RISE OR CATASTROPHIC FALL

A therapist can play a crucial role in helping someone who has experienced a meteoric rise or catastrophic fall navigate the complex emotional, psychological, and social challenges that come with sudden fame or infamy. There are many helpful strategies, such as learning skills to manage stress, boundary setting, exercise, connecting with a support system, and other forms of self-care.

However, the most powerful and versatile thing your client can do is learn how to think differently. This is the basis for Cognitive-Behavioral Therapy (CBT), which is considered the gold standard for psychotherapy (David et al., 2018). More recently, third-wave cognitive-behavioral therapies like Dialectical Behavior Therapy (DBT) and Acceptance and Commitment Therapy (ACT) that emphasize mindfulness, acceptance, non-attachment, and values-based living represent an evolution within the tradition and are now considered EBTs (Linehan et al., 1991; Tjak et al., 2015). These therapies have demonstrated their capacity to help clients manage acute and chronic stress (Joyce et al., 2018).

Drawing from those third-wave CBT therapies, here are five mindsets that you can teach. If mastered, these new ways of thinking can help your clients during times of enormous stress and emotional hardship.

Accept Reality as It Is

Though he was not the first to say it, Japanese writer Haruki Murakami popularized the quote, "Pain is inevitable. Suffering is optional" (Murakami, 2008, p. 44).

It is impossible to live a full, engaged life without pain. However, according to the framework of third-wave CBT approaches, there is a difference between pain and suffering (Vowles & McCracken, 2008; Ye et al., 2024). Suffering is getting stuck in pain, which we do when we fail to accept reality as it is. Instead, we rage against the injustice or the "wrongness" of the situation, causing us to get fused to the pain itself.

Let's use the COVID pandemic as an example. The worldwide pandemic was one of the most disruptive, polarizing, and awful experiences of the past several decades. It affected everyone, but those who did not accept the reality of it and raged against it did far worse than those who practiced radical acceptance. One study found that people who participated in an acceptance intervention reported significant improvements in their general well-being, greater psychological flexibility, and greater ability to cope with anxiety, even if they were still distressed by the pandemic (Shepherd et al., 2022).

Radical Acceptance is when we accept reality as it is, on its own terms, especially when we can do nothing about it. Those who are intentional about acceptance still feel the pain of a stressful situation, but they are far less likely to suffer because they do not get stuck in it. They can move on or, even better, move *through* the pain to live a fulfilling life despite the negative experiences.

To do this, I created the acronym "ACE" that can help your client remember how to practice radical acceptance:

- *Acknowledge Reality:* Say to yourself, "This happened (or is happening or is true), and I cannot do anything to change it."
- *Choose Acceptance:* Say to yourself, "Fighting this or getting stuck on it will not change it and will only make me suffer. Acceptance lets me move forward."
- *Engage Your Life:* Say to yourself, "I will now focus on what really matters to me."

As this self-talk demonstrates, Radical Acceptance is not passive, nor is it resignation or a lack of caring. It is an active and deliberate mindset where you allow yourself to acknowledge and feel the pain of something, but also accept the pain—whether physical or emotional—of something you cannot control, then move through it to get back into your life. Those who practice Radical Acceptance are more mentally flexible and emotionally healthy than those who do not (Brach, 2003). A true acceptance mindset is one of the most helpful ways of practicing self-care.

Become Non-Attached to Outcomes, Things, and Status

Related to the practice of acceptance is the mindset of non-attachment. With this way of thinking, we engage with life while also maintaining the awareness that all aspects of life—circumstances, possessions, relationships, desires, feelings—are transient and impermanent. As a result, we don't attach outcomes, things, or conditions to our sense of self or find our well-being in them. Within this mindset, attachment is a source of suffering, because it leads to craving, clinging, and grasping, which leaves us with dissatisfaction and unhappiness. Non-attachment leads to freedom from suffering.

Non-attachment can involve developing a greater appreciation for the present moment, rather than striving for future outcomes. It can also involve developing healthier relationships with people, based on mutual respect and empathy, rather than codependency or attachment. From a psychological standpoint, non-attachment allows for a more flexible and open engagement with life.

Non-attachment doesn't mean you stop investing yourself in important, life-giving pursuits. It also doesn't mean you don't work hard on personal goals. It means we don't connect our sense of well-being to the outcomes we desire.

I propose this self-talk to help someone learn how to adopt a mindset of non-attachment. It forms the acronym CORE that I developed to help clients remember it:

- *Concede:* Say to yourself, "This moment or circumstance is not permanent."
- *Open:* Say to yourself, "I am open and desire to be unattached to this."
- *Release:* Say to yourself, "This experience is not mine to keep, so I release it."
- *Engage:* Say to yourself, "I will commit to living a full life unattached to impermanent things or circumstances."

There are tremendous benefits to the non-attachment mindset. It reduces overall emotional distress and promotes greater well-being (Whitehead et al., 2019). This mental framework promotes more flexible thinking, which leads to greater problem-solving and less fixation. Those who practice non-attachment show fewer symptoms of anxiety and depression, have less exhaustion and burnout, and are less rigid and perfectionistic (Keng & Tong, 2016; Sahdra et al., 2015). They also perform better in school and at work (Mak et al., 2022).

Adopt a Resilient Growth Mindset

Stanford professor Carol Dweck's simple but revolutionary construct helps us in so many aspects of life, but its application to self-care is especially powerful. Dweck's research found that there are two mindsets that determine success and resilience. The first is a fixed mindset. This is a person's belief that they were dealt a certain hand—good or bad—and that's just how things are. In this way of thinking, the individual feels like they are good at math or bad at public speaking or great at volleyball or terrible at controlling their anger. Whatever the issue, the belief with a fixed mindset is that is just how the person is, with little hope or expectation of change.

A growth mindset focuses on how effort and hard work can make someone better or stronger in a particular area. A growth mindset approaches hard times, mistakes, and setbacks as opportunities for growth, rather than moments of shame. It sees difficulty as a pathway to greater strength and competence. With this mindset, a catastrophic fall would be viewed as a chance to get better rather than just a diminishment (Dweck, 2016).

To develop more of a growth mindset, teach your client to use self-talk that sounds like this:

- "Mistakes are opportunities for growth."
- "Feedback—including negative feedback—helps me become a better person."
- "Every step forward counts."
- "This is a challenging time, but I can use it for my good."

It would be a sad irony if our mindsets were fixed and we could shift a fixed mindset to a growth mindset. Fortunately, that isn't the case. The research shows that exposing someone to the concept of a growth mindset can shift their thinking in that direction. One of the best ways a person can care for themselves during a time of rocky transition is to adopt a growth mindset and use the difficult time as an opportunity to become a stronger and better version of themselves.

Practice Flexible, Dialectical Thinking

Here's an honest question: Are people selfish and disappointing? You probably agreed that they were. Here's another question: Are people generous and delightful? The answer to this is also yes. Both things are true. It's true that the world is a terrible place and a beautiful place. It's true that we should accept ourselves as we are and also desire to change and improve. The ability to acknowledge two competing, hard-to-reconcile sides of a truth is called dialectical thinking.

When people get stressed out, they often become very polarized—very black-and-white in their thinking. The situation is the best or the worst. That person is an angel or a devil. The future is bright or hopeless. A safeguard against this is the practice of dialectical thinking, which leads to greater flexibility. More flexible thinkers cope with stress better (Linehan, 2015).

There are a few practical ways you can help your client practice more flexible, dialectical thinking. Begin by teaching the thinking error of "all-or-nothing thinking," where people or circumstances are seen as either all good or all bad, all right or all wrong. Encourage your clients to practice generating "middle ground" options. Building on that, give them practice in generating several options and possibilities with no evaluation of them, just brainstorming the alternatives.

For example, imagine a client who has been charged with a recent DUI that made national news. Their thoughts might be something like, "Everyone will hate me now." Alternative possibilities are that some people will not like them, some people will feel kindlier toward them, opinion will be split about them, and so on. Just generating the options can help promote more flexible thinking. You can also work through a dialectical vision of the client. Perhaps the client is a good person who made a big mistake that could have hurt others. Maybe the client is a self-centered person who wants to improve themselves. Both sides of that are true and real.

Here are a few examples of dialectical thinking that you might help your client build into their repertoire:

- "Two things can be true at the same time."
- "It's not either/or, it's both/and."
- I can acknowledge both sides without picking one."

Practice flexible, dialectical thinking in sessions with thought exercises that allow a client to hold two opposing views of themselves, others, or circumstances. This can be beneficial to weathering a sudden transition, either up or down in trajectory. This cognitive ability allows for better problem-solving and less tendency to get stuck on certain thoughts. It is a skillset that improves and becomes more effective with practice (Kashdan & Rottenberg, 2010).

Be a Friend to Yourself

Years ago, my father-in-law died, leaving his wife alone in a house on a former working Christmas tree farm on the side of a mountain in rural North Carolina. About a month after the funeral, my wife and I drove to the mountains to check on her mom to make sure she was doing well. Sitting on rocking chairs out on the porch overlooking the beautiful Blue Ridge Mountains, we asked her, "Are you doing okay?"

"I'm doing fine," she said.

"Have you been feeling sad or lonely up here in this house by yourself?"

"No," she replied, "Because I am a friend to myself."

In over three decades as a therapist, I had never thought of that phrasing, but this was what I had been talking to my clients about all those years: You need to be a friend to yourself.

For some people, this is much more easily said than done. They are used to their inner critic badgering and berating them. They don't know what it's like to speak to themselves with kindness and grace.

Loving-kindness meditation focuses on developing feelings of compassion and love toward oneself and others. It involves repeating phrases such as, "May I be happy, may I be healthy, may I be safe, may I live with ease," then extending these wishes to others. The phrases then become, "May you be happy, may you be healthy, may you be safe, may you live with ease."

Research has shown that loving-kindness meditation can increase positive emotions, reduce self-criticism, and improve overall mental health, including during the aftermath of trauma or personal crisis. One study evaluated a trauma-adapted intervention for survivors of interpersonal violence that combined both psychoeducation and mindfulness-based exercises, including loving-kindness meditation. Individuals who had experienced significant trauma participated in eight treatment sessions. The results showed significant reductions in trauma symptoms and increases in well-being, mindfulness skills, and self-compassion (Müller-Engelmann et al., 2019). This practice may not be a good fit for every client, but a solid research base shows that loving-kindness mediation, even in its most elemental practice, can have tremendous benefits for those going through an especially difficult time.

When someone is experiencing a personal crisis, they often don't have the mental or emotional bandwidth to do some extra coping activity, like take a yoga class or work out or keep a mood log. Everything feels too weighty and overwhelming. These five mindsets provide a powerful alternative. They don't require a lot of external effort, so they feel less burdensome. Equipping the person with cognitive skills also extends beyond the present crisis and provides a toolbox for all of life.

EQUIPPING FOR A LIFETIME

Helping someone strapped to the rocket of sudden fame or caught in the whirlpool of a public humiliation or scandal is challenging and multifaceted. The circumstances and your client's personal traits and capacities are so varied that it is impossible to create a one-size-fits-all roadmap. Like all good treatment planning, it needs to be client-centered, tailored to the unique needs of each person. However, teaching new ways to think is always a good part of that plan.

One caution during a crisis: Despite pressure to do so, you should not focus your efforts on image management. That is the purview of celebrity advisors and managers who are committed to mitigating the harm to the wealthy or famous person's reputation. This includes media strategy, messaging, talking points, arranging interviews with soft interviewers, and other impression management tools. These strategies can be antithetical to your work as a therapist, which is first to provide support, but then to help your rich or famous client use the moment to do the deeper work. Strategies designed to deny or dodge or depict are at odds with this. Don't be party to these efforts. Hold out the possibility that the crisis can be an opportunity for growth.

Equip your clients with how to think differently during these difficult times. These mindsets allow them to navigate the experience of fame and infamy but also help them to become a more psychologically healthy person for many years to come.

REFERENCES

Brach, T. (2003). *Radical acceptance: Embracing your life with the heart of a Buddha.* Bantam Books.

David, D., Cristea, I., & Hofmann, S. G. (2018). Why cognitive behavioral therapy is the current gold standard of psychotherapy. *Frontiers in Psychiatry, 9*(4). https://doi.org/10.3389/fpsyt.2018.00004

DeWall, C. N., MacDonald, G., Webster, G. D., Masten, C. L., Baumeister, R. F., Powell, C., Schurtz, D. R., Stillman, T. F., Tice, D. M., & Eisenberger, N. I. (2010). Acetaminophen reduces social pain: Behavioral and neural evidence. *Psychological Science, 21*(7), 931–937.

Dweck, C. S. (2016). *Mindset: The new psychology of success* (Updated ed.). Random House.

Flaskerud, J. H. (2011). Heartbreak and physical pain linked in brain. *Issues in Mental Health Nursing, 32*(12), 789–791.

Garcia, A. (2010, February 19). Tiger Woods press conference: At least he apologized. *Bleacher Report.* https://bleacherreport.com

Joyce, P. R., McIntosh, V. V., Carter, J. D., Frampton, C. M., Wells, J. E., & Olds, R. J. (2018). Long-term follow-up of CBT versus IPT for depression. *Journal of Affective Disorders, 227*, 11–16.

Kashdan, T. B., & Rottenberg, J. (2010). Psychological flexibility as a fundamental aspect of health. *Clinical Psychology Review, 30*(7), 865–878.

Keng, S. L., & Tong, E. M. W. (2016). Riding the tide of emotions with mindfulness: Mindfulness, affect dynamics, and the mediating role of coping. *Emotion, 16*(5), 706–718. https://doi.org/10.1037/emo0000165

Kross, E., Berman, M. G., Mischel, W., Smith, E. E., & Wager, T. D. (2011). Social rejection shares somatosensory representations with physical pain. *Proceedings of the National Academy of Sciences, 108*(15), 6270–6275.

Leyva, A. (2016, June 27). Habitual line-steppers: Tracing Paul Beatty's influences. *The Millions.* https://themillions.com

Linehan, M. M. (2015). *DBT skills training manual* (2nd ed.). Guilford Press.

Linehan, M. M., Armstrong, H. E., Suarez, A., Allmon, D., & Heard, H. L. (1991). Cognitive-behavioral treatment of chronically parasuicidal borderline patients. *Archives of General Psychiatry, 48*(12), 1060–1064.

Mak, W. W. S., Ng, I. S. W., & Wong, C. C. Y. (2022). Nonattachment at work: The mediating role of perceived supervisor support and control at work on well-being among working adults in Hong Kong. *Mindfulness, 13*(2), 271–282. https://doi.org/10.1007/s12671-022-01971-y

Müller-Engelmann, M., Schreiber, C., Kümmerle, S., Heidenreich, T., Stangier, U., & Steil, R. (2019). A trauma-adapted mindfulness and loving-kindness intervention for patients with PTSD after interpersonal violence: A multiple-baseline study. *Mindfulness, 10*(6), 1105–1123. https://doi.org/10.1007/s12671-018-1068-z

Murakami, H. (2008). *What I talk about when I talk about running* (P. Gabriel, Trans.). Alfred A. Knopf.

O'Brien, J. (2023, July 7). The tragic real-life story of Susan Boyle. *Nicki Swift.* https://nickiswift.com

Ord, A. S., Stranahan, K. R., Hurley, R. A., & Taber, K. H. (2020). Stress-related growth: Building a more resilient brain. *The Journal of Neuropsychiatry and Clinical Neurosciences, 32*(3), A4–212.

Perry, K. E. G. (2024, October 19). Bruce Springsteen on Liam Payne death: "It's a business that puts enormous pressure on young people." *The Independent.* https://independent.co.uk

Sahdra, B. K., Ciarrochi, J., Parker, P., Marshall, S., & Heaven, P. C. L. (2015). Nonattachment and mindfulness: Related but distinct constructs. *Psychological Assessment, 27*(3), 1050–1062.

Shepherd, K., Golijani-Moghaddam, N., & Dawson, D. L. (2022). ACTing towards better living during COVID-19: The effects of acceptance and commitment therapy for individuals affected by COVID–19. *Journal of Contextual Behavioral Science, 23,* 98–108. https://doi.org/10.1016/j.jcbs.2021.12.003

Smith, R. (2022, February 10). Ireland Baldwin looks back on Dad Alec calling her a "thoughtless little pig." *Newsweek.* https://www.newsweek.com/ireland-baldwin-dad-alec-calling-her-thoughtless-little-pig-1677944

Swift, N. (2016, February 9). Stars who couldn't handle the pressure of fame. *Nicki Swift.* https://nickiswift.com

Tedeschi, R. G., & Calhoun, L. G. (2004). Posttraumatic growth: Conceptual foundations and empirical evidence. *Psychological Inquiry, 15*(1), 1–18.

Tjak, M. J., Davis, M. L., Morina, N., Powers, M. B., Smits, J. A., & Emmelkamp, P. M. (2015). A meta-analysis of acceptance and commitment therapy for anxiety and depression outcomes. *Journal of Contextual Behavioral Science, 4*(1), 1–12.

Vowles, K. E., & McCracken, L. M. (2008). Acceptance and values-based action in chronic pain: A study of acceptance and commitment therapy. *Pain, 141*(3), 210–219.

Whitehead, R., Bates, G., Elphinstone, B., Yang, Y., & Murray, G. (2019). Nonattachment mediates the relationship between mindfulness and psychological well-being, mental health, and subjective well-being. *Journal of Happiness Studies, 20*(7), 2141–2158.

Ye, L., Li, Y., Deng, Q., Zhao, X., Zhong, L., & Yang, L. (2024). Acceptance and commitment therapy for patients with chronic pain: A systematic review and meta-analysis on psychological outcomes and quality of life. *PLoS One, 19*(6), e0301226. https://doi.org/10.1371/journal.pone.0301226

Chapter 9

Building Healthy Relationships in Wealthy and Well-Known People

One of the longest-running studies in history began in 1938 and tracked 268 Harvard students and a group of less privileged young adults over seven decades, documenting the highs and lows of their lives. John F. Kennedy was among the subjects in the study, as was Ben Bradlee, the *Washington Post* editor who helped break the Watergate story, among other notable people. The results of this massive research project, known as the Harvard Grant Study, tell us what leads to a happy life and what doesn't. For instance, the fastest track to an unhappy life is to develop a drinking problem and neglect your health.

The study's central conclusion was powerful: happiness wasn't about money, status, or fame. Being the president of the United States or a CEO or a multimillionaire didn't matter all that much. Instead, the study found that loving relationships were the key to life satisfaction. Decades of data all pointed in the same direction. People who experienced deep, meaningful relationships were happier, more resilient, and more content.

George Vaillant, the study's lead for over 30 years, concluded, "The seventy-five years and twenty million dollars spent on the Grant Study boil down to five words: 'Happiness is love. Full stop.'" Those with warm, trusting relationships of all kinds consistently reported higher levels of happiness and well-being. Wealth and fame had little to no correlation with long-term happiness.

Stories that emerged from the study reinforce the conclusions. One participant, John, faced career disappointments and health struggles. Despite his setbacks, his close family relationships gave him a sense of fulfillment and contentment. On the flip side, others who had achieved financial success but lacked deep connections often felt lost, reporting feelings of emptiness despite their external success.

The decades-long study illustrates how love and connection help us cope with the slings and arrows of life. People with strong emotional bonds manage stress better, recover from illness faster, and handle life's challenges with greater ease.

DOI: 10.4324/9781003503569-12

These close relationships provided a sense of security and strength that money couldn't match.

The Harvard Grant Study reaffirms what we have really known all along: fulfillment comes not from wealth or fame, but from the love we share with others. The quality of our relationships defines the quality of our lives (Vaillant, 2012).

Clients with fame or fortune are not guaranteed happiness. Without healthy, loving relationships, the chance of living a contented life is low. We may be called on to help them build or repair important relationships. Let's explore the unique threats to their partner relationships, followed by the essential conversations they need to have with their partner and inner circle to ensure the long-term health of their key relationships, then follow with a strategy to build healthier relationships among all family members.

THE STABILITY OF WEALTHY AND WELL-KNOWN MARRIAGES

Celebrity splits and divorces are the lifeblood of tabloids. One popular magazine has a weekly page of celebrity relationship statuses—who got engaged, who got divorced, who made it official, who got back together. If you were to rely only on your newsfeed, you might conclude that celebrity marriages are much less stable than other marriages. Is this true?

The answer is mostly yes, but with some important exceptions. Harry Benson and Rehna Azim examined nearly 500 "A-list" celebrity couples who married between 2001 and 2010. They found the divorce rate was about double that of the baseline population. In particular, they found celebrity marriages often fail early, with much higher divorce rates in the first three years. Musicians had a higher divorce rate than actors, but both fared worse than non-famous people. (Benson & Azim, 2015). Using data from the U.S. Census Bureau, statistician Nathan Yau found that entertainers and performing artists were among the top 25 professions with the highest divorce rate. Notably, dancers and choreographers had a much higher divorce rate than average (Yau, 2015).

Divorce rates vary across groups. Higher income and education levels have been associated with lower divorce rates in some demographics, for example. Research finds that higher net worth and home ownership is associated with lower rates of divorce (Killewald et al., 2023).

Wealthier couples are less likely to get divorced, while famous couples are more likely to get divorced. Not all celebrities are equally at risk. While the evidence suggests that celebrities may face higher divorce rates, individual circumstances vary, and certainly not all celebrity marriages fail. There are many famous couples who have been together for decades. However, when these well-known people get divorced, there are often some contributing factors that are unique to their high-profile status, including:

- *Public Scrutiny:* The constant scrutiny of a celebrity's relationship can put a strain on it. Of all the factors, this is the one that non-famous people have the most difficult time understanding. To get a sense of it, imagine the regular stressors you have in your life, then imagine having to work through those with people ready to take your picture at the gym or at the grocery store. Imagine people writing speculative articles about why you and your spouse were living separately for a month. Imagine having your close friends approached with offers of payment for insider information. The pressures and scrutiny that well-known people face are almost inconceivable to those of us who are not famous. Similarly, being wealthy brings its own unique set of pressures. For both groups, there is pressure related to public image that fame and fortune bring into relationships.

- *Demanding Schedules:* Well-known people often have jobs that take them away from home and involve long hours. As one actor told me, "I'm not always busy. Sometimes there are long stretches where I'm doing practically nothing, but then when I am working, it's nonstop, day and night. Very little sleep. No downtime." When he is home, he goes to the gym, plays golf, and takes a few meetings, but he mostly hangs around the house. He said he's around so much he feels like his kids are almost sick of him being a constant presence. When he is on set, though, he works over 14 hours a day for weeks on end. He has little time to call or videoconference. He falls into bed exhausted, then gets up at 6:00 a.m. the next morning. These types of schedules can put a strain on relationships by making communication difficult and inconsistent. This type of routine disrupts family cohesion for many and makes sustained intimacy difficult.

- *Materialistic Values:* As like attracts like, both wealthy and well-known people are often drawn to partners of comparable or superior status, net worth, and attractiveness. When those are major factors for coupling, it is not surprising that many of these relationships do not weather conflict or stress well. These so-called "materialistic values" (i.e., status, wealth, and attractiveness) are associated with not only higher rates of anxiety and depression, but also great relationship instability and struggles (Kasser, 2002).

- *Surrounded by Attractive People:* Celebrities tend to be more attractive than the average person. It is part of the reason opportunities and offers open up for them. Their coworkers, fellow actors or musicians, might be similarly attractive. This can increase the level of temptation for the famous person and generate uncertainty and anxiety in their partner.

- *Opportunities for Infidelity:* Similarly, being on the road or on set for work can open up far more opportunities for cheating. The suspicious spouse may not be wrong. Their partner really may be at much greater risk of crossing lines and being unfaithful. Like any careers that involve travel, the chances for cheating are increased because of loneliness, having private living accommodations, and new temptations.

- *Relationship Inequities:* In some relationships where one spouse has had greater career mobility, earns more money, or has achieved some fame, more secure partners can celebrate these successes. Others, however, are likely to struggle a great deal with this. The non-famous or low-earning spouse may feel like they are living in the shadow of their partner or having to orient their lives around that partner. Often, this leads to resentment or even depression.
- *Substance Temptations:* Both fame and fortune bring higher risks of substance use because they have more means and greater access. Sometimes, with a substance-abusing partner, their relationships are connected by drug use or drinking, while others are wedged apart by it. In either event, the substance abuse is likely to derail the relationship.

THE FIVE ESSENTIAL CONVERSATIONS

These unique factors can pose threats to the integrity of your client's marriage and family. There are a few important therapeutic conversations that you should be prepared to have with wealthy and well-known clients related to the health of their key relationships.

Wealthy and well-known individuals often face unique pressures and stressors that can have a profound impact on their core relationships. To effectively manage these challenges, there are several important therapeutic conversations that should be considered. This advice, derived from discussions with financial professionals, managers, agents, and other clinicians, provides a partial list of strategies to help navigate these complexities. Each of these conversations is posed as a central question to be answered.

Question 1: How Can We Guard Our Privacy?

Privacy is a massive concern. Individuals in the public eye often struggle with maintaining personal boundaries, as their lives might attract unsolicited interest and scrutiny. This intrusion can strain relationships, as loved ones may also become targets of public attention or criticism. The challenge here is not only managing one's own privacy but also protecting close relationships from the ripple effects of fame or wealth.

The following principles may help a well-known couple or family guard their privacy:

- *Define and Direct:* Advise the couple to define what areas of life are completely off limits. This may include personal struggles, details of home life,

105

and other family issues that are not to be discussed or shared outside of the trusted inner circle. Once those are established, they should direct friends, family members, and supporting professionals to uphold those boundaries.

- *Social Media Safeguards:* Advise them to share only selective, carefully curated content that does not overexpose family details. They should not post vacation or travel pictures in real time to avoid people trying to locate them. Have them consider using secret accounts under different names that allow them to keep up with friends and family in a more authentic way without fear of exposure.
- *Media and Paparazzi Strategies:* Advise them to choose their outing locations carefully. Decide before going out if they will dress in a way that is recognizable or obscured. Build connections with proprietors who will ensure their privacy while dining or during other activities. Cultivate relationships with journalists and other media professionals who understand and respect your privacy needs and boundaries. Give those professionals who play by the rules preferential access while denying formal access to those media outlets and photographers who disregard their boundaries.

Question 2: How Can I Protect and Nurture My Children?

Closely linked to the conversation about privacy is an even deeper conversation about safeguarding one's children and family. There are actually two conversations here. The first concerns safeguarding the well-being of their children. The second is about the unique parenting challenges facing wealthy and well-known parents. In my experience, these parents desire involvement and connection with their children at least as much, if not more, than other parents. Don't believe the myth that most rich and famous parents outsource their responsibilities to nannies and coaches and tutors. Yes, they often have people in all those roles, but these parents still desire a full relationship with their kids.

While wealthy families have to safeguard privacy, the families of well-known people face the biggest concerns related to the privacy and well-being of their children. Celebrities often discuss the profound impact that fame has had on their relationships, especially within their family dynamics. They've shared their struggles to mitigate the negative consequences of their public lives. Beyoncé highlights the importance of keeping familial bonds strong and protected from the public eye: "Jay and I have always made a point to keep our family close and tight. That has been our priority to make sure our kids have a healthy, normal upbringing away from the cameras."

The need for privacy and controlling the intrusion of fame into their personal lives is a recurring theme among celebrities. Sandra Bullock stresses the importance of managing privacy actively: "I learned that if you don't control your privacy, it can be a free-for-all, and that isn't what I want for my family." Ryan Reynolds also acknowledges the inevitability of public interest but asserts a firm stance on maintaining privacy for his children: "We understand that certain aspects of our lives are going to be public, but we fight tooth and nail to keep our kids' lives private." Julia Roberts emphasizes efforts to maintain normalcy despite her career's demands: "We try to create a normalcy in our kids' lives and not just be dictated by my job."

Here are some conversations—posed as questions—about effectively parenting children in these families.

- *Develop Core Values:* Do the parents teach their children the importance of values like kindness, humility, and hard work? Do they highlight the significance of personal effort and character over material wealth to help their children develop a growth mindset?
- *Teach Financial Responsibility:* Do they educate their children about money management? This includes understanding the value of money, earning through allowances or chores, and learning about saving, investing, and philanthropy.
- *Foster Independence:* Do they encourage their children to pursue their interests and make their own decisions within reasonable boundaries? This helps them develop confidence and independence, reducing the potential for entitlement or dependency on family wealth.
- *Promote Social Skills and Empathy:* Do they facilitate opportunities for children to interact with diverse groups and take part in community service? This can help them develop empathy, social skills, and an understanding of life outside their immediate family circle.

You will also want to assess if the parents are modeling the behaviors and values they wish to instill in their character. This goes beyond what they say to their children and touches on how they conduct themselves. Do they show respect for all people? Do they manage stressful circumstances effectively? Do they regulate their own emotions? Do they have healthy relationships with trusted friends and other family members?

Question 3: How Can We Align Our Expectations?

The disparity in lifestyle between wealthy or well-known individuals and their partners, children, or peers can create friction. Differences in daily experiences, financial concerns, and long-term goals can lead to tension.

Some wealthy and well-known people can assume others in their life should comport with their career and lifestyle as a public figure. Others are acutely aware of the need to insulate their family and friends from their life as a public figure. We don't make assumptions, but neither do we assume the wealthy or well-known client has a clear perception of how he is treating people in his life or managing his relationships.

One of my clients told me how he was going to be on set for four months in Vancouver, then do a play in Washington, D.C., for a three-month stint, followed by a monthlong stay in Los Angeles to film a pilot. During those eight months, he would be at home for exactly two weeks. His anxiety about being away from his girlfriend was mounting, preoccupying his thoughts and making it hard for him to concentrate. She was understanding and flexible, he told me, but there's got to be a limit to how much absence a relationship can endure. He feared he was facing a choice between his relationship and his career.

Many well-known people travel much of the year for work. Wealthy people also travel more than most people and their daily lives are full, often with little margin. This can cause fatigue, little time for family or other important relationships, and a feeling of being out of balance. It is one of the chief complaints you are likely to hear in working with wealthy and well-known individuals.

Sometimes the family is frustrated with the schedule of the most wealthy or well-known member, but sometimes that person is frustrated with the rest of the family for not supporting their unique and busy schedule. There is often relationship strife over that person's demanding schedule, with one partner feeling frustrated over the lack of priority for the family, while the other feels resentful of that feedback. "She knew what my schedule was like when she started dating me," one of my clients said. "Now, suddenly, it's a problem and my work schedule is just the same as it was before."

In some ways, these are normal relationship issues that require good communication and a willingness to compromise in order to resolve them. Most couples struggle with trying to align their schedules and work demands with the needs and priorities of the family. These kinds of struggles are more intensified with wealthy or well-known clients, however, mostly because the unusual schedule and time demands are more intense than usual.

The lopsided nature of these relationships, where one person is more well known or generates most of the family's wealth, can put a strain on even the healthiest of these relationships. The imbalanced power dynamic in the family can have significant ripple effects and infect all the family relationships.

For those clients who are public figures, it's hard to toggle between their public and private roles. They may have a public persona that does not at all align with their private style, which may make it hard for others, including family members, to know how to relate to them. There are other wealthy or well-known clients whose public persona is also their private persona, making it even more difficult for others to relate to them. Some find it impossible to separate from their publicly curated persona, which poses an even greater challenge, as those around them find them difficult to get to know or to trust.

Question 4: How Can I Trust Others?

I've been told many stories of wealthy or well-known people who warmed to a new individual or couple, only to be hit up for money. Some trusted a person, then found out the individual shared some personal bit of information on social media. Others have been asked to connect them with other wealthy or well-known people so they can pitch their new business or product. These prominent people learn to keep people at arm's length. One of my clients said,

> I was at this event and these guys seemed pretty cool, but they were all just too eager. They said I should hang out after the event. I just said, "Nah, I'm too tired to go out," but the truth is I know there's only one reason they want to hang with me.

A primary challenge for wealthy or well-known individuals is discerning whether others' intentions in pursuing a relationship are genuine. The constant question of whether friendships or romantic interests are rooted in personal affection or a desire for status and wealth can lead to a sense of mistrust and skepticism. Many have had the experience of allowing themselves to be open and vulnerable, only to be hurt later when they realize another friend or lover desired their bank account or their fame more than them. Others have had ex-partners talk publicly about them and their relationship. This barrier to trust makes it difficult for these individuals to engage openly and vulnerably with others, which is essential for deep, meaningful relationships. The foundation of all meaningful relationships is trust, and for good reasons, it can be in short supply among the wealthy and well known.

Trust lives at the core of every good and close relationship. It is the bedrock of all intimate partnerships, all close friendships, all deep connections. Trust is not a unitary concept, however. Each of us trusts people we've never met all day long. You trust the driver coming toward you not to swerve and hit you. You trust the server not to poison your food. Yet you wouldn't give the driver your PIN number for your bank card. You wouldn't tell the restaurant employee a deeply personal secret.

So we trust in some arenas of life, while not trusting the same person in other important ways. Even in our close relationships, we trust in some ways and not in others. You might trust your partner completely not to cheat on you or to do you harm, but you may not trust them with making good financial decisions or as a good interstate driver or to remember to put their dirty dishes in the sink. Trust is always on multiple continuums, dynamically shifting upward in one area, then downward in another. Likewise, even within the same area, trust can expand or contract. For example, you may have immense trust in a friend to keep confidences, but then the friend has a lapse and shares something that should not have been shared. Your capacity to trust in this way constricts. Let's say that the friend is extremely apologetic and attempts to make amends. Over time, trust rebuilds and expands.

In relationships, we often call this process the "V-shaped rupture and repair," where a breach of trust occurs, followed by honest efforts to repair the relationship, which, if successful, can make the relationship even better than before (Stiles et al., 2004). It's a simple but important concept, as some people can quickly wash their hands of a person who slights them. For wealthy and well-known people, there is some wisdom in tightening the circle of trust, but not so much where no one can make a misstep. The mindset of zero tolerance in relationships often leaves wealthy and well-known people feeling even more isolated and lonely. This hypothetical graph shows the trajectory of a normal healthy relationship where trust drops, then rebuilds, and the level of closeness waxes and wanes.

In the early days of my career, when I worked in community mental health, we did a massive overhaul of the treatment program for our secure residential program. We identified the biggest needs these adolescents had—impulse control, emotional regulation, social skills, and so on—and built treatment plans around those areas of targets. One module we developed was called "Trust Skills." At first, this seemed odd to me, but I ultimately came around to accepting that trust was, indeed, a skill—and a skill that many of our residents didn't have. They trusted the wrong people and didn't trust the right people. They embraced those who ultimately harmed, manipulated, or exploited them, yet were suspicious of those who sought to help them.

The idea that trust was a skill that could be taught and cultivated has stuck with me for my entire career. Those kids were poor and unknown, yet on the other side of the scale, the wealthy and well known often seem to struggle in this area, as well. Trust in relationships among the wealthy and well known can be in short supply, but having these healthy human connections is essential to a flourishing life. With that in mind, here are five principles for engaging your clients in these important conversations about trust.

- *Trust Is Dynamic:* Trust varies in a relationship. It is not static. Like waves, trust goes up and down, depending on many factors. It is on a continuum rather than at a fixed point. As such, a trusted person can gain or lose trust, but the relationship can remain important. Dialectical thinking—the capacity to see the good and bad aspects of the person together—is a crucial skill here, rather than giving into all-or-nothing or highly polarized thinking.
- *Trust Is Multidimensional:* We can trust completely in one area, but not much in another. We can trust people to varying degrees with the management of finances, the wisdom of their advice, keeping confidences, reliability, judgment, clarity and consistency of communication, taking responsibility and non-defensiveness, respect for boundaries, and consistency of their support. We do not trust people equally in all areas, nor should we.

- *Trust Takes Time:* Trust is developed over time as you get to know the person, as you learn about their history, and as you observe them in action with you and with others. Trusting someone completely that you have recently met is unwise. While it may eventually prove to be true that the charming new person is trustworthy, this is also the purview of con men and sycophants, something that wealthy and well-known people do not need in their lives.

- *Trust Requires Some Tolerance of Error:* We all make mistakes. We come up short. We have lapses of judgment and behave selfishly. This is an undeniable part of the human experience. As such, we will never have a deep, emotionally close relationship where there is an absence of frustration and disappointment. As I have found some wealthy and well-known clients quick to end relationships with people who might have erred but who otherwise are able to provide a healthy relationship, I find this part of the discussion essential. Of course, there will be breaches of trust that cannot and should not be repaired, but typically those are fairly clear and considered by most reasonable people as grounds for ending the relationship. However, building in some tolerance for humans to be humans means the person has the chance for more authentic relationships rather than ones where the other people are simply doing and saying whatever will avoid the wealthy or well-known person's rejection.

- *Trustworthy People Have Other Trusting Relationships:* One of the best ways you can know if a person is trustworthy is if they are trusted by others, especially those you can know or observe. A person you can trust should have many other healthy relationships with a track record of trust over long periods of time. Long-term healthy partnerships. Mutually respectful business relationships. Lifelong friendships. Solid relationships with parents or siblings. Observing these relationships and getting their endorsement of the other person is one of the most powerful ways to build trust.

Wealthy and well-known individuals may struggle to trust others' motives, wondering if they're valued for who they are or what they have. Many times, this suspicion is highly adaptive. Trusting the wrong people can have significant adverse effects. As therapists, we may be called on to help these clients discern genuine connections, navigate relationship breaches, and repair damage to important relationships.

Question 5: How Can I Stay Connected to Others?

Despite being surrounded by people, wealthy and well-known individuals can experience profound social isolation. Their unique lifestyle and the responsibilities that come with it can create a divide between them and others. Even close friends and family may not fully understand the pressures they face, and the individual may feel that their wealth or status creates a barrier that others cannot look past. This isolation can be exacerbated by the busy schedules and high-demand environments in which many affluent individuals operate.

Constant travel, demanding schedules, and security concerns can limit opportunities for genuine social connection. Therapists may need to guide conversations with their clients about how to build and maintain healthy social circles. Often these conversations go down two paths. One path is to take inventory of the people who have been in your client's life and provide good, life-giving, safe relationships. These could be "back in the day" friends from high school or college, or it could be friendships established in adulthood. If these healthy and positive people exist, then you will need to talk through how to re-establish these connections and how to make intentional time for them, even when busy.

The other path is to begin conversations about building their social network from scratch. One client, a recording artist, moved to Los Angeles to further his career, but he knew no one, except some brief acquaintances from his label. He ended up connecting with a group of other artists who were more drug-involved. He fell under their influence and struggled for a long time before finally breaking free of those friends. What followed was a yearlong process of building his social network from ground zero. He ended up with much healthier and more reliable friends, but the process took a great deal of initiative and persistence on his part. He told me, only half-jokingly, "I never knew making friends was so hard when you weren't doing drugs." His example raises an important truth of adult friendships: they rarely happen unless you take the initiative.

Years ago, one of my doctoral interns told me, "I've learned so much about making friends since I started leading our high school social skills group."

"Really?" I replied, a little surprised. "What have you learned?"

"Well, when I was living in Boston, I had a lot of friends, but when I came here for the internship, I would meet people and we would hit it off and exchange texts. Each time, it felt like I had made a friend, but every weekend, I would sit around alone with nothing to do. Then I go to our social skills group and all the guys are saying the same things: 'No one ever asks me to do anything' or 'I thought they were my friends, but they never text me or invite me to go out.' Things like that. Then I realized the burden will always be on me. I always have to be the one to ask the other person. I used to take it personally, but now I realize that's just how people are. Everyone is waiting for the other person to take the initiative."

This is even more true with our wealthy or well-known clients. There will be many people trying to push their way into their lives because of a wide range of motives. Out of necessity, your client will need to set limits on or cut out many of those people and their attempts to burrow into the client's life. This leaves them with two options: being lonely, or being the one who takes the social initiative. Taking the initiative allows the wealthy or well-known person to create a sense of social safety while still allowing them to stay connected to important relationships.

The therapist's task is to guide them into constructive steps to create their own circle of safety and then take initiative within that trusted circle.

START, STOP, AND CONTINUE: A FAMILY INTERVENTION

Most of this book focuses on individual therapy with wealthy and well-known people, but there are clearly times when family therapy should be the modality of choice. If you have family therapy training and experience, you will have much opportunity to employ it with these families. A full family therapy is outside our scope here, but I share a fair and effective approach to identifying and interventing in family issues in a way that opens the door to follow-up sessions.

The approach, called "Start, Stop, Continue," serves to generate specific targets that each family member can work on to improve the family's functioning. The intervention is an in-vivo exercise in improving communication and collaboration in both dyads and with the whole family. When done well, it serves to make the family members feel hopeful and encouraged individually and corporately.

"Start, Stop, Continue" is effective because it is action-oriented, which is often appealing to wealthy and well-known families who can have a results-oriented family culture. It also does a good job of not making any person in the family the identified problem. It is fair and produces some change in relating and family engagement quickly, as early as the first session. At a minimum, you must have three family members. At a maximum, it becomes harder to do well if there are over six people, though it is possible.

To explain how it works, let's use a straightforward example: a family with two parents and two kids, a boy and a girl, both teenagers. We'll imagine that the parents are concerned because the siblings fight with each other a lot and can frequently be disrespectful to their parents. You explain you are going to do a very structured session. Every member of the family will be in the spotlight once in each of the three rounds of the session. The first round is called Start, the second is called Stop, and the final round is called Continue. During each round, the person in the spotlight cannot speak or give off any negative nonverbals like eye-rolling or having a disgusted expression. They must simply listen to what is being discussed by the other three family members. You will not speak during their discussion. You will simply be the scribe, the note-taker.

Let's imagine that mom is first in the spotlight—chosen at random. You give the other family members 90 seconds, though this can be adjusted up or down, as needed, as long as it is decided at the beginning of the session. During that minute and a half, the other three say things they wish Mom would start doing. Mom cannot react verbally or nonverbally, even if she disagrees. She must sit and listen, giving good eye contact. You are taking notes throughout, with one page per family member.

113

Each family member is then in the spotlight for the first round as you follow the same procedure. After that round is done, you move onto the "Stop" round with the same instructions, except now the focus is on what each person wants the spotlighted family member to stop doing. Your third and final round is the "Continue" round, focusing on what they hope each spotlighted family member will continue doing. This round should encourage each family member by hearing good feedback about themselves. Use clear instructions to set up this round for success.

Ideally, the three rounds should put each family member in the spotlight in random order. I typically do this by turning over the sheets and shuffling them to reset the order. The randomness sends the message that everyone is on level footing and no one person is singled out to start first or wait until last.

The next series puts each family member in the spotlight again. Let's imagine that Dad is up first in this round. The other three are asked to huddle with each other and come to a consensus about what two things on Dad's list of starts and stops they are going to prioritize. While they are discussing it, you have a little side conversation with Dad. It could be about anything, but the purpose of it is to draw his attention away from their discussion and allow them the chance to talk a little more freely. Once they are ready, they propose the two action steps they feel are most important. It could be two starts, two stops, or one of each. Dad does not have to accept any of these, but that the process always works better when everyone will take some constructive actions.

The two suggestions are proposed to Dad for him to accept or reject. You repeat the same process for each of the family members. By the end, all family members should have had the opportunity to accept two suggestions from the other family members. Hopefully, each person has agreed to at least one of these, if not both. However, if one rejected both, it is acceptable to ask them once more if they want to consider accepting one as a goal for the week. If they persist in rejecting the suggestions, don't react, but continue to give your instructions to the others. They are to try their hardest to work on the one or two things they agreed to do. For example, if Mom accepted the suggestion of "stopping her sarcastic tone when she is frustrated," then this becomes her focus until the next time they all check in.

In the following session, you once again want all family members to attend for the check-in. Structure the session by giving each person the chance to say what they agreed to work on, then ask how they think they did, then ask the other family members how they think they did. Use the material this generates for discussion, being careful not to make any one person feel singled out or overly focused on.

This family therapy process is good for most families, but it is especially strong for the families of wealthy and well-known people because it is immensely fair to all family members and doesn't give preferential treatment to the rich or famous person, nor does it allow for there to be one identified patient.

COMPLICATED RELATIONSHIPS REQUIRE MORE ATTENTION

One of the hidden costs of being wealthy or well known is the toll it takes on relationships. Friendships and partner relationships are more complicated, more fraught. Relationships with children and other family members are also far more challenging. Trust issues are in abundance. On average, they have more work to do on their relationships than many other clients, even when they are strong from the outset. Therapists and other professional helpers can play a key role in helping these clients forge healthy and more resilient relationships or repair ones that have been damaged.

REFERENCES

Benson, H., & Azim, R. (2015). *Celebrity divorce rates.* Marriage Foundation. https://marriagefoundation.org.uk/wp-content/uploads/2016/06/pdf−03.pdf

Kasser, T. (2002). *The high price of materialism.* MIT Press.

Killewald, A., Lee, A., & England, P. (2023). Wealth and divorce. *Demography, 60*(1), 147–171. https://doi.org/10.1215/00703370-10413021

Stiles, W. B., Glick, M. J., Osatuke, K., Hardy, G. E., Shapiro, D. A., Agnew-Davies, R., Rees, A., & Barkham, M. (2004). Patterns of alliance development and the rupture-repair hypothesis: Are productive relationships U-shaped or V-shaped? *Journal of Counseling Psychology, 51*(1), 81–92.

Vaillant, G. E. (2012). *Triumphs of experience: The men of the Harvard Grant study.* Belknap Press of Harvard University Press.

Yau, N. (2015). Divorce and occupation. *FlowingData.* https://flowingdata.com/2017/07/25/divorce-and-occupation/

Chapter 10

Treating Substance Abuse in Wealthy and Well-Known People

Every night Jared drank a half a bottle of wine from the time he got home until he went to bed that evening. On some nights, he'd finish it with a shot of bourbon. It was no problem, he reasoned, because he got into the office every morning on time and his business was doing great. Besides, Jared didn't even have to work if he didn't want to. Work was where he felt most competent, but it was also his biggest source of stress. There was a constant barrage of problems to be solved, employee issues to be addressed, regulatory hassles to be navigated. There were some nights when he questioned why he did this to himself. Why not sell the business and let all this be someone else's problem?

He never thought the drinking was a problem until one of his kids told their mom, "Daddy is always too tired to play with us." In a moment of personal honesty, he realized his children saw him tipsy every night. The idea of giving up his nightcaps was frustrating to him, though. He worked hard and dealt with a lot of nonsense during the day. He deserved this.

His solution was to keep the nightly ritual, but just cut back. Two glasses of wine—a little less—and only one shot of bourbon. This resolution lasted for about two weeks, then he found himself back to where he was before, maybe even a little worse. This continued for over three more months before his wife nudged him one evening. "You're missing out on a lot of great experiences with the kids," she said. "These are years we'll never get back with them. Maybe you should talk to somebody."

When he came into the first session, he told his therapist, "I think I'm fine. I'm just here because I promised my wife I'd talk to someone."

ALCOHOL AND SUBSTANCE USE PROBLEMS AMONG THE WEALTHY

Research reveals a surprising link between wealth and alcohol and substance abuse (Luthar & Barkin, 2012). This was affirmed by many of the mental health and

DOI: 10.4324/9781003503569-13

financial professionals I interviewed. While poverty is associated with addiction, studies show wealthy individuals and children of affluence are also at high risk. Research also finds children from wealthy families are two to three times more likely to develop substance use disorders compared to national averages (Luthar & Barkin, 2012). This applies to both alcohol and illicit drugs.

Wealth permits easier access to substances and creates a culture where problems are masked. An excess of money allows for buying expensive drugs and alcohol without financial constraints. The power and influence afforded to wealthy people can also make them less likely that anyone will question or confront them, allowing the problem to continue for longer. The privacy and insulation afforded by wealth can hide addictions for longer.

Social opportunities and norms among wealthy communities can also encourage substance use. Exclusive parties, events, and certain high-stress industries often have a culture of heavy substance use, making drugs and alcohol more accessible and acceptable.

Despite the advantages of wealth, teens in affluent communities may experience unique pressures and stressors, such as high expectations for success and greater social visibility and lower emotional closeness in family relationships. Children of privilege may experience higher rates of depression and anxiety compared with their less affluent peers (Luthar & D'Avanzo, 1999; Luthar & Kumar, 2018). These mental health struggles can contribute to drinking and using substances as a way of coping with distress. Having more money and greater access only worsens this risk.

Wealthy individuals often face barriers to seeking help for substance abuse, including concerns about stigma, legitimate privacy concerns, and, like Jared, the belief that they should be able to manage on their own. This can delay treatment and exacerbate problems.

ALCOHOL AND SUBSTANCE USE PROBLEMS AMONG THE WELL KNOWN

Over a decade ago, Zac Efron told *The Hollywood Reporter*, "There was something lacking, some sort of hole that I couldn't really fill up." He described his battle with alcohol and substance addiction, saying, "It's a never-ending struggle."

There is limited research that finds higher rates of alcohol and substance problems among well-known people (Just et al., 2016). The constant pressure to be "on," the constant scrutiny, and the fear of losing relevance or fame can lead to significant psychological stress. Substance use becomes a coping mechanism for some, aiming to ease the stress, anxiety, or depression that can come with fame.

For some well-known people, their jobs often take them away from friends and family. These are professional athletes on road games. Actors on set in another city, state, or country. Musicians on tour. They stay in nice hotel rooms, furnished trailers, tricked-out buses, high-end Airbnbs. Despite the high-profile job, they can be isolated and lonely. They are away from their sources of love and support, and even from accountability. Some have crew members who will get them whatever they request. All this represents an enormous risk for substance use or relapse. One touring musician who had a history of struggles with alcohol told me, "It was just me and the hotel room mini-bar every night."

These same traveling artists and athletes can find themselves in situations where the norm is overindulgence. Teammates stay out late at the bar after a game. There's always a party on the tour bus. Someone brings coke to the cast parties. This life might be far different from their life at home, which makes either moderation or sobriety a challenge.

Some research has found higher rates of mental health disorders among creative professionals compared with the general population. A notable study found that individuals in creative professions were more likely to have bipolar disorder. Relatives of patients with schizophrenia, bipolar disorder, anorexia nervosa, and autism were also found to be more likely to work in creative professions, suggesting a genetic or familial link (Kyaga et al., 2011). This predisposition may also make certain well-known people, especially artists of all kinds, more vulnerable to using substances as a way of coping.

Also, certain psychological traits associated with creativity, such as openness to experience, divergent thinking, and sensitivity, may make individuals more susceptible to mental health issues. The intense emotions and experiences that fuel creative expression can also contribute to emotional volatility and psychological distress, which presents a risk for drug and alcohol abuse.

A TREATMENT APPROACH FOR SUBSTANCE PROBLEMS

In the early days of my career, I worked with aggressive teens who were part of a community mental health program. There were no established best practices then. Much of the preferred approaches involved confronting misbehavior and bad decisions, hoping the client would see the error of their ways. This rarely worked. In fact, some clients got worse the more they were confronted or challenged. Their need for control won out over choosing the more pro-social path.

Having been trained in CBT, I knew the model worked for most traditional clients, but only those who owned their problems, showed up consistently, and did their homework. None of this described my clients. I knew I had to find a model that worked for clients who were more reluctant or resistant, who had some kind of problem but seemed unwilling to change it.

As I moved into private practice, I had more teenage and young adult clients who had significant substance problems, but the same approaches seemed to dominate the conventional wisdom at the time: confront, use logic and reason, let them him rock bottom if needed. I continued to search for a better approach.

It was then I learned about Motivational Interviewing. Originally developed as a treatment for alcohol abuse, the heart of the model made it flexible enough to apply to help people overcome a wide range of problem behaviors. For me, it was the first model that made sense. I just wasn't convinced it worked as well as advertised. However, as more and more studies emerge, the consensus was that Motivational Interviewing was a sturdy, evidence-based treatment (Pace et al., 2017).

THE ESSENCE OF MOTIVATIONAL INTERVIEWING

Motivational Interviewing (MI) is a client-centered and collaborative therapy approach that empowers clients to shake free of problem behaviors by leveraging their intrinsic motivation, rather than attempting to impose external motivation through confrontation or criticism. It draws out the individual's own reasons for change, treating ambivalence—the simultaneous desire to maintain and abandon a behavior—as an expected part of the process.

Ambivalence is a common experience in behavioral change. It occurs when individuals are torn between conflicting desires, such as wanting to lose weight while eating dessert after dinner every night. Maybe they want to quit smoking weed, but feel like they need it to sleep well. MI addresses this tension through empathetic exploration, using reflective techniques to help clients articulate and resolve their ambivalence. For instance, a therapist might use a double-sided reflection to acknowledge both sides of a dilemma: "You don't want your drinking to have a detrimental effect on your marriage and family, but you are not yet willing or able to not get tipsy every night," or, "You're saying you want to be healthier and get cleaned up, but you also still feel drawn to coke and other hard drugs, especially when you are on tour."

By presenting both perspectives without judgment, MI creates an opportunity for clients to confront their internal conflicts. This process encourages self-awareness and positions the client as the primary agent of change. Unlike more confrontational approaches, MI lets individuals explore their behavior's positive and negative aspects to increase their own internal motivation for change.

MI's collaborative nature is grounded in client-centered techniques such as reflective listening, open-ended questioning, and affirmations. These strategies let therapists guide clients toward identifying their values, goals, and reasons for change. For example, when working with a client facing alcohol dependence after a public intoxication arrest, an MI therapist would avoid harsh confrontation and finger wagging. Instead, they would help the client explore the enjoyable aspects of drinking alongside its detrimental effects, gently drawing out the client's motivation to make healthier choices.

One of MI's hallmarks is its ability to help clients attribute the decision to change to themselves. When clients perceive their choice as self-directed rather

119

than externally imposed, they are more likely to experience intrinsic motivation and achieve lasting success.

The effectiveness of MI is well documented across diverse populations and behaviors. A meta-analysis of 48 studies found MI superior to other interventions for promoting behavior change in areas such as reduced death rate, lower alcohol dependence, smoking cessation, and less sedentary behavior (Lundahl et al., 2013). Similarly, a meta-analysis of 139 studies on MI for substance use disorders found moderate to large reductions in substance use across various populations and settings (Magill et al., 2018).

Studies also highlight MI's versatility. Research by Barnett et al. (2012) demonstrated MI's success in reducing substance use among adolescents, while Borsari et al. (2021) found it effective in managing opioid use disorders and associated pain. Apodaca et al. (2019) noted that MI's benefits are sustained over time, with reductions in substance use persisting up to 24 months after treatment.

MI often requires fewer sessions than other therapeutic approaches, yet its impact is profound and enduring. A follow-up analysis by Magill et al. (2018) confirmed that clients who participated in MI experienced sustained improvements at 6- and 12-month follow-ups. Furthermore, Lundahl and colleagues (2013) found MI to be as effective as, or more effective than, other standard treatments, including Cognitive-Behavioral Therapy (CBT) and 12-step programs, in reducing substance use and improving treatment retention.

The strength of MI lies in its respect for your client's autonomy and its emphasis on collaboration. By guiding your clients to uncover their own motivations and solutions, MI fosters a sense of ownership and empowerment that significantly enhances the likelihood of long-term success. Whether used as a standalone intervention or integrated with other treatments, MI's evidence-based approach has proven to be a powerful tool for addressing a wide range of behavioral challenges.

The beauty of Motivational Interviewing is that it works best for people who are resistant to changing the problem behavior or ambivalent about it. This is a distinction few therapy models can boast. As a practice, MI relies on a trans-theoretical premise called "The Stages of Change." The model suggests when someone changes a problem behavior, they go through these stages.

1. Pre-contemplation—not considering a change.
2. Contemplation—considering a change.
3. Decision—decided to make a change.
4. Action—taking steps toward change.
5. Maintenance—made the change for a sustained time period, usually six or more months.

Unlike other stage theories, though, it does not assume that once someone has entered a stage, they will remain there or progress forward. The Stages of Change Model says a person might be at the Decision stage (stage 3), but then circumstances conspire to send them all the way back to no longer considering a change (stage 1). The benefit of this way of thinking is it allows for a dynamic assessment of where a client might be at any point in time (Prochaska & DiClemente, 1984).

Research on psychotherapy effectiveness finds that about half of all clients who drop out of therapy do so at the pre-contemplation stage (Prochaska & Norcross, 2018). These are the clients who have not yet decided they are ready, willing, or able to change. Showing up for therapy appointments is great, but they may be in the pre-contemplation stage and not yet ready or willing to change their drug use.

Studies on Motivational Interviewing have found that it works, often in small doses (i.e., number or length of sessions), and can be enhanced by negativity (Hettema et al., 2005). As a result, it works better with resistant clients.

Like all therapies, clinicians differ in how effective they are in using Motivational Interviewing. Accurate empathy is the best predictor of success. A therapist perceived by their client as empathetic will get better results than other, less empathetic professionals. Less effective therapists often rate themselves as being more empathetic than they are and see clients as more engaged than they are (Atzil-Slonim et al., 2019; Lafferty et al., 1989).

Whereas other therapy approaches might forge ahead when presented with a treatment issue, Motivational Interviewing tells us not to regard pre-contemplators or contemplators like they are ready to make a change. Instead, it shifts the focus on creating the fertile ground for change where the client is ready, willing, and able to move forward. It does this by generating "change talk," which includes leading a person to consider the following:

- *Advantages of Change:* "What might be some good things about staying sober when you are on location?"
- *Disadvantages of the Status Quo:* "What are you concerned about if things continue this way with your drug use?"
- *Optimism for Change:* "What makes you hopeful that you could get your drinking back under control?"
- *Intention to Change:* "What do you think you want to do about this now?"

Each of these example questions draws out a particular kind of change talk, but the specific questions you might ask are limitless. If you get an unfavorable or resistant response, you roll away from that part of the conversation in a subtle and non-defensive way. It might go something like this:

Therapist: "What worries you about continuing to drink every night?"
Client: "I'm not worried about it all. I just need to be more careful."

121

Therapist: "I hear you. Let me ask you about when you first started drinking every night. That could help me better understand the role it plays in your life."

In this exchange, the attempt to draw out some change talk around the disadvantage of continuing to drink every night fell flat. It would be a mistake to push the point or argue in favor of it. In doing so, they may be more likely to dig in their heels and hold fast to their no-change position. Instead, you pivot, shifting focus to another potential way into the ambivalence about the problem behavior. As a therapist, you are looking for entry points, but not in a pushy way. If one attempt is rejected, you roll away from the resistance and take another tack.

HOW DO YOU KNOW IF THEY ARE READY FOR CHANGE?

The challenge in Motivational Interviewing is not to move ahead of the client before they are ready. Some other therapy models seem doomed to failure when the therapist whips out the manual before understanding if their client is ready to make a big change. We assume someone would not be in therapy if they didn't want to change, but that is a faulty assumption. People often present in therapy as not quite ready for several reasons.

The question, then, is, how do you know if they are ready to make a change? When are they ready to stop drinking or using? Here are a couple of indicators of your client's readiness that may give you the green light to move forward. Listen for these types of comments or conversations.

- *Decreased Resistance:* Your client stops trying to argue or defend. They no longer dodge, deflect, or avoid. There is a subjective but real feeling that they are no longer fighting the need to change. *I think I'm ready to figure this out.*
- *Resolve:* You hear your client talking about a new determination to change. This isn't just "New Year's Resolution" talk, but a newfound resolve to tackle the issue. *I know I can do it because I've done harder things than this before.*
- *Change Talk:* When you hear your client talk about the advantages of change or the disadvantages of staying in their current state, you may be ready to move forward. *Life would be so much easier if I didn't have to be thinking about when I can get back to my room and drink every day.*
- *Questions About Change:* Your client asks you questions about the decision to change. *If I try again and fail, won't I be more discouraged than before? What do you think I should do to get this under control? Is it normal to feel so conflicted about this?*
- *Envisioning:* If you hear your client imagining what it would be like to be free of this troubling problem, take that as a good sign. *If I could go out of town for*

work and not think of how I can get my hands on some coke, that would be such a big relief!

- *Experimenting:* Sometimes a client has said little, but they report minor efforts to make some changes on their own. These tiny personal experiments suggest they might want to change. *I deleted the contact of the guy I buy Oxy from and I think it helped.*

When you hear your client express one of these indicators, you move toward facilitating the change. You will not be in a hurry, but you'll build on their exploration or engagement, careful not to scare them off by pushing too hard too soon. Your goal is for them to have the experience that they came to this decision to change by themselves. In their view, you were an observer at a minimum and an encourager at most. They were the ones who did the heavy lifting. If you get to this outcome, you are doing well as a clinician.

THE FOUR PILLARS OF MOTIVATIONAL INTERVIEWING

Motivational Interviewing's core principles create the framework and serve as your guide to therapy with a person struggling with an addiction or other problem behavior. While it employs various strategies, it is these principles that provide the backbone of the model and form the spirit of approach. These are the four core principles of Motivational Interviewing:

- *Express Empathy:* Accurate empathy is the bedrock of MI. All therapists think they are outstanding in expressing empathy, but the more important measure is whether the client perceives the therapist as having accurate empathy (Elliott et al., 2019; Watson et al., 2014). Client-rated empathy is the most important measure. Do they feel heard, valued, understood? When this is done well, you are likely to have lower resistance and a great willingness to change.
- *Develop Discrepancy:* This principle involves helping clients recognize the gap between their current behaviors and their core values, ideal self, and personal goals. They want to get sober for their family, but they still want to party on business trips, for example. By illuminating these discrepancies, therapists can guide clients toward increasing the readiness for change. It can be done subtly, almost invisibly, using double-sided reflections and other strategies. When done well, the idea of change feels like a self-discovered decision rather than an imposed mandate. I want my clients to say, "Dr. V was a nice guy, but I decided to stop smoking weed on my own."
- *Roll With Resistance:* In MI, resistance is not met with confrontation or pushiness, but is viewed as a natural response to change. You expect and accept a certain amount of resistance, understand its source, and change

your approach. This flexibility keeps clients from getting locked into not changing their behavior by making it less likely they will argue in favor of the "no change" position.

- *Support Self-Efficacy:* A cornerstone of MI, this principle focuses on bolstering the client's belief in their ability to change. You encourage clients to recognize their own ability and potential, reinforcing the idea that change is not only possible but within their capability. A word of caution, however: sometimes a client lacks the knowledge or skill to help themselves. For example, they might want to control their anger but not have the slightest idea how to do this. It helps to emphasize they can change, but I would always offer help and equip them with skills when they are needed.

The motivational therapist is always moving the client forward on two dimensions: increasing a sense of *importance* that they should tackle the problem, and bolstering their *confidence* that they can change the old pattern. Sometimes a client finds the issue important but doubts they can do it (high importance, low confidence). Other times, the client may not view the problem behavior as that important, but believes they could change it if they wanted to (low importance, high confidence). There are also times when both importance and confidence are low. When addressing importance and confidence in therapy, you are helping the client get to a place where they can say to themselves, "I will do it and I can do it."

To do this well, there are several strategies that can help advance their motivation or confidence. We'll begin with the foundational skills and move to more advanced strategies.

BASIC TECHNIQUE: OARS

The beginning strategies that Motivational Interviewing employs are identical to those most therapists learned in their introductory graduate courses. They are derived from the work of Carl Rogers and his Person-Centered approach to counseling (Rogers, 1942). These foundational skills are open questions, affirmations, reflective listening, and summaries. For ease, they make an easy acronym: OARS.

- *Open Questions:* Asking good open questions is an art form. These questions cast a wide net, giving the client the opportunity to go where they need to go. The best open question is not even a question. It's a directive: "Tell me about . . ." These three words allow you to direct the client while still giving them all the latitude they need. You might say something like, "Tell me about the role of alcohol in your high school years." When you start with "Tell me about" or "Talk about," it tells the person you want them to elaborate.

- *Affirmations:* MI is a respectful and affirming model. Within this framework, you are looking for opportunities to affirm their courage, effort, or positive qualities. You might say, "I respect your recommitment to sobriety after that rough weekend." MI encourages therapists to affirm—but not flatter—their clients in honest ways.
- *Reflective Listening:* One of Carl Rogers's important contributions to the practice of therapy and counseling, reflective listening involves listening well, asking clarifying questions if needed, but then reflecting the essence of what the person just told you. With phrases like, "You're saying you have a desire to stop using, but it's been especially difficult because of all the stress you're under." The goal is to listen well and make the other person feel heard and validated.
- *Summaries:* Summaries are longer versions of reflections where you cover more ground in the statements. You don't just reflect the most recent content, but you give a sweep of a lengthier portion of the conversation. It might sound like, "We started by talking about how being away from your family in Vancouver for three months was hard on all of you. We then discussed how you tried to cope with the loneliness and the temptations you've faced up there. Now that you are home, you're finding some of the old habits have returned and you want to stop them before they hurt your family. Is that a fair summary?" You then use that to launch into a discussion where you co-create a treatment plan together.

These four basic skills provide the backbone and embody much of the spirit of MI. They are gentle, affirming, and engaging. They approach the conversation not as expert-recipient, but as a collaboration. Where MI differs from a pure Rogerian approach is in its directedness, always trying to move the client toward changes in thought and action that will help reduce or arrest the problem behavior. To do that, there are some strategies to help increase the sense of importance and others that help bolster confidence. Let's explore these.

MOTIVATIONAL STRATEGIES TO INCREASE THE IMPORTANCE OF CHANGE

I often have clients who come into therapy because someone else wants them there. This may be a spouse or other family member, a coworker or boss, or someone else in their life. They may have to be there because of some court involvement. In these instances, the client will often show up to therapy with a dim view of the issue to be tackled, believing that others are making more of it than need be. They may continue to insist that the problem behavior is not a problem.

In these instances, you may need to leverage them toward some change talk by using a strategy designed to increase their motivation to work on the problem. These can include:

- *Reviewing a Typical Day:* You ask your client to take you through a regular day with all the highlights from start to finish. You ask them to include when, where, and how much they drink (or use their drug of choice). The hope is that they hear how central the substance use is and reflect on that. If not, you roll away and take a different approach.

- *Looking Back:* You ask your client to discuss how life was before the target behavior was a regular part of life, then contrast that with how life is now with the target behavior having taken up residence. The client may observe the contrast and consider the need for a change.

- *Good Things and Not Good Things:* Motivational Interviewing makes a point of not being judgmental, paying careful attention to language, and being aware that clients are often hypervigilant about criticism. In this spirit, you ask the client to give you an honest account of what is good about their drinking or substance use. After you allow for this to be fairly and thoroughly discussed, you ask what the "not good things" are about the use. It's a subtlety, but an important one. You are not saying, "What's bad about it?" because of the unavoidable negative twinge to that language. Instead, you ask, "And are there any not-good things about it?"

- *Discussing Stages of Change:* Teaching and discussing the stages of change can be a therapeutic intervention. One of my favorite memories of this was a young musician who went to great lengths to tell me how his habitual marijuana use was nothing but good for him. His girlfriend and family were just too uptight about it. Smoking weed helped him be more creative and play more fluidly. Despite my best attempts, I couldn't find a point of entry. Almost as a final Hail Mary, I explained the Stages of Change, then asked where he saw himself, expecting he would say stage 1. Instead, he said, "I'd say I'm around a 1.5." That extra .5 gave me a little open door. "Why a 1.5 and not a 1?" I asked. He then discussed the slightest whiff of ambivalence, which gave us an opportunity to explore further.

- *Values Exploration:* You ask if you can focus on gaining some clarity about their personal values. If needed, you can use an inventory like the one provided in Appendix 1. Following this honest exploration, you lead a discussion about how your client's drinking or drug use aligns with their most highly rated values. For example, say that your client rated "Honesty" as being of very high importance. You might ask, "Do you think your drinking makes it easier or more challenging to live a life marked by fundamental honesty?" If they indicated "Self-Respect" is important to them, you might ask, "Does your drinking strengthen or weaken your self-respect?" Again, as with all motivational interventions, if you get a response that favors no change, you roll away from this form of resistance.

- *Looking Forward:* You invite the client to consider a future without the problem behavior and imagine what life might look like, how it might be better, what it might do for them and the loved ones in their life. With this intervention, you want them to get just a taste of what life might be like if they weren't drinking or using. While they may have had fleeting thoughts about this, they may not have allowed themselves to entertain these ideas or consider them when they are in the grip of their addiction. An honest discussion of what a sober life might look like can be therapeutic for some.

- *Exploring Ready, Willing, and Able:* Sometimes it's worth explaining that any time a person prepares to change a habit, they have to consider whether they are ready to make that change, whether they are willing to make that change, and whether they believe they can make that change. The therapist then guides the client to consider each of these three dimensions, hoping the discussion might strengthen the pro-change side of their internal conflict and ambivalence.

- *Decisional Balance:* In other contexts, this is called a cost-benefit analysis. This involves writing the reasons to stop in one column and the reasons to continue drinking or using in another. I prefer to weight the variables from 1 to 5, with a rating of 5 being most important and a score of 1 being not very important. The weighting gives a little more variance. And what do you do when the cost-benefit analysis seems to suggest continuing to drink? You roll away from it and come in from another angle.

MOTIVATIONAL STRATEGIES TO IMPROVE CONFIDENCE IN MAKING A CHANGE

There are also some strategies that might improve your client's confidence in his ability to make a change. You would use these types of approaches when he reports an uncertainty that he could have success in tackling the problem behavior.

- *Confidence Ruler:* You ask the client to rate how confident they are from 1 to 10, with 10 being most confident, that they could stop drinking. No matter what they say, you contrast that by asking why they gave it that score and not a 1. For example, if they say, "I'd give it a 3," you don't say, "Why not a 6 or 7?" Instead, you say, "You gave it a 3. Why not a 1?" This puts them in the position of having to argue the side of why they might be able to change if they set their mind to it. In the rare chance they say a 1, you say, "You're not feeling optimistic about that yet," and then shift to another focus.

- *Reviewing Past Successes:* For a client who feels stuck and unable to move forward, you might inquire about times in their life when they managed the problem well, even for a very brief period. That time becomes framed as a little victory rather than evidence that they will always relapse or that they have no ability to change.
- *Personal Strengths and Supports:* You might ask a client to generate a detailed list of the personal qualities and strengths they have, followed by the social supports they have. What do they have going for them, and who's in their corner? You then leverage that conversation to see if it might strengthen their sense of confidence that they might be able to make a change this time.
- *Brainstorming:* If you reach a stuck point, sometimes it is worth having a genuine brainstorming time. In keeping with the spirit of a good brainstorm, you don't critique or problem-solve the options that get generated. It is a strategy to thaw out the frozen spot by shifting focus to possibilities and options.
- *Reframing Past Experiences:* Often a person who has struggled with substances or drinking for a long time will look back over their past and see nothing but failure. For them, it's just one relapse after another, just one failed promise on top of the next. This intervention reviews past experiences, but reframes them so they can be more helpful. Instead of one failure after another, you might frame it as someone who kept getting back up after he had been knocked down, which is something to be proud of.
- *Hypothetical Change:* You paint a picture of a future where they have had solid success with managing the problem behavior. Then you ask, "How did it happen? How did you do it?" This causes them to shift their thinking about what might work for them.
- *Considering Radical Change:* If your client has tried lesser measures—outpatient therapy, AA, change of social circle, and so on—and nothing has gained any traction, then it may be time for a discussion about making a big change. Move out of town. Check into rehab. Switch jobs. Is there some big lifestyle change that might make it more likely that they stop the problem behavior? One of my clients switched from touring to studio work as a radical change that reflected his desire to get his drug use under control. Even discussing radical options can be a strong intervention because it sends the message that a serious issue requires a serious solution.

AVOIDING THE COMMON PITFALLS OF A MOTIVATIONAL APPROACH

My psychotherapy training was in the CBT tradition. I was taught how to structure sessions that move into teaching and practicing skills. There's a place for that, but when someone is wrestling with a problem that has tremendous upsides (pleasure, social connection, numbing of negative emotions, etc.) and tremendous downsides (harm to relationships, legal trouble, damage to one's body, etc.), you'd be wise not to barrel into the CBT or other skill-building work before you reckon with the ambivalence that such a dilemma brings. Bypassing ambivalence is a serious error, and one that is likely because of your own anxiety about making progress, creating safety, or just using the time well.

Another error from a Motivational Interviewing perspective is giving too much or too little direction in therapy. If you give too much direction, you risk moving too quickly and stripping them of their agency to generate solutions and problem-solve. If you don't give enough direction, you may make them feel frustrated about the lack of tangible help or hopeless about their ability to get what they need out of therapy.

A rule of thumb is that if I am asked directly for guidance or advice, I'll give it. If I have a client who says, "I know I need to control my anger to save my relationship, but I don't have any idea how I could do that," they are unlikely to find it helpful to hear a response like, "Well, I'm sure you can come up with some good solutions." This client is ready to learn the skills to manage anger, and you should provide them. The same is true for substance use, drinking, or other addictive behaviors, of course. If a client is asking for tangible help and does not know what to do, then give them the help they need. Teach them a skill. Give them direction. Teach a mindset.

Being neither too directive nor not directive enough is sometimes an impossible balance to achieve. You should seek your client's feedback regularly, if not every session. Some clinicians use a model called Feedback Informed Treatment (FIT) that asks for the client to evaluate the therapist at the end of every session (Miller et al., 2016; Seidel, 2012). For substance use work, this is an excellent practice to adopt.

A HIGH-STAKES TASK

Countless celebrities and wealthy people have died from their alcoholism and substance abuse. It has claimed the lives of remarkable talents like Whitney Houston, Matthew Perry, Michael Jackson, Amy Winehouse, Jim Morrison, Prince, Philip Seymour Hoffman, Jimi Hendrix, River Phoenix, John Belushi, Janis Joplin, Heath Ledger, and many others. There are others who survived their drug abuse, but didn't emerge unscathed, including Demi Lovato, Ozzy Osbourne, Stevie Nicks, and scores of others. As Johnny Cash said, "I was taking the pills for a while and then the pills started taking me" (Gross, 2004, p. 35).

The stakes are high when working with clients who struggle with substance abuse. Because of their easy access, their unique pressures, and their enabling sub-cultures, wealthy and well-known people are especially vulnerable to developing drug and alcohol addictions (Patrick et al., 2012). Because our understanding of the human brain and the mechanisms of addiction are developing, you can never know all there is to know as a therapist, nor can you ever have all the skills you'll need to be your most effective. Instead, if you work in this area, carry yourself with the humble attitude of being a lifelong learner and an ever-improving therapist.

REFERENCES

Apodaca, T. R., Longabaugh, R., & Magill, M. (2019). Advances in the science of motivational interviewing: A review of key research emerging from the Harvard Center on the development of adolescent treatment interventions. *Psychology of Addictive Behaviors, 33*(5), 457–468.

Atzil-Slonim, D., Bar-Kalifa, E., Fisher, H., Lazarus, G., Hasson-Ohayon, I., Lutz, W., Rubel, J., & Rafaeli, E. (2019). Therapists' empathic accuracy toward their clients' emotions. *Journal of Consulting and Clinical Psychology, 87*(1), 33–45. https://doi.org/10.1037/ccp0000354

Barnett, E., Sussman, S., Smith, C., Rohrbach, L. A., & Spruijt-Metz, D. (2012). Motivational Interviewing for adolescent substance use: A review of the literature. *Addictive Behaviors, 37*(12), 1325–1334. https://doi.org/10.1016/j.addbeh.2012.07.001

Borsari, B., Li, Y., Tighe, J., Manuel, J. K., Gökbayrak, N. S., Delucchi, K., Morasco, B. J., Abadjian, L., Cohen, B. E., Baxley, C., & Seal, K. H. (2021). A pilot trial of collaborative care with motivational interviewing to reduce opioid risk and improve chronic pain management. *Addiction, 116*, 2387–2397. https://doi.org/10.1111/add.15401

Elliott, R., Bohart, A. C., Watson, J. C., & Murphy, D. (2019). Empathy. In J. C. Norcross & M. J. Lambert (Eds.), *Psychotherapy relationships that work: Evidence-based therapist contributions* (3rd ed., pp. 245–287). Oxford University Press. https://doi.org/10.1093/med-psych/9780190843953.003.0007

Gross, T. (2004). *All I did was ask: Conversations with writers, actors, musicians, and artists.* Hachette.

Hettema, J., Steele, J., & Miller, W. R. (2005). Motivational interviewing. *Annual Review of Clinical Psychology, 1*, 91–111.

Just, J. M., Bleckwenn, M., Schnakenberg, R., Skatulla, P., & Weckbecker, K. (2016). Drug-related celebrity deaths: A cross-sectional study. *Substance Abuse Treatment, Prevention, and Policy, 11*(1), 40. https://doi.org/10.1186/s13011-016-0084-z

Kyaga, S., Lichtenstein, P., Boman, M., Hultman, C., Långström, N., & Landén, M. (2011). Creativity and mental disorder: Family study of 300 000 people with severe mental disorder. *British Journal of Psychiatry, 199*(5), 373–379. https://doi.org/10.1192/bjp.bp.110.085316

Lafferty, P., Beutler, L. E., & Crago, M. (1989). Differences between more and less effective psychotherapists: A study of select therapist variables. *Journal of Consulting and Clinical Psychology, 57*(1), 76–80.

Lundahl, B., Moleni, T., Burke, B. L., Butters, R., Tollefson, D., Butler, C., & Rollnick, S. (2013). Motivational interviewing in medical care settings: A systematic review and meta-analysis of randomized controlled trials. *Patient Education and Counseling*, *93*(2), 157–168. https://doi.org/10.1016/j.pec.2013.07.012

Luthar, S. S., & Barkin, S. H. (2012). Are affluent youth truly "at risk"? *American Psychologist*, *67*(3), 222–235.

Luthar, S. S., & D'Avanzo, K. (1999). Contextual factors in substance use: A study of suburban and inner-city adolescents. *Development and Psychopathology*, *11*(4), 845–867.

Luthar, S. S., & Kumar, N. L. (2018). Youth in high-achieving schools: Challenges to mental health and directions for evidence-based interventions. In A. W. Leschied, D. H. Saklofske, & G. L. Flett (Eds.), *Handbook of school-based mental health promotion: An evidence-informed framework* (pp. 441–458). Springer.

Magill, M., Apodaca, T. R., Borsari, B., Gaume, J., Hoadley, A., Gordon, R. E. F., Tonigan, J. S., Moyers, T., & Longabaugh, R. (2018). A meta-analysis of motivational interviewing process: Technical, relational, and conditional process models of change. *Journal of Consulting and Clinical Psychology*, *86*(2), 140–157.

Miller, S. D., Bargmann, S., Chow, D., Seidel, J., & Maeschalck, C. (2016). Feedback-informed treatment (FIT): Improving the outcome of psychotherapy one person at a time. In W. O'Donohue & A. Maragakis (Eds.), *Quality improvement in behavioral health* (pp. 247–262). Springer International Publishing/Springer Nature. https://doi.org/10.1007/978-3-319-26209-3_16

Pace, B. T., Dembe, A., Soma, C. S., Baldwin, S. A., Atkins, D. C., & Imel, Z. E. (2017). A multivariate meta-analysis of motivational interviewing process and outcome. *Psychology of Addictive Behaviors: Journal of the Society of Psychologists in Addictive Behaviors*, *31*(5), 524–533. https://doi.org/10.1037/adb0000280

Patrick, M. E., Wightman, P., Schoeni, R. F., & Schulenberg, J. E. (2012). Socioeconomic status and substance use among young adults: A comparison across constructs and drugs. *Journal of Studies on Alcohol and Drugs*, *73*(5), 772–782. https://doi.org/10.15288/jsad.2012.73.772

Prochaska, J. O., & DiClemente, C. (1984). *The transtheoretical approach: Crossing the traditional boundaries of therapy*. Dow Jones/Irwin.

Prochaska, J. O., & Norcross, J. C. (2018). *Systems of psychotherapy: A transtheoretical analysis* (9th ed.). Oxford University Press.

Rogers, C. R. (1942). *Counseling and psychotherapy: Newer concepts in practice*. Houghton Mifflin.

Seidel, J. (2012). Using Feedback-Informed Therapy (FIT) to build a premium-service, private-pay practice. In C. E. Stout (Ed.), *Getting better at private practice*. https://doi.org/10.1002/9781118089972.ch18

Watson, J. C., Steckley, P. L., & McMullen, E. J. (2014). The role of empathy in promoting change. *Psychotherapy Research: Journal of the Society for Psychotherapy Research*, *24*(3), 286–298.

Chapter 11

Treating Narcissism in Wealthy and Well-Known People

In our third session, a 28-year-old client named Brad repeated his litany of business successes, the same ones he had told me each time we had met.

"I sold my first company for 10 mil," the young man said. "I plan to sell this new one for no less than 50. So I've done pretty good and I'm not even 30 yet." I'd heard this script twice before, word for word. I assumed he was saying it again because I had not reacted enthusiastically enough or because this was the autopilot mode he quickly got into with his conversations. Either way, I was intent on communicating that I heard him, but I would not fawn over him.

In therapy, I pay attention to the "pull" someone has on me. Do they set me at ease, or does my stomach knot up when I'm with them? Do they make me want to rescue them? Am I kept at arm's length? Do I want to keep them at arm's length? Do they make me want to avoid diving into the harder issues? Everyone has a certain "pull" on us that we are wise to observe in ourselves. Brad's desire was for me to show how impressed I was with him, but the pull he had on me was to feel irritated and withholding. I had to be mindful of both his desire and my response to it and not lean too hard in either direction.

"You've been very successful in business so far," I said with simple reflection. Yet he didn't take it as a reflection. He perceived it as a jab at him, an injury.

"What do you mean 'so far'? You think this has just been dumb luck or something?"

"I mean that you have been successful in business," I said, dropping the objectionable words.

"Hell, yeah, I've been successful," he said, chastening me. "I'm not even 30. This is just the start for me." The fact he had made a lot of money before he was 30 was important to him because he referenced it in each session.

"You have built a distinguished career in business at an early age," I said.

"Yeah, some business magazine wants to interview me. I'll probably do it. I haven't decided yet. The company is getting a lot of attention. We just got

DOI: 10.4324/9781003503569-14

another $3 million in investments. I've got the former CEO of a Fortune 500 company on my board. Shit like that."

"So it must be confusing to be that successful in business, but struggle in your relationships," I said. He had come in because his latest girlfriend had dumped him, just like the one before, and the one before that.

"I don't struggle," he said. "These women are just two-faced. When they find out how much money I have, they are all sweet and flirty, but after they get me to be with them, they show their true colors. Every time. *Every time*," he repeated for emphasis.

In his telling, he was always the victim of these unscrupulous, gold-digging women. He had no role in the demise of the relationships, except for being too nice, too trusting, too generous. They tricked him. They emotionally abused him.

In a rare moment of vulnerability in a later session, he let an admission slip.

"My father is such an asshole," he said. "No one likes him. He's just so self-centered and he acts like he's entitled to everything. They have to seat him right away in the restaurant. They have to let him board with the first group at the airport. Everyone has to take his call, no matter what they are doing right then. He's like that with everything. My biggest fear is that I'll turn into a giant asshole like him if I'm not careful."

Here was an opportunity if I played my hand right, which is always the challenge of working with a narcissistic client. If I pushed too hard, I might never see him again. If I didn't push hard enough, he would not able to hear me. In fact, there was a good chance he would take a softer response as an endorsement. I wanted to stay in the game, but not at the expense of effectiveness.

I took the opportunity with Brad. What followed was a series of sessions wrestling with his ambivalence about being self-promoting and emotionally callous, which he often valued, and not wanting to be like his dad, which is something that terrified him.

As we've seen, the research finds wealthy and well-known people are more narcissistic on average than the general population. A series of four studies found the wealthy have a greater sense of entitlement and more narcissistic personality traits (Piff, 2014). This is a consistent finding across the research.

The same is true of well-known people. A study of 200 celebrities found they are significantly more narcissistic, based on self-report, than the general population. Reality show contestants had the highest narcissism scores, followed by comedians, actors, and then musicians. It also did not matter how long they had been in the entertainment industry, suggesting their narcissism preceded their fame and was not the product of their fame (Young & Pinsky, 2006).

In an interview, Ben Affleck, a two-time Oscar winner, was asked about whether narcissism was inherent in wanting to be an actor. He said, "Narcissism is the part of my personality that I am the least proud of, and I certainly don't like to see it highlighted in everybody else I meet." Later, he added, "You have these qualities in you that are awful, and the best you can do is to try to be aware of them and actively try to diminish them" (Sischy & Abou-Sabe, 2014).

So how do you help a narcissist try to become aware of their narcissism and actively try to diminish these traits? It's difficult. It requires patience and persistence. First, let's explore what narcissism really is, what causes it to form, the two different variations of it, and then how you can be helpful to a narcissistic client.

WHAT IS NARCISSISM?

All humans are self-interested, a fundamental trait essential for survival. We call this "normal narcissism," a healthy level of self-esteem and self-regard necessary for psychological well-being. It enables us to maintain self-respect, assert our needs, and pursue personal goals without compromising empathy or healthy relationships.

However, when narcissism becomes excessive, it can morph into a pathological form, characterized by extreme self-centeredness, entitlement, and a lack of empathy. Pathological narcissism can harm or destroy personal and professional relationships. While it may temporarily fuel ambition, it ultimately undermines long-term success and happiness.

Understanding the distinction between normal and pathological narcissism is crucial. By recognizing the signs of excessive self-absorption, we can strive for a balanced approach that prioritizes both self-interest and the well-being of others.

If narcissism exists on a spectrum, with everyone displaying some narcissistic traits, Narcissistic Personality Disorder (NPD) represents the most toxic and severe form of these traits, leading to significant interpersonal problems, especially when the person is not treated as special or does not get their way. The diagnostic traits for NPD include:

- *Grandiose Sense of Self-Importance:* Individuals with NPD often exaggerate achievements and talents, expecting recognition as superior. Some narcissists are more covert, subtly revealing their "impressiveness," while others, like Brad, are overt and easy to spot.
- *Preoccupation With Fantasies:* These individuals obsess over visions of unattainable perfection in success, power, beauty, or love. For instance, clients may claim they will be the world's most successful actor (as I've had at least one client claim) or will have the biggest tech startup in history.
- *Belief in Being Special:* They insist that only other special or high-status people can understand them, often creating challenges for helping professionals who are flattered into believing they were chosen for their "world-class" abilities.

- *Need for Excessive Admiration:* A constant demand for attention and validation is central to NPD. For example, Brad repeatedly brings up the same talking points, driven by a relentless need for positive feedback and flattery.
- *Sense of Entitlement:* This manifests as unreasonable expectations of special treatment. The standard rules don't apply to them. Helping professionals may face demands for special accommodations, which will be discussed in greater detail later.
- *Interpersonal Exploitation:* Narcissists often exploit others to achieve their goals, whether in business or personal relationships. This can extend to the therapeutic relationship, where therapists may be pressured to write misleading court letters, waive fees, or cross boundaries.
- *Lack of Empathy:* Narcissists often struggle to recognize or care about others' feelings. While some may have the cognitive ability to understand others' struggles, they lack the emotional capacity to care. This has significant implications for therapy.
- *Envy or Belief That Others Are Envious:* Narcissists may feel rivalry or resentment toward others perceived as more successful. This can lead to strange fixations on the careers of others, sometimes turning into public or personal rivalries.
- *Arrogant Behaviors or Attitudes:* Narcissists often display snobbish, disdainful behavior toward those deemed inferior, though this is harder to observe in therapy. They are notorious for treating support staff poorly, as highlighted by countless online posts rating wealthy clients' behavior in public settings.

A person doesn't need to have full-blown NPD to display these traits. Even subclinical narcissism, where symptoms are less severe, can still cause significant problems that need to be addressed.

Some individuals mask deep-seated insecurities with narcissistic behaviors, while others, especially those from wealthy or famous families, believe they are genuinely entitled to special treatment, so the disorder can be a product of either too little or too much self-regard. The presentation of narcissism varies widely, from covert (masked symptoms) to more overt forms.

HOW NARCISSISM FORMS

Historically, psychiatry and psychology often blamed parents, particularly mothers, for the development of mental health problems. However, some children in entitled families do not become narcissists because of their temperament, while others from warm, empathetic families may develop narcissistic traits. There is no perfect correlation between the development of narcissism and family experiences or parenting style.

While parenting style plays a role, it's just one piece of the puzzle. Genetics, environment, and life experiences collectively shape narcissistic traits. In extreme cases, this results in NPD, which is notoriously resistant to therapy. Here are some common factors that contribute to the development of unhealthy narcissism.

Genetic Predisposition

Genetics play a significant role in the development of narcissistic traits, making some individuals more prone to these patterns (Luo et al., 2014).

- *Sensitivity to Reward:* High sensitivity to reward can lead to an excessive focus on positive feedback, central to narcissism (Buckels & Trapnell, 2013).
- *Low Emotional Regulation:* Difficulty managing emotions can contribute to narcissism as a defensive mechanism to protect self-esteem (Blay et al., 2024).
- *Assertiveness and Aggression:* Temperament leaning toward assertiveness or aggression, without empathy, can lead to narcissistic behavior (Barry & Kauten, 2014).
- *High Extraversion:* While not negative in itself, high extraversion combined with low empathy can foster narcissistic traits (Paulhus & Williams, 2002).
- *Low Agreeableness:* A lack of concern for others can make an individual more vulnerable to narcissism (Miller & Campbell, 2008).
- *Reactivity and Sensitivity:* High sensitivity to environmental stimuli, especially criticism, can contribute to vulnerable narcissism (Pincus & Lukowitsky, 2010).
- *Low Adaptability:* Trouble adapting to changes in routines or expectations can lead to narcissistic behaviors as a way to assert control (Howes et al., 2020).

Temperament alone does not determine whether someone will develop narcissistic traits. It is the interaction between temperament, environment, perception, and other life experiences that influences the manifestation of narcissism.

Parenting Styles

Parenting behaviors can either promote or reduce narcissistic tendencies. Early life experiences with caregivers significantly impact narcissism. Two extreme patterns linked to its development are:

- *Excessive Admiration:* Overly flattering and praising children can inflate their sense of self-importance and entitlement, as can communicating that they are overly special (Brummelman et al., 2016).
- *Neglect or Criticism:* Harshly critical or neglectful parenting can lead to narcissism as a defense mechanism against feelings of inadequacy (Horton & Tritch, 2014).

Sometimes, children experience both excessive praise and criticism, making it difficult to reconcile being treated both as special and as inadequate. This paradox can set the stage for a lifetime of narcissistic behavior as well.

Social and Cultural Factors

Social and cultural forces, especially in the United States, often cultivate narcissism. With its emphasis on affluence, individualism, and the fascination with fame, the United States promotes unhealthy self-absorption.

Research identified the United States as the second most narcissistic country globally, trailing only Russia. One study measured the gap between a nation's self-perception and how others viewed it. For the United States, this gap was a striking 23 points, signaling a grandiose national identity exceeded only by Russia (Zaromb et al., 2018).

Being raised in a narcissistic culture is a risk factor for personal narcissism. Similarly, growing up in environments that foster entitlement—such as elite institutions or privileged upbringings—are also strong predictors of narcissistic traits (Twenge & Campbell, 2009).

Trauma and Abuse

Trauma and abuse can also lead to narcissism. The traumatized child creates a false self—one that is big, invincible, and in control—to cope with a frightening world. Narcissism, in this sense, serves as a powerful strategy for survival, although it often leaves a trail of interpersonal destruction. Others become frightened or insecure and self-loathing, becoming what we term "wounded narcissists." Not all traumatized children grow up to have narcissistic traits, however. Some go down a different path developmentally, becoming more other-centered.

TWO TYPES OF NARCISSISM

Not all narcissists are the same, of course, nor do they arrive there because of the same influences. There is not universal agreement about the subtypes of narcissism. Cain and colleagues (2008) concluded there are two types: overt and covert. Pincus and Lukowitsky (2010) categorized the variants as agentic and communal. Wink (1991) said there are three types, called grandiose, vulnerable, and exhibitionistic. Akhtar and Thomson (1982) proposed four pathological subtypes: arrogant, shy, aggressive, and manipulative. Ronningstam (2005) also claimed there are four, but he conceptualized them differently. He called them oblivious, hypervigilant, oblivious-extraverted, and oblivious-introverted. Millon argued for five subtypes called unprincipled, amorous, compensatory, elitist, and normal (Millon & Davis, 2000).

Some of these taxonomies appear to incorporate traits or symptoms that fit other personality disorder profiles better. As examples, Wink's exhibitionistic

137

style is probably more aligned with Histrionic Personality Disorder, while Akhtar's aggressive type is more similar to Antisocial Personality Disorder. Despite this lack of full agreement, there is close to a consensus among major researchers that unhealthy, maladaptive narcissism seems to be best divided into two major types, grandiose and vulnerable (Zajenkowski & Szymaniak, 2021). Here are succinct descriptions of each:

1. *Grandiose Narcissism:* This type is characterized by overt expressions of feelings of superiority and entitlement. Individuals with grandiose narcissism are extroverted, are domineering, and seek attention and admiration aggressively. They often have an inflated sense of self-importance and a lack of empathy for others. This is typically our stereotypical concept of narcissism.

2. *Vulnerable Narcissism:* Also known as covert narcissism, this type is characterized by hypersensitivity to evaluation, introversion, defensiveness, and a constant need for reassurance. Vulnerable narcissists may appear shy or withdrawn and have a strong sense of entitlement and inadequacy. They are often preoccupied with fantasies of success or power, but also have intense feelings of shame and inadequacy. This type of narcissist is much harder to spot. Based on clinical observation, wealthy and well-known people are more likely to be grandiose narcissists, but you will also see the defensive, fragile, or wounded narcissist who desires reassurance and flattery.

THREE ASSUMPTIONS IN WORKING WITH NARCISSISTIC INDIVIDUALS

I have several assumptions when working with narcissistic clients. While not true of all highly narcissistic people, these themes emerge often enough that they are worth expecting from the outset, then being pleasantly surprised if they prove not to be true. Here are three assumptions:

- *Assumption 1: Narcissists often do not come into therapy desiring to change.* Instead, they want others to change. For them, therapy can become a platform to complain about the behavior of others and how mistreated they feel by them. Inherent in this is their desire to be validated in how wrongly the other person treated them. You are assessed in their eyes as good if you allow them to frame it this way and bad if you attempt to challenge this frame.

- *Assumption 2: Many narcissists do not see narcissism as a problem.* They see it as a feature, not a bug. As they view it, their lack of empathy, their need to win and feel superior, and their sense of entitlement work well for them. Why should they change it? When their relationships don't work out, then it's the other person's fault. Many of these clients may even readily accept or suggest the label of narcissist, not viewing it as a mostly negative feature.

- *Assumption 3: Some narcissists can be incredibly charming and disarming.* They have a ready smile as they look you in the eye. They may call you by your first name when they greet you. Some narcissists are unpleasant to be around, of course, but many are among the most disarming people you've ever met. As such, you may lower your defenses or be tempted to collude with them. Add fame and wealth on top of that and it makes this even harder.

ASSESSING NARCISSISM

There are normed psychological instruments that measure narcissism, such as the Narcissism Personality Inventory (NPI) and the Millon Clinical Multiaxial Inventory (MCMI) among others, but the assessment of narcissism might be more easily done by using the information you gain from your initial diagnostic interview and follow-up sessions combined with the subjective experience of being in the room with the person, which can be extremely clinically relevant.

A fascinating phenomenon is how comfortable it often feels for the narcissistic person to identify in this way, as if it were a neutral or positive descriptor. On a social media platform, I saw a post from a young influencer of his "personality testing" results. It was presented as a graph with nearly all the personality disorders. It said he was "100%" on the narcissism scale. The point is not whether the results were legitimate, but how untroubled he was with broadcasting this information. For him, it seemed to be just another post designed to draw attention and interest.

Over the years, I have found a nonchalance among many therapy clients, particularly young men, regarding their narcissism. While they might not always be proud of it, they easily own the possibility of it. As one of my young adult clients asked me, "I agree I'm a narcissist, but why is that bad?"

Narcissism can be seen by some as a competitive edge or a sign of aspiration. As a result, this offers both an opportunity and a challenge in therapy. The challenge is to make a compelling case that this is something in need of change. The opportunity is that it allows you to put the issue on the table quickly and directly.

In a series of 11 experiments with over 2,200 participants, researchers asked them one simple question: "Are you a narcissist? Note that the word 'narcissist' means egotistical, self-focused, and vain." They asked the individuals to rate themselves from 1 (not very true of me) to 7 (very true of me). They found their responses correlated highly with the 40-item Narcissistic Personality Inventory (NPI). One of the study's coauthors, Brad Bushman, said, "People who are narcissists are almost proud of the fact. You can ask them directly because they don't see narcissism as a negative quality—they believe they are superior to other people and are fine with saying that publicly" (McNamee, 2014).

139

While I would not find the Single Item Narcissism Scale (SINS) sufficient as a measure for a true psychological assessment, it can be a clinically useful tool because of its brevity (i.e., an average of 20 seconds to complete versus 13 minutes for the NPI). Based on the findings of a replication that found a mean score of 2.16 and a standard deviation of 1.41, it might make sense to regard self-ratings higher than 4 to be revealing (van der Linden & Rosenthal, 2016).

How can this simple question be useful in the treatment process? When I use it, I employ it in response to something they said, especially when the client has a glimmer of awareness that they may have some narcissistic qualities. The question then allows the issue to be put on the table quickly and succinctly. It might go something like this:

You just said, "I'm sure some people would say I'm pretty narcissistic myself." What do you think? If you had to rate yourself from 1 (very low) to 7 (very high), what would you give yourself in response to the question, "I am a narcissist," if the word narcissist means egotistical, self-focused, vain?

If he rates himself a 5–7, I might say something like, "That's probably higher than most people. Tell me more about why you rated it there." Again, keep in mind that this is only one source of data, and you may have other evidence that your client is highly narcissistic, even if they rate themselves as a 2 or 3 on this scale. There is no magic in the question or the scale. The point is to use this as a clinical tool that may give you a way in, rather than as a thorough assessment measure.

Assuming you can come to some agreement that he probably possesses more narcissistic traits than most, this opens a conversation about whether they perceive that as good or bad, beneficial or detrimental. If you can establish it as partly negative, you are over one of the high hurdles in this work. From there, talk in terms of agreement between the two of you, like it was his idea that you now align with. You can also talk about this acknowledgement as a sign of strength. Always appeal to strength, rather than weakness or diminishment. You could say something like:

You definitely see the narcissistic tendencies in yourself. That's pretty strong to acknowledge that. Some people can't do that. And it also sounds like you realize it has probably helped you in some important ways, like in your career, but it has a downside, especially in your relationships. I imagine our goal is to keep the good of it, which is your determination and drive, but lose the bad of it, which is the way it sometimes affects your relationships. Is all that correct?

Once you agree and align, move into changing these old relationship patterns. This simple question and the straightforward conversation might position you to address the narcissistic qualities directly. From there, a lot of the work becomes CBT- and DBT-based. You'll employ tools for interpersonal effectiveness and rescript old habits of interacting and solving problems.

While this direct approach to addressing narcissism is effective for some clients, others are too defensive or lack sufficient insight. For those, you will need to take a different tack. Here, consider using an approach based on the outstanding model of Schema Therapy, an evidence-based treatment for difficult-to-treat conditions.

TREATING NARCISSISM

Treating mental health problems is challenging work, but some conditions are more difficult to treat effectively than others. Eating disorders, attachment disorders, severe bipolar disorders, and Borderline Personality Disorder are among the toughest. Narcissism is definitely on that list. Narcissists rarely come into therapy unless they are under duress—a partner threatening to leave, a legal charge, a requirement of the sports league, being kicked out of the band, the diagnosis of an incurable sexually transmitted disease. When they show up, they come in with thick defensive walls and either try to monopolize the conversation or stonewall. They blame and lash out at everyone else. They push boundaries and test limits. The work is arduous.

For therapists who have been trained in short-term models, you will either need to reconsider those assumptions or avoid taking on more narcissistic clients. Their narcissism is years in the making and, as we've discussed, the product of multiple factors. As such, it will take time to make significant progress. This requires the helping professional to do two things in tension: build a trusting and warm relationship while setting boundaries where the narcissist does not get the chance to do as he pleases. Narcissists exit when they don't get their way, so this makes maintaining the long-term relationship challenging.

Therapists who are most effective in working with highly narcissistic clients do two things well, regardless of their theoretical orientation: they establish and maintain clear boundaries early in the therapy relationship, and they can tap into genuine empathy, despite the challenge of doing so with a narcissistic individual (Gabbard, 2009). Here's what that can look like.

Establish Clear Boundaries

Narcissistic individuals test limits in nearly all relationships and settings. Most of the time, they are attempting to establish control and dominance. To do good work, you must clearly define the professional boundaries of your relationship from the start. This includes what your role is and is not, when and how you can be contacted or communicated with, late charges and no-show fees, when and where the appointments can be held, and how you will both be expected to treat each other. Give a rationale for why this is good for your working relationship.

All this can be done in a way that is warm and kind without sounding cold or off-putting. These boundaries ensure respect and mutual understanding and foster a healthier relationship. When your client tests the limits or pushes the boundaries, you refer to your earlier conversations.

Develop and Express Empathy

Accurate empathy is a fundamental element of effective psychotherapy (Elliott et al., 2019). The research consistently finds this to be a significant predictor of clinical outcomes, regardless of the therapeutic model or specialized treatment intervention (Lambert & Barley, 2001). As such, you meet the client with empathy. They got arrested for assaulting a photographer? You're sorry to hear they have found themselves in such a tough situation. They got herpes after sleeping with a fan? That's an awful gut-punch. You're so sad that happened. They got canceled on social media for reports of racist and sexist comments? You know they have got to be going through such a hard time.

To be clear, this is not where you will stay. Your goal is for them to fully own their misbehavior, correct it for the future, and even make amends. But that is not where you start. You start with empathy, not confrontation. This is an enormous challenge when you face behavior you find distasteful or offensive. I find racist attitudes difficult to sit with, especially since I have one Hispanic and two Black young adult children and spent the formative years of my career serving primarily minority clients. However, if I am to be helpful to this client and have any chance at all of reducing their racist attitudes, I must lean into empathy. In doing so, I will in no way endorse the racism. Instead, I'll shift to the client's felt experience.

Some therapists worry they will be misunderstood as minimizing or validating his attitudes. This rarely happens, but it is a strategic risk I will take. I keep my eye on the long-term goal of using our therapeutic relationship to help shape their attitudes and develop their own empathy. Take this exchange with a client as an example:

Dave: When you first came to see me, you were in a down place. You were really hurting and felt mistreated. We've talked about how you felt my support and my care for you in all this. I'm glad you felt that because I knew it was such a tough time and you are a person who deserves kindness and respect.

Client: Yeah, I appreciate that.

Dave: So now, you've experienced what that feels like and I was wondering whether you've thought about what that might look like for you to show understanding and respect to others, especially with those who might be challenging for you.

Client: I don't know. I haven't thought about it.

Dave: When we first started, I remember you saying how quick everyone was to turn their back on you. Even some people who knew you ran away from you and judged you.

Client: Yeah, that's how they are.

Dave: But when you and I started talking, we didn't focus on your mistakes. We focused on how this deeply affected you.

Client: Yeah.

Dave: And the reason we did that was because you were hurting and you needed that. You deserved to be treated with empathy and kindness. So I'm wondering if you might consider which way you would like to live: being a person who criticizes and judges people, or being a person who wants to put more empathy and kindness out there, even when it's tough to do that.

Client: I don't know. I just hate how people are.

Dave: Being harsh and judgmental?

Client: Yeah. I hate that, but I know it's so easy to do.

Dave: It's understandable why someone would be that way, because it's so easy. And for you, it's easy because you have felt so mistreated and abandoned.

Client: Right.

Dave: I'd agree it's easy to be that way. The question is, how do you want to be?

Client: I guess I don't want to be like that.

If he did not want to contemplate this further, I would follow the Motivational Interviewing principle of rolling away from resistance. I would simply reset and then open up another direction for the conversation. I was glad he engaged, and this became the dominant theme for the rest of the session.

You can also help build empathy by using other real-life situations, including stories in the news or personal stories from the client. First, practice taking the perspective of those involved. This is a purely cognitive process. What might the participants have been thinking? Feeling? Why?

The next step is to move to the affective or the emotional experience. This is harder to do. You might ask them to identify with a participant in the story. Have you ever felt like that? What did it feel like, and have you ever felt anything like that before?

USE SCHEMA THERAPY PRINCIPLES AND STRATEGIES

Schema Therapy, developed by Dr. Jeffrey Young in the 1980s, is an integrative model of psychotherapy designed to treat individuals with pervasive and chronic psychological disorders, particularly those resistant to other treatment approaches like Cognitive-Behavioral Therapy (CBT). By blending elements of CBT with psychodynamic concepts, gestalt therapy, emotion-focused therapy, and attachment theory, Schema Therapy addresses deeply entrenched patterns of thinking, feeling, and behaving—known as "schemas" or "lifetraps." These schemas, often developed in response to unmet emotional needs during childhood, may initially serve as adaptive coping mechanisms but tend to become maladaptive in adulthood, contributing to enduring emotional and relational difficulties.

Research has consistently demonstrated Schema Therapy's efficacy in treating personality disorders, chronic depression, and other complex psychological conditions. For example, a randomized clinical trial found that clients with personality disorders, including Narcissistic Personality Disorder (NPD), experienced significant recovery rates with Schema Therapy compared to treatment-as-usual approaches. This study also revealed lower dropout rates and sustained improvements in depressive symptoms, social functioning, and overall well-being (Bamelis et al., 2014).

Schema Therapy has proven particularly effective for Borderline Personality Disorder (BPD). A large-scale study involving almost 500 participants across five countries concluded that Schema Therapy was both effective and safe for treating BPD, with high retention rates (Arntz et al., 2022). Two meta-analyses further confirm its efficacy. These studies suggest that even less intensive forms of Schema Therapy yield substantial improvements, with many clients no longer meeting diagnostic criteria for BPD after treatment (Nadort et al., 2009; Zhang et al., 2023). Additionally, combining individual and group formats appears to enhance its effectiveness (Arntz et al., 2022).

Schema Therapy is particularly well suited for individuals with NPD, which is often rooted in schemas of inadequacy, abandonment, or entitlement. The therapeutic process focuses on identifying and modifying these maladaptive schemas while developing healthier ways of coping and relating. By addressing the underlying emotional needs driving narcissistic behaviors, narcissistic clients have a greater chance to develop emotional regulation, greater empathy, and more authentic self-esteem.

The "Defectiveness" schema, which involves feelings of inadequacy, or the "Entitlement" schema, which can manifest as an inflated sense of self-worth, are common targets in Schema Therapy for NPD. Through guided exploration, clients understand the origins of these schemas and their impact on relationships and self-concept.

Schema Therapy's success often hinges on the therapist's training and application of experiential techniques. Studies indicate that therapists trained with hands-on exercises and applied experiences achieve better client outcomes than those relying solely on theoretical instruction (Bamelis et al., 2014). Despite its growing recognition, Schema Therapy is less widely practiced than CBT or Motivational Interviewing, though its adoption is increasing (David et al., 2018; Louis et al., 2021).

One of the most striking findings in Schema Therapy research is the durability of its effects. For instance, researchers observed that clients maintained their treatment gains even three months post-therapy, underscoring its long-term benefits (Koppers et al., 2020). This sustained improvement, combined with its adaptability to various disorders, highlights Schema Therapy's potential to address ingrained emotional and behavioral challenges effectively.

As Schema Therapy continues to gain traction within the mental health community, its comprehensive approach offers a powerful framework for treating complex cases. By integrating multiple therapeutic principles into a cohesive model, it provides a versatile and effective alternative for individuals whose needs may not be fully met by other evidence-based treatments.

A SCHEMA THERAPY–INFORMED APPROACH

While I have found the full Schema Therapy model to be helpful, what I will discuss here is more of a "Schema Therapy–Informed" or "Schema Therapy–Based" approach. This may be just as effective as the full model for some individuals. If this seems appealing, I'd encourage you to seek formal training in the model to round out your knowledge and skill. For now, this streamlined approach may be helpful in your work with narcissistic clients.

Begin the schema work by asking if your client wants to go deeper than just focusing on behaviors and surface emotions. If they say no, respect that and move to another focus. If they say yes, have them take a brief inventory that will help your discussion.

The principle authors of Schema Therapy have their own inventories available online. I am offering one that I created based on their earlier work; you can reference it in Appendix 2. In my experience, this single item per schema inventory has been as helpful as other inventories that require a person to rate four or five items per schema. I have not yet established reliability or validity data for this tool, so use the more concise inventory with that caution. After your client completes the inventory, follow up by asking them to elaborate on the items rated "Completely True" or "Mostly True."

Ask curious follow-up questions to establish themes. For example:

Did you see yourself as competent or incompetent in that time of life?
Did you feel more connected or isolated?
Did you feel like you were successful or a failure?
Did you feel loved or disregarded?
Were you confident or unconfident?

Ask them to elaborate. See if they can share a couple of significant memories connected to this experience. Spend time getting a good picture of how they saw themselves and how they perceived others during each key developmental stage of early life.

145

Similarly, how did they see others? Get more specific with your questions. Perhaps they felt competent in sports, but incompetent with academics. Maybe they felt confident around adults, but not around peers. They may have seen others as rejecting or excluding. There are almost endless possibilities of how they viewed themselves and others.

Whether or not we use an inventory, if I need a more well-rounded picture, I may also prompt them with something broad like this to make sure I am not missing major themes:

Tell me about how you saw yourself and how you think others saw you in elementary school. In middle school. In high school.

Don't rush these conversations. Listen well and find the major themes, then weave them into a coherent narrative. A summary might sound like:

When you were a kid, your family gave you the message you were special and the way they treated you and the opportunities and experiences you had, even at an early age, seemed to prove that was true. But at school, you had a hard time making friends. The one friend you had stopped talking to you in middle school for no reason, as far as you could tell. You went off to boarding school hoping it would be better, but it was just more of the same. So now, when you rated yourself on the inventory, you said it was "completely true" that you felt special and entitled to special treatment, but also isolated and disconnected from others. You also said you have impossibly high internal standards of performance where you feel you always have to push harder and harder to prove yourself to others, to surpass them. And all of that worked really well when you were younger, but now you realize that it all comes with a cost. The cost is exhaustion, disconnection, and self-doubt covered up by pushing even harder. Does that sound right?

Invite them to give honest feedback about the summary, describing what feels correct, what feels incorrect, and what needs to be clarified or revised. Once you come to some agreement, introduce the idea of schemas with a setup that could sound like this:

There's a concept that many people have found to be helpful. It's called "schema." It refers to a pattern of thoughts, feelings, bodily reactions, memories, behaviors all bundled together that formed when a person was younger. Most of the time, they form to meet some unmet need. It helps a kid respond and survive in the presence of something bad or the absence of something good. The problem is later, even after that need may have been met or the schema isn't helpful, it continues to run. In fact, when you try to challenge it, it fights for survival because it believes it is protecting you.

Personify it just slightly to make it seem both part of them and also "other" than them, then talk about their probable schemas. The goal is to help them understand the schema concept and framework and align in the decision to dismantle their maladaptive schemas.

> *Based on what you have told me and how you responded to the survey, it seems like you may have two, maybe three, old schemas that started early and continue today. The first is called Entitlement, where you have grown up feeling like you are special and others should recognize that. Does that seem correct? (Then allow for discussion here.) The second is called Isolation, where you feel disconnected from people, not really part of any group, and different in ways that make it hard to fit in. Does that seem to fit? (Allow for discussion here.) Finally, there is a schema called Unrelenting Standards. This is where you feel you are always pushing yourself to meet impossible standards, often to the point that it robs you of the ability to slow down, relax, and enjoy life and your accomplishments. How does that fit for you?*

These three schemas are just examples. All clients will have a different constellation of probable schemas. I try to identify one to three and then have more in-depth conversation and assessment to find consensus on at least one of them. The dismantling of these agreed-upon schemas becomes our focus if I can get an affirmative response to this question:

> *Now that we've identified them and you know they will probably fight us if we challenge them, is that something you are willing to do?*

Once you agree and align, then move forward with pulling this old schema apart and replacing it with a new pattern. Don't move too quickly until there is general agreement about what pattern you are targeting. Again, the key word is "pattern." A schema is a complex *pattern* of thought, emotion, reaction, memory, and behavior that gets activated under certain conditions. To change it, the pattern and its component parts need to be well understood.

Much of the work here can then fall more readily into the CBT tradition, where you help identify the patterns of thought, the patterns of action, the core beliefs, and the behaviors that flow from this. You collaboratively map out the pattern, then find practical ways to change it cognitively, affectively, and behaviorally. Schema Therapy allows for a wide range of therapeutic approaches, however, including psychodynamic, attachment-based, and Gestalt work, but it functions best when it creates an accessible, easily understood framework that can then be attacked with cognitive-behavioral strategies. However, make room for good psychodynamic work here if that fits your style.

I value many things about Schema Therapy, including how it focuses therapy on a construct rather than a diagnosis. While some clients have no problem being referred to as a narcissist, others who are more vulnerable narcissists may resist the term and be reluctant to own that diagnostic label. However, understanding how life experiences and personal wiring caused them to develop a protective pattern is almost never met with resistance. This is especially true when we explain that the pattern (i.e., their schema) was adaptive and helpful early on, but now continues past its effectiveness. In fact, it now hurts and undermines them. Most clients can make sense of this.

A MOST CHALLENGING CONDITION

Therapy to help mitigate the effects of narcissism is often challenging and requires a patient therapist skilled in navigating the complex interpersonal dynamics of the condition. A well-boundaried and empathetic approach, combined with a strong therapeutic alliance and a solid framework like Schema Therapy, is hopeful and has the hope of improving the person's relationship style and quality of his interpersonal relationships.

REFERENCES

Akhtar, S., & Thomson, J. A. (1982). Overview: Narcissistic personality disorder. *American Journal of Psychiatry*, *139*(1), 12–20.

Arntz, A., Jacob, G. A., Lee, C. W., Brand-de Wilde, O. M., Fassbinder, E., Harper, R. P., Lavender, A., Lockwood, G., Malogiannis, I. A., Ruths, F. A., Schweiger, U., Shaw, I. A., Zarbock, G., & Farrell, J. M. (2022). Effectiveness of predominantly group schema therapy and combined individual and group schema therapy for borderline personality disorder: A randomized clinical trial. *JAMA Psychiatry*, *79*(4), 287–299. https://doi.org/10.1001/jamapsychiatry.2022.0010

Bamelis, L. L., Evers, S. M., Spinhoven, P., & Arntz, A. (2014). Results of a multicenter randomized controlled trial of the clinical effectiveness of schema therapy for personality disorders. *The American Journal of Psychiatry*, *171*(3), 305–322. https://doi.org/10.1176/appi.ajp.2013.12040518

Barry, C. T., & Kauten, R. L. (2014). Nonpathological and pathological narcissism: Which self-reported characteristics are most problematic in adolescents? *Journal of Personality Assessment*, *96*(2), 212–219.

Blay, M., Bouteloup, M., Duarte, M., Hasler, R., Pham, E., Nicastro, R., Jan, M., Debbané, M., & Perroud, N. (2024). Association between pathological narcissism and emotion regulation: The role of self-mentalizing. *Personality and Mental Health*, *18*(3), 227–237. https://doi.org/10.1002/pmh.1613

Brummelman, E., Thomaes, S., & Sedikides, C. (2016). Separating narcissism from self-esteem. *Current Directions in Psychological Science*, *25*(1), 8–13.

Buckels, E. E., & Trapnell, P. D. (2013). Narcissism and the motivation to engage in prosocial behavior. *Personality and Individual Differences*, *54*(5), 652–656.

Cain, N. M., Pincus, A. L., & Ansell, E. B. (2008). Narcissism at the crossroads: Phenotypic description of pathological narcissism across clinical theory, social/personality psychology, and psychiatric diagnosis. *Clinical Psychology Review*, *28*(4), 638–656. https://doi.org/10.1016/j.cpr.2007.09.006

David, D., Cristea, I., & Hofmann, S. G. (2018). Why cognitive behavioral therapy is the current gold standard of psychotherapy. *Frontiers in Psychiatry*, *9*(4). https://doi.org/10.3389/fpsyt.2018.00004

Elliott, R., Bohart, A. C., Watson, J. C., & Murphy, D. (2019). Empathy. In J. C. Norcross & M. J. Lambert (Eds.), *Psychotherapy relationships that work: Evidence-based therapist contributions* (3rd ed., pp. 245–287). Oxford University Press. https://doi.org/10.1093/med-psych/9780190843953.003.0007

Gabbard, G. O. (2009). Transference and countertransference in the treatment of narcissistic patients. *Psychiatric Annals*, *39*(3), 129–136.

Horton, R. S., & Tritch, T. (2014). Clarifying the links between grandiose narcissism and parenting. *Journal of Research in Personality*, *53*, 1–5.

Howes, S. S., Kausel, E. E., Jackson, A. T., & Reb, J. (2020). When and why narcissists exhibit greater hindsight bias and less perceived learning. *Journal of Management*, *46*, 1498152. https://doi.org/10.1177/0149206320929421

Koppers, D., Van, H., Peen, J., & Dekker, J. J. M. (2020). Psychological symptoms, early maladaptive schemas and schema modes: Predictors of the outcome of group schema therapy in patients with personality disorders. *Psychotherapy Research*, *31*(7), 831–842. https://doi.org/10.1080/10503307.2020.1852482

Lambert, M. J., & Barley, D. E. (2001). Research summary on the therapeutic relationship and psychotherapy outcome. *Psychotherapy: Theory, Research, Practice, Training*, *38*(4), 357–361. https://doi.org/10.1037/0033-3204.38.4.357

Louis, J. P., Ortiz, V., Barlas, J., Lee, J. S., Lockwood, G., Chong, W. F., Louis, K. M., & Sim, P. (2021). The good enough parenting early intervention schema therapy based program: Participant experience. *PLoS One*, *16*(1), e0243508. https://doi.org/10.1371/journal.pone.0243508

Luo, Y. L., Cai, H., & Song, H. (2014). A behavioral genetic study of the Dark Triad of personality and moral development. *Twin Research and Human Genetics*, *17*(6), 583–594.

McNamee, D. (2014, August 6). Narcissism can be diagnosed "with a single question." *Medical News Today*. https://www.medicalnewstoday.com/articles/280718

Miller, J. D., & Campbell, W. K. (2008). Comparing clinical and social-personality conceptualizations of narcissism. *Journal of Personality*, *76*(3), 449–476.

Millon, T., & Davis, R. (2000). *Personality disorders in modern life*. Wiley & Sons.

Nadort, M., Arntz, A., Smit, J. H., Giesen-Bloo, J., Eikelenboom, M., Spinhoven, P., van Asselt, T., & van Dyck, R. (2009). Implementation of outpatient schema therapy for borderline personality disorder with versus without crisis support by the therapist outside office hours: A randomized trial. *Behavior Research and Therapy*, *47*(11), 961–973.

Paulhus, D. L., & Williams, K. M. (2002). The Dark Triad of personality: Narcissism, Machiavellianism, and psychopathy. *Journal of Research in Personality*, *36*(6), 556–563.

Piff, P. K. (2014). Wealth and the inflated self: Class, entitlement, and narcissism. *Personality and Social Psychology Bulletin*, *40*(1), 34–43.

Pincus, A. L., & Lukowitsky, M. R. (2010). Pathological narcissism and narcissistic personality disorder. *Annual Review of Clinical Psychology*, *6*, 421–446.

Ronningstam, E. (2005). *Identifying and understanding the narcissistic personality*. Oxford University Press.

Sischy, I., & Abou-Sabe, K. (2014, April 16). New again: Ben Affleck. *Interview Magazine*. https://www.interviewmagazine.com/film/new-again-ben-affleck

Twenge, J. M., & Campbell, W. K. (2009). *The narcissism epidemic: Living in the age of entitlement*. Free Press.

van der Linden, S., & Rosenthal, S. A. (2016). Measuring narcissism with a single question? A replication and extension of the Single-Item Narcissism Scale (SINS). *Personality and Individual Differences*, *90*, 238–241.

Wink, P. (1991). Two faces of narcissism. *Journal of Personality and Social Psychology*, *61*(4), 590–597.

Young, S. M., & Pinsky, D. (2006). Narcissism and celebrity. *Journal of Research in Personality*, *40*(5), 463–471.

Zajenkowski, M., & Szymaniak, K. (2021). Narcissism between facets and domains. The relationships between two types of narcissism and aspects of the Big Five. *Current Psychology*, *40*, 2112–2121.

Zaromb, F. M., Liu, J. H., Páez, D., Hanke, K., Putnam, A. L., & Roediger, H. L. III. (2018). We made history: Citizens of 35 countries overestimate their nation's role in world history. *Journal of Applied Research in Memory and Cognition*, *7*(4), 521–528. https://doi.org/10.1037/h0101827

Zhang, K., Hu, X., Ma, L., Xie, Q., Wang, Z., Fan, C., & Li, X. (2023). The efficacy of schema therapy for personality disorders: A systematic review and meta-analysis. *Nordic Journal of Psychiatry*, *77*(7), 641–650. https://doi.org/10.1080/08039488.2023.2228304

Part IV

The Therapist's Own Work

Chapter 12

Doing Your Own Work Around Money and Fame

In graduate school, the unspoken but very real message permeating our training was that a desire for a high income was greedy and inappropriate. We were to be motivated purely by our desire to help people because we wanted to make a difference in their lives, whether as academics and researchers or as practitioners. There was never a discussion of career finances or income. No one I knew in our field had taken even a single business course or seminar while in undergraduate or graduate school. No professor or mentor ever talked about it as part of our preparation to be mental health professionals. This attitude toward money was never voiced, but it was heard loud and clear. This message seeped its way into my work, especially in the earlier years of my career.

From the time we are young, we get messages about money. Over our lifespans, these messages are sent by our parents, our extended family, our neighbors and classmates, media and social media, our coworkers and friends. To some extent, everyone has a philosophy of money, even if they don't articulate it. These are beliefs and attitudes and opinions about money. As examples: How frugal should you be? Should you desire to be wealthy? What good does money bring to your life? What negatives does it threaten to bring? Do you talk about money with your peers? How do you communicate about money in your partner relationship? Do you discuss family finances in front of your children or personal money management with your children? How much do you value generosity? Do you live by a budget? Should you live by a budget? How do we communicate or hide our wealth status? Is your money a source of pride or a source of shame? How do you behave when you feel financially secure? How do you behave when you feel financially insecure?

There are dozens of other questions that elicit the beliefs, attitudes, and opinions we have internalized about money across our lifespan. Some people cannot articulate what messages they have received about money. Others are painfully aware. As therapists working with wealthy clients, we should take stock of our own ideas about money.

DOI: 10.4324/9781003503569-16

Our own relationship with money often parallels our human relationships and attachment style. For example, those with fearful and insecure attachments in their human relationships may be more fearful and insecure around issues of money. Ed Coambs, author and past president of the Financial Therapy Association, is a pioneer in this field. "Many people have an unconscious relationship with money," he told me, adding:

> To engage with ourselves and others in more empathic and authentic ways as it relates to money, we must recognize that we each have a wide range of experiences with money that started long before we were born, that we were exposed to before we could even understand the concept of money, that continue to shape and influence us during our lifetime, and that will shape future generations through the money message we pass on.[1]

We begin by reflecting on our own family of origin and the message we received about money. To model the process, I'll share part of my own story.

IDENTIFYING FAMILY OF ORIGIN ISSUES SURROUNDING WEALTH

My parents were 18 and 20 when they got married in the early 1960s. I was their first child, born two years later, making them parents in their early 20s. As a working-class couple, they had very little money, yet in those days, they could afford a two-bedroom house with an unfinished attic that ended up becoming an additional two bedrooms. They had a car and all the minor luxuries of middle-class living. My father parlayed his training as an electrician to a job with the Navy, getting in on the ground floor of the computer revolution. Despite having only a GED, he retired from a job that required a master's degree as the minimum qualifications for his replacement. My mother began selling Avon products, then got a promotion to district manager, then became the East Coast training director for the company.

They went from having little money to both making comfortable levels of income, moving us from lower middle class to upper middle class over the course of my childhood. Since they married so young, no one had ever taught them about how to think about their money well. They often went out to eat and spent freely on clothes, decorative items, and other non-essentials. They acted like they didn't have a care in the world about their finances—at least, that is how it seemed.

Yet, by the time they were in older adulthood, they had no investments, no money in savings, and very few assets. Their house became cluttered with pointless possessions, yet we rarely took any major vacations or traveled to see the world as a family. By the time my dad died, my mom was living month to month on Social Security and half of my father's pension. She had no retirement savings, investment accounts, or other sources of net worth besides their house.

Unfortunately, they transferred this lack of financial wisdom and intentionality to me. Neither of them ever talked to me about how to manage my money because neither of them knew how to do it well for themselves. The implicit messages to me included:

- We don't have to worry about money.
- If you want something, you should get it.
- Money is for now, not for the future.
- Buying things now is more important than saving for bigger life experiences.
- Managing money is complicated and uninteresting, so there's no point in trying.
- Investing is something only wealthy people do.

There were other messages, but these were among the most important. You can see how their lack of anxiety around money could be a good thing, but how the shortsightedness about it and the lack of planning was harmful. I began my young adulthood accepting these assumptions. Not until my middle adulthood years did I identify these beliefs and challenge them. I still work on being more future-oriented with money, investing it well, and prioritizing experiences over possessions.

According to Ed Coambs,

Doing our own work in regard to financial therapy means that we acknowledge and work through the reality that we have had painful experiences—control, manipulation, loss, mixed messages, judgments, shaming, etc.—around money that has led us to make adaptations to the way we live with money, ourselves and others. These adaptations may have worked as short-term survival strategies but will not lead us to longer-term financial well-being. We can and do make personal and cultural policies and laws that reflect original money points of pain.

You have your own story about money, shaped by the messages said or inferred by your parents and peers. Coambs suggests we introspect with honest questions about our relationship with money and wealth. He said, "Asking self-reflective questions is one of the most powerful things you can do to explore your relationship with money." He gave examples of the kinds of questions we might ask ourselves, including:

- Why do I have this (emotion, behavior, thoughts, sense of self, sense of other) related to a money topic?
- Is there another way I could experience this that would be more helpful?

- What experiences have I had with money that shaped me but are now no longer helpful for me?
- If money could talk to me, what would it want to tell me?

Coambs encourages us to generate our own personal inquiries related to money and finances. "Coming up with your own self-reflective questions can also be very powerful and liberating," he said. I recommend that you create some quiet time for yourself and take his advice.

OUR RELATIONSHIP WITH FAME

Early messages about money are universal, while messages about fame are not. Since fame is not a life experience familiar to most people, few people received family messages about the role of fame in their lives. Most of us have opinions about it, though. Some of us desire it, while others of us disdain it. However, we should reflect on our own attitudes toward it before we work with anyone who is famous or who has been affected by fame.

There are undoubtedly some therapists who desire to have famous clients. They fill their websites and social media accounts with claims of working with well-known (but unnamed) clients, or they market themselves to celebrities. If you are doing this or have the impulse to do this, pause and reflect. What is the lure of this for you? A study by Ashe and McCutcheon (2001) explored motivations for wanting to be close to famous people. They found that people often seek proximity to celebrities because they believe that fame and success will rub off on them, enhancing their social status, self-worth, and, for some, professional reputation and success. This "borrowed fame" provides a sense of importance and recognition.

Other research examined the psychological motivations behind the desire for fame, finding that people seeking fame often experience lower levels of psychological well-being. The study suggested that the desire for fame is linked to external validation and self-esteem issues, with participants reporting a heightened need for admiration and recognition. People with a higher need for fame showed higher-than-average symptoms of narcissism (Ang, 2025).

Sean Redmond's work on celebrity culture shows how media portrayals glamorize fame, intensifying a desire in many to experience the attention and admiration it brings. While few of us know fame firsthand, his findings reveal that many are drawn to the famous to boost their own social standing or self-esteem (Redmond, 2014).

Stewart and Giles (2020) came to the same conclusion. Their research found that those who seek proximity to famous people do so to gain boosts in social standing and self-esteem. Another study explored deeper reasons people desire to associate with famous people. The research suggested that seeking proximity to famous people fulfills unconscious desires for power, prestige, or validation, often compensating for feelings of inadequacy or early unmet needs for attention and admiration (Houran & Lange, 2004). This is not true of all therapists who desire to see famous clients, but we should all contemplate what needs the desire to be associated with famous people meet in us.

There are also undoubtedly some therapists who desire to be famous themselves. Perhaps you are one of them. You aspire to gain a huge social media following or become a fixture on news or talk shows. Again, the research paints a bleak picture of fame-seeking. When fame becomes a top value, people often experience dissatisfaction in other areas of their lives. In fact, when people strive for fame and gain some measure of it, they often feel less fulfilled than before (Green et al., 2017). They also end up lonely and isolated more often (Stever, 2011). If the idea of becoming the next celebrity shrink seems appealing to you, reflect on your real motives, contemplate the cost of the pursuit, and reevaluate whether it will be good for you and your family. If so, make sure that you have strong interpersonal relationships and people in your life who will not only keep you grounded, but tell you the truth when you drift.

DEALING WITH YOUR OWN STUFF RELATED TO MONEY AND FAME

I was well into adulthood, far into my career, before a financial planner coached me how to think about money. If I had a philosophy of personal finances before then, it was, "You can buy it if you have the money for it." This financial professional said, "Money is about mindset and behavior," he said. "If you took ten people who are poor and ten who are rich, wipe out all their assets and give them each $100,000, in five years, most of the ones who were poor will be poor again and most of the ones who are rich will be rich again."

"Explain that," I said.

"Because people who have never learned how to manage money make $25,000 and they spend $25,000, then they make $40,000 and they spend $40,000, and then they make $60,000 and they spend $60,000. The result is the same. No savings. No net worth."

"I get that," I said.

"The people who are good with money make $25,000 and they spend $25,000, then they make $40,000 and they spend $30,000, and then they make $60,000 and they spend $40,000, and so on. They take the money they are saving and they invest it in something smart. Does this make sense?" he said.

"Yes, but it's so easy to spend that money when he knows it's there," I said.

"Exactly," he said. "And that's what keeps people trapped."

This had happened to me. I lived on an intern's salary, then a post-doc salary, then an entry-level salary, then a senior clinical salary, then a growing private practice salary. At each level, I was spending what I was making. It's hard to do otherwise. This was the financial legacy I had inherited from my parents.

Even as the owner of a successful business, I never had an extravagant lifestyle, but I also spent what I made. With the help of some wise financial professionals, I built a new philosophy of money. By the time I sold my businesses, I had a different mindset about money. I'm grateful I did because it would have been so easy to continue the old pattern. I don't find it hard to understand how people who come into a lot of money—first year professional athletes, lottery winners, inheritance beneficiaries, and others—could burn through it so quickly. Money is about mindset and behavior, not how much you have.

It has been important for me to reflect on my own history with money and the kinds of messages I received about it. In my earlier developmental years, I believed the purpose of money was to allow you desired possessions and experiences. I never thought bigger than that. As I have processed this, I realize that this set me up neither to be impressed with money nor to be envious of it. In some ways, this has prepared me well to work with wealthy clients. I neither idealize nor devalue them. Their money rarely impresses me or evokes negative feelings in me.

My relationship with fame is a little more complex. I've had a more ambivalent relationship with the desire to be famous. When I was in high school, my best friend and I loved radio disc jockeys and decided we would pursue careers in broadcasting. I chose my college because they offered a broadcasting major. I picked up a shift at the campus station, then some part-time work at a National Public Radio station, then a commercial radio station. It didn't take me long to figure out that this was not the career for me. The work was tedious. The coworkers were unpleasant. And though this was the 1980s, we were getting the first hints that radio might be a dying industry. I switched majors to psychology during my sophomore year, which ended up being a great fit for me. I continued to do part-time work in radio, though, and when I went to graduate school, it became one of my primary ways of supporting myself. I ended up working about seven years on air.

A few years after graduate school, I began collaborating with a friend on what would become my first book. I have continued to write since then, making this my tenth book. Books often lead to speaking engagements, podcast interviews, and broadcasting opportunities, all of which I've had done many times over a 30-year career.

As I've sorted out my stuff, I've realized I have a high need to communicate, but a low need to be famous. You could have a lifetime career in radio and be unrecognizable to the public. The same is true with writing. Public speaking rarely makes you recognizable to a wide swath of the population. These platforms, along with podcasting and video production, have allowed me to share ideas and communicate to audiences of various sizes while maintaining relative anonymity.

Over the years, I have observed the perils of fame from the perspective of my clients. The more famous they become, the less normal their lives become.

The more well known they are, the less connected they often feel. They've had to shrink their relationships to a tight inner circle. It's caused me not to desire fame, having seen the toll it takes. Yet, if I'm being honest, I enjoy being on stage, whether as a conference keynoter or doing magic (yes, that's a thing!). I enjoy knowing that people have listened to my thoughts on a podcast or a video. I've found it's difficult to tease out my motive. How much of my motive is a thirst to communicate, a desire to move people, or a longing to persuade others? And how much of that is enjoying the attention, the positive strokes, the affirmation? How much of my enjoyment in working with well-known clients or those in their orbit is finding pleasure in the proximity? How much of it is just how my career has developed over the years? I reflect on these ideas a lot.

I share all this introspection to say it's good for you to do the same. Do you desire to work with wealthy or well-known clients? You should ask yourself why. It's unlikely you'll have a purity of motive, but you should examine yourself. If you find you are drawn to wealthy or well-known clients because of the vicarious social and professional standing it might give you, please resist. If you find having these clients is a self-esteem booster, steer clear.

The reasons for avoiding work with these clients when your motive is unhealthy are both obvious and subtle. It makes the work about meeting some unmet need in yourself. It also clouds your objectivity that you will need more than ever.

I have a contract with a professional sports league to see players who have run into trouble. The intent behind having only approved or paneled clinicians is smart. It keeps players who are mandated into treatment from finding a therapist who is unqualified or smitten with professional athletes. When they first approached me, they asked me to complete a lengthy application. Not knowing what they were looking for, I responded to a question asking about my level of interest in that sport and that league. I said I had only a fleeting interest in it, watching games from time to time. I thought that would doom my application, but I learned later it was what they were looking for. They didn't want therapists who were fans because fans are not impartial, especially when things get tough with a client. You should do the same for yourself. Don't strive to be a therapist to clients for whom you might otherwise be a fan.

GETTING OUR OWN FINANCIAL HOUSE IN ORDER

Doing our own work ensures we are being wise with our own personal finances. In the same way that conducting marital therapy while your own partner relationship is in shambles is not wise, working with individuals around money issues when your own financial situation is poorly managed is also not advisable. It's best to learn about money and practice good money management. Drawing from research and the advice of financial professionals, here are some key areas you will need to address:

- *Living Within Your Means:* Spend less than you earn. This basic habit keeps you from building up debt just to cover everyday expenses and positions you to save for future goals. Accumulating debt is a key sign of poor financial health, and the only way to prevent that is by ensuring your monthly spending is less than your monthly income.

- *Emergency Fund:* Maintain a solid emergency fund that covers three to six months of living expenses to ensure you're ready for the unexpected—whether it's job loss, medical bills, or urgent home repairs. To calculate your goal, take your total income from last year's tax return and divide it by four. That amount is the minimum you should have set aside in a secure emergency fund. For example, if you earned $100,000, your target should be between $25,000 and $50,000 reserved for genuine emergencies.

- *Savings Goals:* Set clear savings goals and contribute to them regularly, whether it's for retirement, a down payment on a home, or other major expenses. This shows both financial discipline and the ability to plan ahead.

- *Manageable Debt:* Keep a low debt-to-income ratio and avoid the weight of excessive credit card debt, loans, or other financial burdens. Necessary debts, like a mortgage, are fine as long as you can afford to pay them back.

- *Retirement Savings:* Contribute to retirement accounts like 401(k)s, IRAs, or other pension plans. The sooner and more consistently you invest in your future, the better positioned you'll be when the time comes to retire.

- *Investment and Growth:* Invest your money to build wealth over time is a mark of financial maturity. Know your risk tolerance and maintaining a diversified investment portfolio that aligns with your long-term goals.

- *Insurance Coverage:* Carry the right insurance, whether it's health, life, disability, homeowner's/renter's, or auto, to guard against major financial setbacks.

- *Estate Planning:* Have a will, a living will, and maybe a trust, depending on your circumstances. This ensures your assets are handled according to your wishes when you die.

- *Financial Literacy:* Develop a solid grasp of basic financial principles, such as how interest works, the value of saving, and the fundamentals of investing. Learn and apply that knowledge to your financial decisions.

Achieving and maintaining financial health is an ongoing process that requires regular review and adjustments to your habits and goals.

LEARNING THE LANGUAGE OF WEALTH AND FAME

With matters of finance and wealth, do you know what initials like EBITDA, IPO, and ROI stand for? Do you know what a Roth IRA or a P/E ratio means? Do you know the difference between a venture capitalist and a private equity firm? If not, you're not alone. Many helping professionals are not well versed in the language of wealth.

With fame and celebrity, do you know how an agent differs from a manager? Do you know what bank-end deals or option agreements are? What's the difference between Above the Line and Below the Line with film credits? What does a key grip or a gaffer do? With athletes, do you know what it means to be a free agent or to have a collective bargaining agreement? Again, mental health professionals are often unaware of what many of these terms mean.

I've prepared two glossaries of some words and phrases you should know. You can see both of them toward the back of the book. There is no expectation that you have an MBA-level money and wealth vocabulary. However, the more terms and phrases that are part of the daily world of wealthy or famous clients, the more effective you will be. You'll never know all the vocabulary of these worlds because you are not living in them every minute of every day like your clients are, but the more you know, the more attuned you can be in your work.

Doing your own work involves understanding the relationship you have with money and how you bring that into your work with wealthy clients—or any clients. It also involves equipping yourself with the knowledge and the vocabulary to understand the world of the wealthy person. These steps will elevate your skill in working with wealthy clients.

EXTENDING EMPATHY

Years ago, a psychologist I liked and respected said of his therapy clients, "I believe everyone is always just trying their best." Even though I admired the man, I didn't agree with him then, and I don't agree with him now. I don't believe everyone always tries their best. I know I'm not always trying my best at all moments. Such a sentiment, which I've heard echoed by other therapists, strips people of their agency and responsibility. If a person who is making rotten choices is just trying their best, then who are we to challenge or prompt them in a different direction?

In the same way that I can be selfish or take the path of least resistance, wealthy and well-known people can, as well. I would argue that it is harder for someone who is used to privilege to allow themselves much discomfort. I was on a business trip at a resort when I observed a wealthy man and his son in a cart being driven by a resort staff member. The worker stopped the cart and hopped out so he could help an older woman who was struggling to get her luggage to the concierge station. The wealthy man seethed. He shouted out, "We need to get to our room." The worker kept the smile on his face and said, "I'll be right there," which only infuriated the wealthy man more as he shook his head in disgust. I am certain you'll agree that the rich man was not doing his best in that moment. He was impatient and self-centered, oblivious to the legitimate needs of the older woman. He was also modeling some pretty awful attitudes for his son.

It's easy to see these and dozens of other examples and become very judgmental toward wealthy or well-known people. With judgment comes a diminishment of empathy, which is the bedrock of therapy. The goal, then, is not to believe the untruth that we are all doing our best all the time, but neither is it to hold the view that it is our responsibility to pass judgment.

We come to this work seeing the rich and famous as neither godlike nor monstrous. They are humans with some rare privileges that can both benefit and undermine them. Above all else, they should be afforded the dignity due all humans. If you struggle with idealizing or devaluing wealthy or well-known people, either this work is not for you or you need to do some deeper work on yourself before you take on these clients. You must see them as fully human, with both beautiful and ugly qualities, but still deserving of your respect and genuine empathy. Before you take on these clients, make sure you have done your own work on any issues that may lead you to envy or fame-seeking or judgmental attitudes so you can show them genuine empathy.

NOTE

1 All quotes from Ed Coambs are from personal communication, June 14, 2024.

REFERENCES

Ang, C. S. (2025). Unravelling fame-seeking motive and narcissism: The roles of problematic internet use and acculturation to Western culture. *Behaviour & Information Technology*, 1–13. https://doi.org/10.1080/0144929X.2025.2462258

Ashe, D. D., & McCutcheon, L. E. (2001). Shyness, loneliness, and attitude toward celebrities. *Current Research in Social Psychology*, 6(9), 124–133.

Green, M. C., Hefner, V., & Gleason, T. R. (2017). The impact of celebrity status on youth development: Celebrity worship and the emergence of fame-seeking behavior. *Journal of Adolescent Research*, 32(4), 431–449. https://doi.org/10.1177/0743558416630818

Houran, J., & Lange, R. (2004). Delusions of grandeur: The need for uniqueness and the influence of celebrity worship and fantasy proneness on paranormal beliefs. *Personality and Individual Differences*, 36(7), 1419–1429.

Redmond, S. (2014). *Celebrity and the media*. Palgrave Macmillan.

Stever, G. S. (2011). Fan behavior and lifespan development theory: Explaining para-social and social attachment to celebrities. *Journal of Adult Development*, 18(1), 1–7.

Stewart, S., & Giles, D. (2020). Celebrity status and the attribution of value. *European Journal of Cultural Studies*, 23(1), 3–20.

Chapter 13

Ethical Issues and Practical Considerations in Working with Wealthy and Well-Known People

Affluence and fame pose unique clinical challenges that demand highly skilled and well-prepared therapists, while also raising intricate ethical dilemmas when working with these wealthy and high-profile clients. These ethical considerations often stem from the status of these clients and their unique needs and circumstances. They may also come from a sense of entitlement on their part or a failure to remain objective on your part.

My favorite phrase about ethics in therapy comes from the work of Thomas Skovholt and Len Jennings in their book *Master Therapists: Exploring Expertise in Therapy and Counseling*, based on their interviews with peer-endorsed master therapists. They found the true masters are ethical, but they operate from what they term "a nuanced ethical compass." Of these therapists, they write, "There is not an immediate turn to ordinary rules or what others will think. If this means risk-taking, then they very seriously consider the risk" (Skovholt & Jennings, 2004, p. 137). Working with wealthy and well-known clients demands this kind of high-level and nuanced thinking.

You may face circumstances with these clients that you have never had with other clients. Being rigid about your response might feel safer, but it might not always be best. Following are some of the ethical issues and practical considerations you may have to navigate well.

JURISDICTIONAL ISSUES

Imagine you are working with a musician who is having trouble with anxiety. Sometimes his panic attacks are debilitating and last for over an hour. His job requires him to be on stage and perform before thousands of people. On some nights when he feels anxiety creeping in, he drinks a little too much before a show. There's been some chatter on social media, especially Reddit, that he has a drinking problem.

DOI: 10.4324/9781003503569-17

His tour takes him through 20 states. You're only licensed in one of them. He needs you most when he is on the road, but you aren't licensed in most states where he'll be traveling. Can you see him during his tour? What if he is having an emergency, like a panic attack so intense those around him are contemplating taking him to the hospital? What if he texts you before a show in another state saying he is worried about drinking too much? Can you text him back?

What about a professional baseball player who could play in as many as 162 games across up to 28 states each season? Must he get a new therapist in each state where he plays? What if he is using therapy as a part of his personal efforts to prevent relapse on painkillers or if he is going through a rough time being separated from his family?

What if you are a therapist seeing a depressed child from a wealthy family from New York that will travel from Vail, Colorado, to Martha's Vineyard to San Diego over six weeks during the summer? They will be in three different states, gone for a month and a half. They need their child to be seen while they are away. Who can see this child? Will you agree to see him for continuity of care, or will you decline because you are not licensed in those other states?

These jurisdictional issues are among the greatest ethical and legal challenges facing therapists who work with wealthy and well-known clients. By law, therapists cannot practice in states where they are not licensed. However, with our increasingly mobile, technologically connected society, these artificial barriers now make far less sense.

State-level licensing boards provide good safeguards and protections for the public. Without them, it would be the Wild West, with little to no accountability. However, if a client is based in your state and the relationship has been initiated in the state where you are licensed, but travels regularly to other jurisdictions because of work or other lifestyle demands, then it also seems wise to allow continuity in the therapeutic relationship. For most clients, therapists are not interchangeable.

We all have to play by the rules, but in my view, the rules need to change. Each of our professions should support full and automatic reciprocity across states for licensed professionals in good standing. Imagine if states didn't have reciprocity for driver's licenses. Let's say you lived in Los Angeles and wanted to drive to Santa Fe, but Arizona didn't recognize your license. What if they threatened to charge you with a crime if you drove into the state without an Arizona license? Well, now you'd have to drive to Las Vegas, up into Utah, across into Colorado, then down into New Mexico to get there. That makes little sense. Instead, we understand that being licensed in one state should suffice for licensure to drive in another state, even if the standards or tests are different.

The same should be true for mental health licensure for the practical considerations we just explored. As it stands, a therapist seeing a traveling client may face legal risks if they provide services to that client in a state where the therapist is not licensed. Yet, there are many clients who are constantly in other states and other jurisdictions who deserve access to a therapist when they are away from home (Taube et al., 2023).

A person in these circumstances—and a hundred other situations—cannot be reliably seen by any therapist when they travel. Without an interstate compact between all states for all mental health disciplines, you are restricted from seeing the client when they travel out of your state. The closest we have is PsyPact in psychology, which is an interstate compact that allows tele-therapy in participating states. While most states have signed the compact, several have not as of this writing, including some larger states where artists and athletes often travel for work. More recently, the Interstate Counseling Compact was passed, allowing licensed professional counselors the option of practicing telehealth across state lines.

As of this writing, you cannot see a client who travels to states where you are not licensed or approved for practice, but the deeper issue is that this has become untenable and unfair in our current culture. I encourage you to advocate for interstate compacts in all disciplines among all states, or, as Dan Taube and his colleagues advise, for a national professional licensing system. We don't protect the public by restricting a resident's access to services when out of the state. I would argue that it can do harm to that client and the community with whom the client is connected when we don't allow them to have easy access to their trusted therapist.

CONFIDENTIALITY AND PRIVACY

Confidentiality and privacy are foundational to therapy but take on added complexity when working with wealthy and well-known clients. These individuals' public visibility and unique societal roles amplify the ethical challenges surrounding confidentiality. High-profile clients face a heightened risk of privacy breaches due to media scrutiny, public curiosity, and opportunists seeking to exploit sensitive information. This reality underscores the need for therapists to adopt robust confidentiality protocols.

Therapists should consider enhanced privacy measures, such as non-disclosure agreements (NDAs) for staff, advanced security protocols for electronic health records, and ongoing training in privacy laws and ethics, which change with advancements in technology and social media. For prominent clients who prefer in-person therapy, additional considerations may include alternative entrances, private waiting areas, and strategic scheduling to reduce exposure. For instance, when contracting with a professional sports league, representatives assessed my practice's setup to ensure it could accommodate these needs. Our Charlotte and Nashville offices include separate waiting areas and entrances, allowing clients to avoid public waiting spaces if desired. Although these measures are seldom requested, having them available provides peace of mind.

Many therapists lack the resources or room for such accommodations. In smaller practices, confidentiality can be safeguarded by spacing out appointments to avoid overlaps or allowing high-profile clients to wait in their cars until notified. Ask clients about their preferences and do your best to meet their needs, though not always their wishes.

The potential exposure of high-profile clients in a public waiting area illustrates the importance of special accommodations. While a typical client may blend into a crowd, a recognizable artist or athlete risks having their presence shared on social media or discussed publicly, compromising their confidentiality. This reality justifies accommodations like private waiting spaces, separate entrances, and staggered appointments.

Train your support staff to be vigilant against unauthorized photography or recording in waiting areas. While such incidents are rare, I have used moments when clients recognize a public figure as an opportunity to stress their moral obligation to respect privacy, reminding them that everyone deserves confidentiality at a therapist's office.

Requests for offsite therapy to protect confidentiality present another challenge. Some clients may request sessions in unconventional settings, such as tour buses, private homes, hotels, or backstage areas. While flexibility can sometimes be appropriate, these requests should be evaluated carefully. Factors to consider include your therapeutic approach, client boundary concerns, and whether accommodating the request fosters a sense of entitlement. Personally, I rarely if ever agree to offsite sessions, particularly in private residences or hotels, though you may make exceptions for someone unable to leave their home or specialized therapy models, such as in-home play therapy for children. Navigating these decisions requires thoughtfulness and ethical rigor.

Wealthy clients who lack public recognition typically do not require enhanced privacy accommodations, as providing them may inadvertently reinforce entitlement issues. Treating all clients identically is neither practical nor fair. Fairness means tailoring care to meet individual needs, not that everyone gets identical consideration.

In solo or small-group practices, where resources may be limited, therapists can still take steps to protect client privacy by spacing appointments and being vigilant about potential risks. Balance this with the need for limits on wealthy clients who may seek special treatment without genuine need. For well-known clients, however, special accommodations are often essential to create a safe therapeutic environment where they can focus on their mental health without fear of exposure.

DUAL RELATIONSHIPS

Maintaining relationship boundaries with prominent clients can be a challenge, especially when they extend invitations to social events or propose opportunities outside the therapeutic context. The American Psychological Association (APA) Ethics Code and similar guidelines caution against dual relationships that could impair objectivity, confidentiality, or effectiveness (APA, 2017). This guidance is particularly relevant when working with clients who may offer you opportunities for connection, community involvement, or collaboration.

The APA defines dual relationships as situations where a therapist simultaneously has a professional relationship and another type of relationship with the same individual, such as being a business associate, family member, or social acquaintance. While dual relationships are not universally prohibited, the ethical standard advises avoiding them if they could reasonably impair the therapist's objectivity or harm the client. They leave room for some types of dual relationships. As the code states: "Multiple relationships that would not reasonably be expected to cause impairment or risk exploitation or harm are not unethical" (APA, 3.05a).

Similarly, the American Counseling Association (ACA) Code of Ethics warns against counseling relationships with individuals for whom the therapist cannot maintain objectivity. The ethical standards permit sequential roles or role changes—such as transitioning from individual therapy to family therapy—if managed carefully to avoid harm (American Counseling Association, 2014). The key principles across these ethical codes are caution and ensuring no harm to the client.

Consider an example: a well-known actress who has benefitted from therapy and has formed a high opinion of you asks you to join the planning committee for her nonprofit and speak at a fundraiser aimed at destigmatizing mental illness. While this cause aligns with your passions, the situation creates overlapping ethical issues: a potential dual relationship (as a committee member and speaker) and concerns about the client's confidentiality. Should you accept the offer? Declining may seem like the simplest answer, but it's worth deeper reflection.

A core principle of ethical decision-making is that ethics serve to protect the client, not the therapist. While personal discomfort—such as dislike of public speaking or awkwardness in dual roles—is valid, it is not an ethical basis to decline. The central ethical question is not your discomfort, but whether your involvement could harm them.

In this scenario, begin by educating the client about potential challenges. Clients rarely anticipate how dual roles might affect them. Explore questions such as:

- How might this new dynamic complicate our therapeutic relationship?
- What would it be like for you to see me in a different role?
- How can we address any negative impacts that arise from this arrangement?
- Is there someone else better suited for this role to preserve our therapeutic relationship?

After discussing these angles, if you remain uncertain, err on the side of caution. For instance, while the client is actively in therapy, it might be prudent to

167

decline. However, once therapy has concluded, you may feel more comfortable exploring such opportunities.

Dual relationships can arise in other contexts, too. Imagine a software developer who offers to help create a therapeutic app idea you've been longing to develop. He proposes a barter for therapy sessions. This would lead to overlapping roles, such as app collaborator and therapist, potentially blurring boundaries and complicating the therapeutic dynamic. Even if the client is enthusiastic, they might not foresee how awkward or counterproductive such an arrangement could become.

The safest approach is generally to avoid dual relationships during active therapy. After therapy concludes, these considerations may shift. Ethical decisions require nuanced thinking, balancing caution with a thoughtful, client-centered approach. Prioritize the client's well-being and consider all potential risks to navigate these challenges effectively.

PUBLIC SCRUTINY & PROFESSIONAL RISK

Stutz, Jonah Hill's documentary, features his therapist, Dr. Phil Stutz, in a unique and intimate exploration of their therapy sessions together. The stated goal was to bring Dr. Stutz's therapeutic ideas and methods, which Hill found so helpful and life-giving, to a bigger audience (Hill, 2022). This creative endeavor, while innovative and enlightening for many, also opens up several avenues for public scrutiny, criticism, and complaint. Writing for *Medium*, Mark Dalton writes,

> There is obvious massive ethical boundary issues here between the two and it certainly comes across that Stutz is viewed more as a friend to Jonah and not his therapist. Boundaries were so obvious when Jonah sat down early into the movie and told Stutz he felt pressure to lie to him about how the documentary is going.
>
> (Dalton, 2023)

Psychotherapist and author James Davies is quoted in *Vice* as saying, "Stutz rejects much that's associated with good therapeutic work—maintaining boundaries, not giving advice and not relying on untested theories," and adds, "For his approach, (Stutz) claims an almost transcendental status, as might a shaman, diviner or necromancer" (Sharma, 2022).

To be fair, reviews and analysis for the film were more positive than negative. For example, Dr. Cheralyn Leeby, a licensed marriage and family therapist, wrote for *Psychology Today*, "Stutz successfully demonstrated how his vulnerability, authenticity, and transparency invited the radical notion of mutual healing. Could this become a new trend?" (Leeby, 2023). However, any time a therapist becomes associated with a well-known person in public, they can become the subject of criticism. Since confidentiality belongs to the client and not the therapist,

Hill has every right to expose his working relationship with Stutz. Many celebrities have shared their experiences in therapy, sometimes referring to them anonymously but sometimes calling them by name, like Howard Stern talking about his therapist, Dr. Lou. When the therapist becomes connected with the high-profile person, the therapist will face new scrutiny and ethical challenges. While it is the client's decision to talk about you in public, I advise you to say you do not prefer this if the topic comes up. I would not bring it up preemptively (which would be very presumptuous), but only if you are asked.

It is not inherently unethical to be identified as a prominent person's therapist, but it will heighten scrutiny of you and expose you to greater risk of not only criticism, but ethical complaints.

DEALING WITH THE TEAM

Working with wealthy or well-known clients often involves interacting with their agents, managers, personal assistants, or other professional staff, who frequently serve as gatekeepers. These individuals are often your first point of contact, reaching out to vet you for their client and assess your fit and accessibility. Typically, you won't know who the client is until the vetting process is complete. A typical call might sound like this:

> I'm Darren Brown, calling on behalf of a client. He's a professional athlete going through some difficulties and is finally open to therapy. You've been highly recommended, and I'd like to take a few minutes to see if you might be a good fit.

Often, these inquiries don't lead to follow-ups. The client may change their mind, opt for another provider, or have therapy deprioritized due to scheduling conflicts. In most cases, you won't learn who the client was. While this is largely beyond your control, one critical factor you can influence is how you approach and build rapport with the representative.

Therapists are trained to uphold boundaries and safeguard confidentiality, but when working with high-profile clients, gatekeepers like agents and managers play a central role. Establishing a good relationship with them doesn't mean compromising ethical standards or breaking rules. You still require signed releases and protect all confidential information. The key lies in your posture toward the gatekeeper—how you engage with them, not just what you do.

Consider this analogy: I specialize in working with young adult men, many of whom come to therapy reluctantly, often at the urging of a parent or significant other. A parent—often the mother—usually makes the initial contact. To gain the trust of both the client and their parent, I aim to demonstrate openness and competence without betraying confidentiality. For example, if a parent emails me unsolicited concerns, I share the content with my client, emphasizing that

169

information coming to me is not confidential, but only the information I share. This transparency builds trust while keeping everyone informed.

The same principle applies to working with managers and other gatekeepers. Early on, you should establish openness and collaboration. For instance, acknowledging their insights with a simple comment like, "I really appreciate your perspective—it's helpful," can go a long way. If they press for confidential information, I might respond with, "To maintain trust with my client, I'll need his permission to discuss this with you. How would you feel about me asking him?" This approach sets clear boundaries without alienating the gatekeeper. If they back off, it's often a sign they already knew they were crossing a boundary.

Gatekeepers come in various personality styles, but two stand out. The first is the "bulldog"—a forceful personality who relies on intimidation to achieve their goals. The challenge is to remain calm and firm without becoming either overly compliant or combative.

The second type is the "charmer," socially adept and skilled at gaining compliance through warmth and flattery. This type requires heightened vigilance, as their approach can subtly coax information or favors. With either personality, the goal is to strike a balance: assertiveness without rigidity, and collaboration without overstepping ethical limits.

Navigating these dynamics requires clarity, professionalism, and a firm commitment to ethical standards while maintaining a collaborative posture that fosters trust and respect.

GETTING PULLED INTO COURT MATTERS

When high-net-worth or celebrated individuals face relationship conflicts, a therapist's role can become significantly more challenging and precarious. You may be asked to provide a letter or testify on your client's behalf in legal matters, such as child custody disputes or criminal proceedings. These situations require careful navigation and strategic decision-making.

If asked to weigh in on a child custody matter, it is wise to decline. Offering an opinion—no matter how favorable—can be problematic because your perspective is inherently limited. You have access only to your client's version of events, their self-perception, and their account of their former partner and child. Critical information from other parties or contexts is missing. Whether your client is wealthy, well known, or otherwise, if you are serving as their individual, couples, or family therapist, refrain from providing written or verbal testimony regarding custody. Engaging in such matters significantly increases your risk of facing a professional complaint.

If you receive a subpoena related to a legal matter, it's important to understand that you do not have to comply immediately by providing testimony or releasing records. Most subpoenas are signed by an attorney rather than a judge. In these cases, you can retain your own attorney to challenge or quash the subpoena.

Unless a judge issues a direct order, you are not obligated to share records or testify. During this process, keep open communication with your client, emphasizing that while you want to support them, it would be unethical for you to involve yourself in the proceedings.

Proactively addressing these potential challenges early in therapy can help establish boundaries. For clients navigating separation or divorce, explain your role and limitations at the outset. Make it clear that as their individual therapist, your responsibility is to represent their best interests in therapy—not to provide opinions or recommendations on child custody issues. Clarify that custody evaluators, who maintain an objective stance, are the appropriate professionals to make such recommendations to the court. Reinforce that your role is inherently subjective, as you have not gathered all sides of the story.

Even with clear communication and documentation, such as having your client sign an agreement acknowledging that you will not participate in custody disputes, conflicts may still arise. A determined or aggressive attorney may view you as a potential asset to their case and attempt to involve you, even against your expressed boundaries. Early conversations and signed agreements can help establish expectations, but they may not entirely prevent attempts to draw you into legal proceedings when tensions escalate.

By maintaining clear boundaries, enlisting legal support when necessary, and prioritizing ethical standards, you can navigate these complexities while protecting both yourself and your professional integrity.

PUBLIC STATEMENTS AND ADVERTISING

You should not solicit a client to make public statements on your behalf or give you endorsements, but you also need to be cautious about how you represent your practice and expertise. Any statements that might cause people to suspect who you have seen in therapy are off limits, as are statements boasting that you are some kind of "celebrity therapist" or something similar.

Because no one will know who your clients are, they will also not know whether your public statements about your work are true or not. You could highlight your "extensive experience" working with those in the entertainment industry in your online bio when you've only seen one or two people on the periphery. It is easy to bend the truth and make public statements that are misleading at best or outright lies at worst.

Keep these public statements toned down until you reach a point in your career where this is clearly true of you, not aspirationally true. As such, this may require years of practice before you are established in this space. Before then, make public statements that represent where you are in your career, not where you want to be.

You may also face a well-known client who wants to make public statements about you and your work together. The client may have seen enormous benefits from therapy with you and want to tell the world about it. As appealing as this sounds, I would not encourage these kinds of statements. However, your client has full agency and autonomy. You cannot limit their public statements. Making general comments about the benefits of therapy or saying how good their therapist is can be helpful, but once you are named, it can create some unforeseen difficulties in your working relationship. It may also produce some unexpected complications in other areas of your professional practice.

RECEIVING GIFTS

You are seeing a professional athlete who has gotten a DUI. He has late cancelled or no-showed more appointments than he has kept. He has lied to you at least twice. What happens when that guy gives you playoff tickets one week, then requests a letter to the court sharing how well he is doing in his therapy?

The ethics code for psychologists does not directly address gift giving from clients to their therapist. The American Counseling Association addresses this in their most recent code of ethics, saying,

> Counselors understand the challenges of accepting gifts from clients and recognize that in some cultures, small gifts are a token of respect and gratitude. When determining whether to accept a gift from clients, counselors consider the therapeutic relationship, the monetary value of the gift, the client's motivation for giving the gift, and the counselor's motivation for wanting to receive or decline the gift.
>
> (American Counseling Association, 2014)

This is a wise start and tells you what factors to consider, but it gives little practical guidance for counselors and therapists in how they should navigate these ethical moments. I propose a simple standard: receive the gift unless it is apparent it will negatively affect the therapeutic relationship or bias your judgment. In the example of the professional athlete, I would not receive the gift because it could be an attempt to bias my feedback to the court. Perhaps this was not his intent, but because I have that concern, I would not accept the gift. If the tickets were of significant value, I also would not accept the gift. However, if he brought me a small souvenir or trinket and I did not perceive it as an attempt to curry favor with me, then I might accept it.

Rejecting a present can be embarrassing for the giver, so a personal policy of not accepting any gifts is not without its therapeutic risks. I encourage you to accept small gifts that seem to be authentic expressions of connection and gently decline gifts that are of significant value, or that risk causing you to lose objectivity, or that could attempt to nudge your behavior.

With wealthy clients, there may be a temptation to accept more expensive gifts because it represents no hardship for them. However, I would still discourage against this. There is no clear threshold for what constitutes a lavish gift, but if it makes you feel uncomfortable or questioning, pay attention to that. The client's net worth is not what should determine your decision to accept or reject the gift.

To help you in your general decision-making about accepting gifts, consider these guidelines. You should be able to say yes to each of these questions before you accept the gift:

1. Are any gifts allowed by the ethics code of my profession?
2. Is the gift of low monetary value?
3. Is this client's gift giving an infrequent behavior?
4. Do you believe the gift is given without an ulterior motive?
5. Is it likely receiving the gift will have no adverse impact on the therapy relationship?

In addition, consider whether the client is from a culture where giving gifts is an important part of the relationship. We are more likely to see this in many Asian, Hispanic, and Middle Eastern countries (Komter & Vollebergh, 1997). If this is the case, err on the side of accepting the gift. If you are not sure, engage your client in a respectful cultural conversation.

TERMINATION AND CONTINUITY OF CARE

Prominent people do not let people into their orbit casually. Younger celebrities have been coached to be cautious, while older rich or famous people have learned the hard way. Over the years, they've had seemingly trustworthy people disclose private comments or actions. They've had people worm their way into their lives for personal gain. They've seen people become jealous of them and their attention. As such, when they allow themselves to have a trusting relationship with others, they often want to keep those relationships intact. Many established celebrities have had the same agent for decades. Many well-known people are still only best friends with people they knew before they became famous.

In the same way, a wealthy or well-known client may want to stay with their therapist in an open-ended relationship. For some practitioners, this poses no problem at all. Their therapeutic model, in fact, may lend itself to therapy over longer periods of time. For others, such an open-ended, long-term relationship might contrast with your typical way of operating where you are used to a goal-directed, solution-focused, evidence-based approach. Those therapists may bend for the prominent client in ways they might not otherwise.

173

The APA Ethics Code reads, "Psychologists terminate therapy when it becomes reasonably clear that the client/patient no longer needs the service, is not likely to benefit, or is being harmed by continued service" (APA Ethics Code 10.10). The ACA Ethics Code is almost identical in its wording (American Counseling Association, 2014). Following these guidelines, we must terminate when the need for benefit of therapy no longer exists or where continuing might harm or undermine the client.

However, the notion of "need" or "benefit" may develop over time. What they came in for may differ from what they need later. Depending on your style and model, you may decide to discuss termination with the client once their original goals are met. If they came in because of PTSD symptoms and they are no longer experiencing them, perhaps it may be time to wrap up. However, some clients benefit from ongoing therapy check-ins and desire to continue. In these instances, it's wise to acknowledge the original goals are met and then discuss whether you should set new goals. A new goal might be more open-ended, such as "Process life stressors and discuss strategies for managing them." Therapy can then continue in a way that allows it to be ongoing or as needed, while still having an agreed-upon goal.

I had some key client statistics pulled for the year 2023. We found I averaged eight sessions per client, but if you dug deeper, there were some people that I saw four to six times, and others I saw all year long. I typically operate within a solution-focused CBT framework, employing strategies from ACT and Motivational Interviewing. We focus on the goal and then wrap up when we are done. However, I have other clients, prominent or not, whom I have seen for long stretches of time. More often, I will not see them continuously, but we'll have a run of sessions one year and then another run of sessions a couple of years later. I tell them I want them to think of me as more like the family doctor than a specialist. You may not see me every week for years, but the door is always open to you if you need to pop back in. As a result, I may slide them to an inactive status after a stretch where they have not come in, but I will easily reactivate them as needed.

FINE-TUNING YOUR ETHICAL COMPASS

There are other unique ethical issues you will encounter in your work with wealthy and well-known people. Navigating these ethical issues requires you to have a strong grounding in your professional ethical codes, while fine-tuning your nuanced ethical compass. You may have witnessed other therapists who seem rigidly committed to some "rule" without respect for the subtleties of the situation. This inflexibility comes from one of two sources. First, this is the way graduate students are trained. It is easier to ensure consistency with hard and fast rules. *Never have a dual relationship with a client. Never see a client outside of your office. Always follow a lock-step evidence-based treatment protocol.* These absolutes allow graduate programs to create safety and quality control in training young therapists, but they don't always speak to the needs of the unique situations you will encounter in your practice.

Second, this inflexibility comes from fear. The anxious brain wants certainty, sameness, order. Following ethical guidelines like they are rigid rules produces a false sense of safety. Erring always on the side of caution makes the venture feel less risky. While I have not done certain things like see a client in their home or hotel room, I have had colleagues who have acted ethically and professionally and made a different choice. I might also make a different choice for myself in the future. For example, if a client became ill or was injured and didn't want to or could not use tele-therapy, I would consider visiting the client. For me, I don't want to base my decision on fear. I want my choice to be driven by what is in the ultimate best interest of the client.

I had one prominent client who came to my office the first time to tell me the story of a tragedy that affected his family and how I might best help his young adult son. In a matter-of-fact way, he said, "So I want you to come to our house every week and see him. You can sit out in the sunroom and it's plenty private out there." I declined for several reasons. First, he began dictating the frame and practice of how I would do my work, which is something he seemed accustomed to doing. For me to agree would risk playing into his sense of entitlement and unhealthy needs for control. Second, his son was able-bodied, had his own car, and could come in, so there was no good reason to grant this request. This was before tele-therapy was in wide use. In an identical circumstance today, I would offer the tele-therapy option since it is available to almost all clients and would not be a special consideration or privilege.

It's wise to seek supervision or consultation when faced with complex ethical decisions where you must maintain a clear focus on the welfare and autonomy of your client. However, it's also best practice not to disclose the name or provide identifying information to your colleague if it is unnecessary. Even among professionals, the fewer people who know who you are talking about, the better. It also keeps our need to impress others with the fact you are seeing a rich or famous client in check, which is an essential discipline and practice.

THERAPIST ATTITUDES AND MOTIVES

I was part of a lunch conversation that turned to the state of the economy and the current political climate with a group of friends. One guy at the table joked, "I think we should eat the rich." This line, attributed to Jean-Jacques Rousseau, the political philosopher and a leader in the French Revolution, was coined when 98% of the citizenry of France was part of the lower class. On social media, the hashtag #eattherich pops up with some regularity. I laughed along with the rest of the group at the comment, but later, I reflected on how easy it is for us to disrespect and caricature wealthy people.

175

Psychologist Jamie Traeger-Muney, who specializes in work with wealthy clients, told *The Guardian*, "You can come up with [a] lot of words and sayings about inheritors, not one of them is positive: spoiled brat, born with a silver spoon in their mouth, trust fund babies, all these things," She adds, it's "easy to scapegoat the rich" (Kasperkevic, 2015). In some quarters, there is a clear anti-rich sentiment that would be easy to fall into as a therapist.

We may have empathy at the ready for underprivileged people but find it hard to kindle for the rich. There's no dispute that the wealthy have far more advantages, privileges, and resources than others, but that shouldn't relieve us of our human obligation to regard them with empathy, as we should all people, especially those who are struggling. This doesn't mean they can't be challenged or have limits set on them. Indeed, both those things are necessary parts of excellent therapy. We should push back on our own preconceptions and judgments to be the best helpers possible.

Psychotherapist Clay Cockrell reflects, "Over the years, I have developed a great deal of empathy for those who have far too much." His compassion stems from the unique struggles faced by the wealthy, which often go unnoticed or misunderstood. He details at least six challenges they face:

One of the most profound challenges is the difficulty they experience in trusting their relationships. Wealth introduces the constant question of authenticity—how can they discern whether someone is a genuine friend or lover, rather than an opportunist seeking personal gain?

Cockrell finds common issue is a loss of purpose. After spending years or even decades building their empires, some wealthy individuals find themselves adrift when their enterprises no longer require their involvement. Selling a business or achieving financial independence can leave them questioning what to do with the rest of their lives to find a renewed sense of purpose and drive.

The wealthy are also more susceptible to specific mental health problems. Conditions such as Narcissistic Personality Disorder, anxiety, and certain eating disorders are disproportionately prevalent among this population, highlighting the psychological toll of wealth and privilege.

Cockrell sees parenting as another source of difficulty. Wealth often allows them to overindulge their children or shield them from hardships they themselves endured. While they are well intentioned, these behaviors can unintentionally undermine their children's development and resilience.

Isolation among the rich is a significant burden, Cockrell observes. Many wealthy individuals lead lives with few genuine connections or loyal friends. Their ability to relate to others becomes increasingly limited, and their social circles often shrink to a handful of people—or none at all.

Finally, this lack of authentic connection often diminishes empathy. With fewer deep relationships and limited opportunities for true intimacy or trust, the wealthy may struggle to understand or connect with the experiences of others, leaving them emotionally distant and less empathetic.

Cockrell writes, "It can be very difficult to watch these individuals struggle with the toxicity of excess, isolation, and deep mistrust" (Cockrell, 2021).

To be clear, it is neither more noble nor less honorable to want to work with wealthy or well-known clients. In my career, I worked for years with the poorest of clients, and I've also served rich individuals and their families. I've had clients with recognizable faces and those who are known only to a few people. Both extremes of wealth and fame have their unique challenges, as do those in the middle.

If you work with wealthy and well-known clients—or aspire to work with them—take an inventory of your motives, values, and goals. With issues of wealth especially, you must keep judgmental impulses in check. You must also push against impure motives of wanting some vicarious association with affluent or famous people. Both extremes of judging wealth and fame or seeking proximity to them will interfere with your ability to be effective as a therapist.

FINAL THOUGHTS

After a man who was both famous and wealthy died unexpectedly, his young adult son came to see me in therapy. "It's hard enough to have your dad die, but the toughest part for me is having so many people talk about him like they knew him," he said. "These stories on TV and online, none of them sound like him. Some people are saying positive things about him that aren't true and others are saying negative things about him that aren't true either."

"Tell me why that is the toughest part of this," I said.

"Because he always said he hated being treated like he wasn't a real person and they are still doing the same thing after he has died. They are acting like he was just a made-up character and they can do as they please with him."

How hard it must be to live a life where people can strip you of your humanity because of your status. Prominent people can become works of fiction, two-dimensional beings, caricatures. When, in fact, the opposite is true. They are, at once, flawed, beautiful, and complicated.

Wealthy and well-known people pose unique challenges for therapists and other helping professionals. When they become clients, they bring a great deal of hidden complexity to the entire enterprise of therapy. Our charge is to meet them in their flawed, beautiful, complicated humanity and to do our best work.

REFERENCES

American Counseling Association. (2014). *ACA code of ethics*. https://www.counseling.org/resources/aca-code-of-ethics.pdf

American Psychological Association. (2017). *Ethical principles of psychologists and code of conduct (2002, Amended June 1, 2010, and January 1, 2017)*. https://www.apa.org/ethics/code

Cockrell, C. (2021, November 22). I'm a therapist to the super-rich: They are as miserable as *Succession* makes out. *The Guardian*.

Dalton, M. (2023, January 5). Jonah Hill's tribute to his therapist: *Stutz*. *Medium*.

Hill, J. (Producer & Director). (2022). *Stutz* [Film]. Netflix.

Kasperkevic, J. (2015, October 17). Wealth therapy tackles woes of the rich: "It's really isolating to have lots of money." *The Guardian*.

Komter, A., & Vollebergh, W. (1997). Gift giving and the emotional significance of family and friends. *Journal of Marriage and Family*, *59*, 747–757.

Leeby, C. (2023, January 28). Film review: The therapeutic relationship in *Stutz*. *Psychology Today*.

Sharma, R. (2022, December 23). What an actual therapist thinks of Jonah Hill's Netflix doc. *Vice*.

Skovholt, T. M., & Jennings, L. (2004). *Master therapists: Exploring expertise in therapy and counseling*. Allyn & Bacon.

Taube, D. O., Shapiro, D. L., Harster, K., Cruitt, P., & Maddux, J. (2023). Problems with the interjurisdictional regulation of psychological practice. *Professional Psychology: Research and Practice*, *54*(6), 389–402.

Verhaagen Personal Values Inventory

Your Name: _____ Today's Date: _____

There are no right or wrong answers. This is for personal understanding and follow-up conversation about your personal values. Be as honest as you can.

How much IMPORTANCE does this value hold for you?

	Importance to Me				
	Not important	*A little important*	*Moderately important*	*Highly important*	*The most important*
1. **Achievement:** The drive to accomplish goals and excel in one's pursuits.	❏	❏	❏	❏	❏
2. **Adaptability:** Being flexible and open to change in response to new situations or challenges.	❏	❏	❏	❏	❏
3. **Adventure:** Embracing new experiences, risks, and challenges.	❏	❏	❏	❏	❏
4. **Authenticity:** Staying true to oneself, values, and beliefs in all situations.	❏	❏	❏	❏	❏

(*Continued*)

(Continued)

	Importance to Me				
	Not important	*A little important*	*Moderately important*	*Highly important*	*The most important*
5. **Balance**: Maintaining harmony between work, relationships, and personal well-being.	❑	❑	❑	❑	❑
6. **Community:** Valuing connection, collaboration, and contributing to a group or society.	❑	❑	❑	❑	❑
7. **Compassion:** Demonstrating kindness, understanding, and care for others.	❑	❑	❑	❑	❑
8. **Courage**: Acting bravely in the face of fears, challenges, and uncertainty.	❑	❑	❑	❑	❑
9. **Creativity**: Valuing originality and innovative thinking to solve problems or express oneself.	❑	❑	❑	❑	❑
10. **Curiosity**: A desire to explore, learn, and understand the world around us.	❑	❑	❑	❑	❑
11. **Determination:** Persisting in the pursuit of goals despite hardships or obstacles.	❑	❑	❑	❑	❑
12. **Discipline**: Exercising self-control and focus to achieve what is important.	❑	❑	❑	❑	❑

(Continued)

(Continued)

	Importance to Me				
	Not important	*A little important*	*Moderately important*	*Highly important*	*The most important*
13. **Empathy:** Understanding and sharing the feelings and perspectives of others.	❑	❑	❑	❑	❑
14. **Excellence:** Striving to deliver the highest quality and perform to the best of one's ability.	❑	❑	❑	❑	❑
15. **Fairness:** Upholding justice, equality, and impartiality in all actions.	❑	❑	❑	❑	❑
16. **Freedom:** Prioritizing independence, autonomy, and personal choice.	❑	❑	❑	❑	❑
17. **Fun:** Enjoying lightheartedness, playfulness, and moments of joy.	❑	❑	❑	❑	❑
18. **Generosity:** Willingness to give time, energy, or resources to help others.	❑	❑	❑	❑	❑
19. **Gratitude:** Recognizing, appreciating, and being thankful for life's blessings.	❑	❑	❑	❑	❑
20. **Harmony:** Creating peace and balance within relationships and environments.	❑	❑	❑	❑	❑

(Continued)

(Continued)

	Importance to Me				
	Not important	*A little important*	*Moderately important*	*Highly important*	*The most important*
21. **Honesty**: Being truthful, transparent, and trustworthy in words and actions.	❑	❑	❑	❑	❑
22. **Humility**: Showing modesty and recognizing the value of others' contributions.	❑	❑	❑	❑	❑
23. **Humor**: Finding joy and laughter in life's moments, even during challenges.	❑	❑	❑	❑	❑
24. **Innovation**: Pioneering new ideas, solutions, and creative progress.	❑	❑	❑	❑	❑
25. **Integrity**: Consistently aligning actions with values, principles, and beliefs.	❑	❑	❑	❑	❑
26. **Kindness**: Acting with care, consideration, and friendliness toward others.	❑	❑	❑	❑	❑
27. **Learning**: Having a commitment to lifelong learning and acquiring new knowledge.	❑	❑	❑	❑	❑
28. **Legacy**: Leaving a positive and lasting impact for future generations.	❑	❑	❑	❑	❑
29. **Love**: Valuing deep, meaningful relationships with those we care about.	❑	❑	❑	❑	❑

(Continued)

(Continued)

	Importance to Me				
	Not important	*A little important*	*Moderately important*	*Highly important*	*The most important*
30. **Loyalty**: Remaining steadfast, faithful, and reliable to commitments or relationships.	❏	❏	❏	❏	❏
31. **Mindfulness**: Being fully present, aware, and engaged in the current moment.	❏	❏	❏	❏	❏
32. **Optimism**: Focusing on the positive and maintaining hope for the future.	❏	❏	❏	❏	❏
33. **Patience**: Maintaining calm and understanding during delays, challenges, or frustrations.	❏	❏	❏	❏	❏
34. **Perseverance**: Persisting with effort and dedication despite adversity.	❏	❏	❏	❏	❏
35. **Purpose**: Living with intention and a clear sense of direction or meaning.	❏	❏	❏	❏	❏
36. **Reliability**: Being consistently dependable, responsible, and trustworthy.	❏	❏	❏	❏	❏
37. **Resilience**: Bouncing back and adapting in response to challenges or setbacks.	❏	❏	❏	❏	❏
38. **Respect**: Demonstrating regard for the worth, dignity, and perspectives of others.	❏	❏	❏	❏	❏

(Continued)

(Continued)

	Importance to Me				
	Not important	*A little important*	*Moderately important*	*Highly important*	*The most important*
39. **Self-Respect:** Valuing oneself and maintaining a healthy self-image.	❏	❏	❏	❏	❏
40. **Service:** Contributing time, skills, or resources to support others or a larger cause.	❏	❏	❏	❏	❏
41. **Simplicity:** Prioritizing a less complicated, intentional, and meaningful life.	❏	❏	❏	❏	❏
42. **Spirituality:** Seeking a connection to something greater and searching for purpose and meaning.	❏	❏	❏	❏	❏
43. **Trust:** Having confidence in the reliability, character, or integrity of others.	❏	❏	❏	❏	❏
44. **Well-Being:** Prioritizing physical, mental, and emotional health and wellness.	❏	❏	❏	❏	❏
45. **Wisdom:** Applying knowledge, experience, and good judgment to life's decisions.	❏	❏	❏	❏	❏
46. **Wonder:** Appreciating the awe, beauty, and vastness of life and the world.	❏	❏	❏	❏	❏

How I See Myself and Others

Name: _____ Age: _____ Date: _____

	Not True	Somewhat True	Mostly True	Completely True
Abandonment—Others are likely to abandon me during my times of greatest need.	❑	❑	❑	❑
Approval-Seeking—I focus so much on gaining approval or attention from others that I don't have a true sense of myself.	❑	❑	❑	❑
Defectiveness—I am defective, inferior, or "less than" others. If people really knew me, they would find me to be unlovable.	❑	❑	❑	❑
Dependence—I require others to get through everyday life. I often feel helpless and incompetent.	❑	❑	❑	❑
Deprivation—Others are not going to be able to give me emotional support, understanding, or protection when I need it.	❑	❑	❑	❑
Enmeshment—I am so emotionally entangled with others, like my parents, that I haven't been able to become my own person.	❑	❑	❑	❑
Entitlement—I am special, superior to others, and I should be able to do what I want.	❑	❑	❑	❑
Failure—I have failed, will inevitably fail, or have not achieved as much as my peers. I feel less successful than others.	❑	❑	❑	❑

(Continued)

(Continued)

	Not True	Somewhat True	Mostly True	Completely True
Inhibition—I hold back on expressing my thoughts or feelings so others won't disapprove of me.	❑	❑	❑	❑
Insufficient Self-Control—I don't have enough self-control and it causes me not to achieve my own goals or desires.	❑	❑	❑	❑
Isolation—I am isolated from the rest of the world, different from other people, and not part of any group or community.	❑	❑	❑	❑
Mistrust—Others will try to hurt, humiliate, cheat, manipulate, or take advantage of me if given the chance.	❑	❑	❑	❑
Negativity—I focus on the negative and overlook the positive. I expect things will go wrong.	❑	❑	❑	❑
Punitiveness—I believe people should be punished harshly for their mistakes. I tend to get angry and feel intolerant of others.	❑	❑	❑	❑
Self-Sacrifice—I focus so much on meeting the needs of others that I rarely get my own needs met.	❑	❑	❑	❑
Subjugation—I always give over control to others in relationships so they don't get mad at me or leave me.	❑	❑	❑	❑
Unrelenting Standards—I have impossibly high internal standards of performance that make it hard to enjoy things.	❑	❑	❑	❑
Vulnerability—I have an intense fear of imminent and inevitable catastrophe that will negatively affect me or those I love.	❑	❑	❑	❑

A Glossary of the Language of Wealth

This glossary aims to provide clear definitions of key financial terms for mental health and other non-financial professionals working with wealthy individuals or families. These terms can be helpful in understanding the financial landscape and effectively communicating with clients about their work, family circumstances, or financial well-being.

Active Income Income earned from direct work, such as wages, salaries, and commissions.

Amortization Gradually paying off a debt or the cost of an asset over time.

Annuity A financial product that provides a steady stream of income, often used for retirement.

Arbitrage Profiting from price differences by simultaneously buying and selling the same asset in different markets.

Asset Allocation Strategically dividing investments among different types of assets (like stocks, bonds, and cash) to manage risk and potential returns.

Asset Management The professional management of a client's investments and financial assets to achieve specific goals.

Assets Valuable possessions owned by an individual or organization, such as cash, property, and investments.

Balance Sheet A financial statement showing a company's assets, liabilities, and overall financial health at a particular point in time.

Bankruptcy A legal process for individuals or businesses unable to repay their debts.

Bear Market A period of declining stock prices, often characterized by widespread pessimism.

Blockchain A secure and transparent digital ledger that records transactions across a network of computers.

Bonds Debt securities representing loans made to borrowers, typically governments or corporations.

Bull Market A period of rising stock prices, driven by investor optimism.

Capital Expenditure (CapEx)   Funds a company invests in acquiring or improving physical assets (like buildings or equipment).

Capital Gain   Profit earned when an asset is sold for more than its purchase price.

Capital Loss   A financial loss incurred when an asset is sold for less than its purchase price.

Capital Market   Financial markets where long-term securities (like stocks and bonds) are traded.

Cash Flow   The movement of money into and out of a business, reflecting its liquidity and financial health.

Certificate of Deposit (CD)   A savings account with a fixed interest rate and a specific term, often with penalties for early withdrawal.

Certified Financial Planner (CFP)   A professional certified to provide comprehensive financial planning advice.

Commodity   A basic good used in commerce, such as gold, oil, or agricultural products.

Credit Limit   The maximum amount a lender allows a borrower to spend on credit.

Credit Risk   The possibility that a borrower may not be able to repay a loan.

Credit Score   A numerical rating reflecting an individual's creditworthiness based on their credit history.

Cryptocurrency   A digital currency that uses cryptography for security and often operates independently of central banks.

Debt-to-Income Ratio (DTI)   A measure of an individual's total debt compared to their gross income.

Deflation   A general decline in the prices of goods and services, often indicating economic slowdown.

Derivative   A financial contract whose value is derived from the performance of an underlying asset (like stocks or bonds).

Diversification   Spreading investments across different assets to reduce overall risk.

Dividend   A portion of a company's profits distributed to shareholders.

Dividend Yield   The annual dividend per share divided by the stock price, indicating the dividend's percentage return.

Dow Jones Industrial Average (DJIA)   A stock market index tracking the performance of 30 major U.S. companies.

Economic Bubble   A situation where asset prices significantly exceed their actual value, often leading to a market crash.

Estate Planning   The process of preparing for the management and distribution of assets after death.

Exchange-Traded Funds (ETFs)   Investment funds traded on stock exchanges, holding a basket of assets like stocks and bonds.

Family Office   A private entity that manages the financial affairs of wealthy families.

FICO Score   A widely used credit score ranging from 300 to 850.

Financial Derivatives   Contracts whose value is derived from underlying assets, such as options and futures.

Financial Independence   Having sufficient income to cover living expenses without relying on employment or external support.

Financial Literacy   The knowledge and skills needed to make informed financial decisions.

Financial Planner   A professional who helps individuals create and implement financial plans to achieve their goals.

Fixed Income   Investments that provide regular, fixed interest payments, such as bonds.

Hedge Fund   A pooled investment fund that uses various strategies (including short selling and leverage) to seek high returns.

Inflation   The rate at which the general price of goods and services increases over time.

Interest Rate   The cost of borrowing money, expressed as a percentage of the principal.

Investment Strategy   A plan for achieving financial goals through investing, tailored to individual risk tolerance and time horizon.

IRA (Individual Retirement Account)   A tax-advantaged retirement savings account.

Leverage   Using borrowed money to increase potential investment returns.

Lien   A legal claim on property to secure the repayment of a debt.

Liquidity   How easily an asset can be quickly converted into cash without significant price loss.

Liquidity Risk   The risk of not being able to easily sell an asset for cash at a fair price.

Margin Call   A demand from a broker for an investor to deposit additional funds to cover losses.

Market Capitalization   The total market value of a company's outstanding shares.

Monetary Policy   Actions taken by a central bank (like the Federal Reserve) to control the money supply and interest rates.

Mutual Fund   A professionally managed investment fund that pools money from investors to purchase a diversified portfolio of securities.

Net Worth   The total value of an individual's assets minus their total liabilities.

Portfolio   A collection of financial investments, such as stocks, bonds, and other securities.

Rebalancing   Adjusting a portfolio's asset allocation to maintain the desired risk and return profile.

Return on Investment (ROI)   A measure of the profitability of an investment.

Risk Tolerance   An individual's ability and willingness to accept investment risk for the potential of higher returns.

Roth IRA   A retirement savings account where contributions are made after taxes, allowing tax-free withdrawals in retirement.

Short Selling   Selling borrowed securities with the expectation of buying them back at a lower price to profit from the price decline.

Stock Options   Contracts that give the holder the right (but not the obligation) to buy or sell a company's stock at a predetermined price.

Trust A legal arrangement where assets are held by a trustee for the benefit of beneficiaries.

Valuation The process of determining the worth of an asset or company.

Venture Capital Funding provided to startups and high-growth companies.

Volatility The degree of price fluctuations of an asset over time, indicating its risk level.

Wealth Management A comprehensive service for high-net-worth individuals, combining investment advice, tax planning, and estate planning.

Will A legal document outlining how an individual's assets will be distributed after their death.

Working Capital The difference between a company's current assets and current liabilities, reflecting its short-term financial health.

A Glossary of the Language of Fame

The worlds of fame, especially in entertainment, sports, and the arts, come with their own vocabulary. Here are terms and definitions that are commonly used by agents, managers, producers, technical crew, and other professionals in the industry:

Above-the-Fold The most prominent position in print media, websites, or promotional materials, often reserved for major celebrities or headlines.

Above the Line Key creative personnel on a project, such as directors, producers, lead actors, and screenwriters.

Agency Package A bundled deal where an agency offers a project (script, actors, director) to a studio or network for production.

A-List The most famous and in-demand individuals in the entertainment industry.

Agent A professional who negotiates contracts and secures work for entertainers, earning a commission.

Audition A trial performance to showcase skills and compete for a role.

Back-End Deal An agreement where personnel receive a share of project profits in addition to their initial payment.

Below the Line Crew members responsible for technical and noncreative tasks, like lighting, sound, and set design.

Billing The order and prominence of credits, often determined by negotiations that are informed by star power, box office track record, and similar factors.

B-Roll Supplemental footage used in film, TV, or video production to complement the main shots.

Box Office Revenue from ticket sales for movies or live events, a measure of commercial success.

Call Sheet A daily schedule for cast and crew, with shooting times, locations, and other details.

Cameo A brief, often uncredited appearance by a well-known person.

Casting Call The process of inviting and selecting performers for roles.

Casting Director A professional who finds and recommends actors for roles.

Clout   Influence and power within the entertainment industry.

Cold Read   A type of audition where an actor reads from a script without prior rehearsal.

Completion Bond   Insurance guaranteeing a film's timely and on-budget completion.

Craft Services   The department providing food and beverages to cast and crew.

Cover Shoot   A photoshoot for a magazine cover, often featuring a high-profile model or celebrity.

Dailies   Raw, unedited footage reviewed daily to assess filming progress.

Day Player   An actor hired for a short-term, daily role.

Demo Reel   A short video compilation showcasing an actor's, model's, or performer's past work and range of talent.

Development   The early stage of a project involving idea exploration, scriptwriting, and securing funding.

Development Hell   A prolonged period where a project is stuck in development.

Distribution   Making films, TV shows, or other productions available to the public.

Entourage   A group of people who accompany and support a celebrity.

Equity (Actors' Equity Association)   A labor union representing actors and stage managers in live theater, ensuring fair wages and working conditions.

Executive Producer   A producer primarily focused on the financial and business aspects of a project.

Fashion Week   A series of events held in major cities where designers showcase their new collections.

Feature Film   A full-length film, typically over 60 minutes.

Filmography   A list of films associated with an actor, director, or crew member.

Gaffer   The chief electrician responsible for lighting on a set.

Go-See   An appointment where models meet with clients or agencies to show their portfolio and discuss potential work.

Greenlight   Approval from a studio or financier to begin production.

Grip   A crew member who sets up equipment for cameras and lighting.

Guild   An organization representing professionals in a specific field (e.g., Writers Guild of America).

Headliner   The main performer or star attraction of an event, show, or concert.

Headshot   A professional photograph of an actor used for casting and promotion.

Hiatus   A break in a production schedule, often between seasons of a TV show.

Hit   A successful show, film, song, or performance that gains widespread popularity.

House Seats   Reserved seats in a theater for VIPs, friends, family, or industry professionals.

In the Can   A term indicating that filming or production for a project is complete.

Indie   A project (film, music) made outside the mainstream studio system.

Logline   A concise summary of a story highlighting the central conflict.

Lookbook   A collection of photos used by fashion models, designers, or photographers to showcase work, style, or branding.

Looping/ADR   Re-recording dialogue for audio quality or content changes.

Manager   A professional who guides an artist's career, offering strategic advice and opportunities.

Martini Shot   The final shot of the day during filming.

Model Release   A legal document signed by a model, giving permission for their image to be used in photos, videos, or advertisements.

NDA (Non-Disclosure Agreement)   A legal contract preventing the sharing of confidential information.

On-Call   A status where performers or crew are ready to work at short notice.

Option   A temporary agreement to purchase rights to a script, novel, etc., for a film or TV production.

Paparazzi   Freelance photographers who pursue celebrities for candid photos.

Pilot   The first episode of a proposed TV show, used to gauge network or audience interest.

Pitch   A presentation of an idea for a film, TV show, or project to attract funding or approval.

Portfolio   A collection of a model's or performer's best photographs or work samples.

Post-Production   The final stage of filmmaking, including editing, sound design, and visual effects.

Pre-Production   The planning phase before filming, including casting, budgeting, and location scouting.

Press Junket   A series of interviews, screenings, and promotional events for a film, show, or album release.

Principal Photography   The main period of filming.

Publicist   A professional who manages and shapes a celebrity's public image.

Red Carpet   A media event at premieres, awards shows, or galas where celebrities pose for photos and conduct interviews.

Rebalancing   Adjusting promotional efforts or career priorities to maintain success.

Residuals   Payments to performers, models, or creatives for the reuse of their work.

Rider   A list of requests or requirements specified by performers in their contracts.

Runway   The platform or stage where fashion models walk to showcase a designer's clothing collection.

Royalties   Ongoing payments to creators for the continued use of their work.

Screen Test   A filmed audition to evaluate an actor's suitability for a role on camera.

Showrunner   The lead executive producer responsible for the creative direction and management of a TV show.

Sizzle Reel   A short, fast-paced promotional video highlighting a project, product, or person.

Slate   The process where actors introduce themselves during auditions by stating their name, agent, and role being read for.

Social Media Influencer   A person with significant online following who can sway audiences.

Spec Script   A script written without a contract, in the hopes of being purchased or produced.

Spin-Off   A new show or project derived from an existing one, focusing on different characters or stories.

Stage Name   A pseudonym used by performers or entertainers instead of their real name for professional purposes.

Storyboard   A sequence of sketches illustrating the planned shots and scenes.

Stunt Coordinator   The professional who designs and oversees the performance of stunts.

Table Read   A read-through of a script by actors to prepare for production and clarify the narrative.

Talent Scout   A professional who identifies and recruits performers, artists, or athletes.

Tear Sheet   A page from a published magazine or ad featuring a model or performer, used as proof of professional work.

Trailer   A promotional video for a film or show, showcasing highlights to attract audiences.

Trust   A legal arrangement for managing an artist's rights or assets.

Typecast   The practice of repeatedly casting an actor in similar roles based on their previous work.

Understudy   A performer who learns the role of another actor and is prepared to step in if needed.

Voice-Over (VO)   Recorded narration delivered by someone not seen on screen.

Walk-On Role   A small part in a film, TV show, or theater production, often with no spoken lines.

Wardrobe Fitting   A session where models or actors try on costumes to ensure proper fit and appearance for a production.

Work-for-Hire   A legal term indicating that the creator of work (e.g., photos, scripts) does not retain ownership, as the employer or client owns the rights.

Wrap Party   A celebration held to mark the end of filming or production.

Writer's Room   A collaborative space where a team of writers creates scripts for a TV show.

Zoom Audition   A virtual audition conducted via video conferencing platforms that become more commonplace during the pandemic but has continuing regularly since then.

Index

Acceptance and Commitment Therapy
(ACT) 9, 94
addiction 40, 49, 71, 74, 80–82, 117, 123,
127, 130
addictive behaviors 10, 129
anxiety 8, 19, 24, 26, 30, 42, 49, 50, 53,
55–56, 59, 67, 81, 89, 95–96, 104,
108, 117, 129, 155, 163, 176
artists 5, 42, 68, 103, 112, 118, 165
athletes 3–5, 9, 42, 61, 66–67, 82, 90,
117–118, 158–159, 161, 165–166,
169, 172

behavioral challenges 120, 145
benefits of being rich 4, 6, 9, 13–14,
23–33

celebrities, celebrity 4–8, 16–18, 47,
61–63, 65–72, 83, 89–91, 99, 101,
103–104, 106, 129, 133, 156–157,
161, 169, 171, 173
challenges of being rich 34–60
children in wealthy families 47–60
child stars 74–84
Cognitive-Behavioral Therapy (CBT) 9,
55, 71, 94–95, 120, 128–129, 141,
143–144, 147, 174
cognitive flexibility 10, 95, 97
confidentiality 5, 54, 165–170

debt 15, 29–30, 42, 58, 160
depression 8, 24–26, 49–50, 52–53,
55–56, 67, 81, 89, 96, 104–105, 117,
144, 164
Dialectical Behavior Therapy (DBT) 9–10,
94, 141

emotional regulation 9, 110,
136, 144
empathy 29, 31, 37–39, 44, 57, 96, 107,
121, 123, 134–136, 138, 141–144,
161–162, 176
ethical challenges 163–177
evidence-based treatment (EBT) 9–10,
94, 119, 141, 145, 173

fame 3, 6–9, 12, 16–19, 61–72, 74–84,
89–94, 102, 104–106, 108, 117, 133,
137, 139, 156–158
family dynamics 50, 106
financial health 42, 160

high-net-worth individuals 5, 15,
19, 170

identity 69, 76, 77, 79, 81, 83
isolation 41, 43–44, 49, 66, 89,
110–112, 118, 146, 147,
157, 176

materialism 8, 104
Motivational Interviewing (MI) 9, 71, 119–129, 143–144, 174, 177
MusiCares 5

narcissism 36–39, 43–44, 57, 67, 132–148, 156, 176

PsyPact 5, 165

Q-Score 17–18

radical acceptance 71, 95
reality show contestants 3, 62, 64, 90, 133
relationship issues 6, 44, 81, 102–115

Schema Therapy 9–10, 141, 143–147
social media 3, 5, 16, 18–19, 61–66, 69, 75, 77, 92, 106, 109, 139, 142, 153, 156, 157, 163, 165–166, 175
substance abuse 4, 6–7, 9–10, 30, 40, 44, 48–49, 52–55, 59, 70, 72, 74, 76, 79–81, 83, 89–90, 105, 112, 116–130

wealthy people 3–4, 6, 23–32, 34–45, 47–59, 108, 117, 129, 175–177
well-known people 3, 5–10, 61–72, 74–84, 103–105, 108–109, 117–118, 129, 133, 138, 156, 159, 165–169, 171–173

For Product Safety Concerns and Information please contact our EU
representative GPSR@taylorandfrancis.com
Taylor & Francis Verlag GmbH, Kaufingerstraße 24, 80331 München, Germany

9 781032 815589